CHILDREN'S RELIGIOUS BOOKS

GARLAND REFERENCE LIBRARY
OF THE HUMANITIES
(VOL. 689)

CHILDREN'S RELIGIOUS BOOKS
An Annotated Bibliography

Patricia Pearl

GARLAND PUBLISHING, INC. • NEW YORK & LONDON
1988

Library of Congress Cataloging-in-Publication Data

Pearl, Patricia.
Children's religious books.

(Garland reference library of the humanities ; vol. 689)
1. Bible—Juvenile literature—Bibliography.
2. Religions—Juvenile literature—Bibliography.
I. Title. II. Series.
Z7759.P4 1988 [BS539] 016.2 87-14374
ISBN 0-8240-8531-0 (alk. paper)

Cover design by Valerie Mergentime

Printed on acid-free, 250-year-life paper
Manufactured in the United States of America

CONTENTS

PREFACE

The purpose of this book is to give an overview of children's religious literature, hitherto a neglected field. No prior lists of this length have been attempted. Except for an examination library in the beginning stages at Baylor University, no large library collections in this area even exist, although a surprisingly large number and variety of publications are available. Because the output of Protestant Christian publishers is large, the bibliography may seem weighted in that direction, but Roman Catholic, Jewish, Hindu, and Bahai publishing houses are included, as well as many trade publishers.

The principal criterion for selection is that the work have some overt religious theme. If those books with implicit spiritual or good-versus-evil themes were included, the size of the bibliography would be unmanageable. Because this field of literature is relatively unexamined, mediocre and modest material has been included to give the user some idea of what is available. Obviously denominational curriculum material is excluded. Illustrations are judged according to standard criteria for picture books. The annotations mention writing quality that is particularly good or bad. Otherwise the text of the book may be assumed to be adequate for its purpose.

The age range of the list is from preschool through sixth grade, but some young adult and adult material with appropriate subjects and interest level for upper elementary children is included.

The bibliography is intended to be current, reasonably comprehensive, and critical. The availability of titles has been verified in the 1985-86 *Books in Print* and 1986 publishers' catalogs. Items for review have been examined in public, academic, church, and synagogue libraries and gathered from publishers. They are evaluated in terms of scope, authority, bias, style of writing, and quality of illustration. Citations refer to the editions actually examined, but often other hardcover and paperback copies of the titles exist.

The bibliography is arranged by subject and then by author. Two or more titles dealing with the same area are set off under a specific heading. Pagination and age level recommendations are included to help with usage. "Unpaged" does not necessarily mean the book is short. Scripture references keyed to the text are a valuable tool for religious educators and thus have been noted in the annotations. If more than two titles in a fiction series are listed, the books are treated as a group, provided that the protagonist, setting, and writing style remain generally the same throughout.

For easier identification of titles the names of illustrators, compilers, retellers, editors, etc., are used as authors if no actual author is specified in the book. Fiction and fictionalized biography are blended with nonfiction in most of the subject areas, although occasionally if there is a great deal of material, fiction may be made a separate category.

No attempt has been made to cross-reference, because the material overlaps so extensively. Christian church history naturally includes Christian biography and holidays such as Thanksgiving, Halloween, and Valentine's Day. Jewish life incorporates Jewish holidays. Theology is inseparable from the Bible. Christian life and Christian devotional materials are logical partners. Only in the cases of Christmas and Easter have any "see also" suggestions been given. St. Patrick's Day materials are listed with the life of that saint.

Potential users of this bibliography are educators and researchers in the fields of religion and children's literature; public, academic, and school libraries; church and synagogue libraries; and those in general who choose religious books for children or look for material on specific religious topics.

Children's Religious Books

I
THE BIBLE

GENERAL WORKS

1. Bullock, Henry M. *Young Reader's Bible: The Holy Bible, Revised Standard Version.* Nashville: Abingdon, 1946. 900p.

   The *RSV* text is unchanged but is arranged in a large readable format, with several type faces and sizes. Colored line drawings are scattered throughout to add interest. Each book has a short, lucid explanation and contains an introduction on Bible history and usage and color maps. Upper grades.

History

2. Doney, Meryl. *How Our Bible Came to Us: The Story of the Book That Changed the World.* Illus. Peter Dennis. Belleville, Mich.: Lion, 1985. 44p.

   Lively, clever, thorough presentation of facts about the Bible contains statistics, brief summaries of the types of books included, some Old and New Testament writers, historical time lines for both, the evolution of writing and paper, Bible versions through the centuries, various translators, etc. Plentifully illustrated. Done in an informal style. Fourth grade and up.

3. Flournoy, Fran. *The Very Best Book of All.* Photog. Robert Cushman Hayes. Cincinnati: Standard, 1982. unp. Happy Day Series.

   Misty, softly colored photographs of pretty children exploring all kinds of books, especially their favorite, the Bible, which tells them about God's love and care for everyone. Preschool to kindergarten.

4. Henderson, Felicity. *Learning About the Bible*. Illus. Michael Grimsdale. Belleville, Mich.: Lion, 1984. 30p.

   Simplest facts about the Bible and what it tells about God. Brief descriptions of the Old and New Testaments and how they are all part of one true story, how God is eternally loving and caring, how the Good News has spread worldwide. Contains watercolors of modern children and Biblical scenes. Early elementary.

5. McElrath, William N. *Bible Guidebook: Clear and Basic Help on What the Bible Is and How to Use It*. Illus. Don Fields. Nashville: Broadman, 1972. 144p.

   Easily read, interesting, written from a Baptist perspective. Condensation and commentary are given for every book of the Bible, along with useful advice on Bible translations, aids, reading schedules. The book contains a time line and has an alphabetical arrangement. Fourth grade and up.

6. Nystrom, Carolyn. *What Is the Bible?* Illus. Wayne Hanna. Chicago: Moody, 1982. unp.

   Simple how, what, when, and why of the Bible, as it was written through God's inspiration of people such as Samuel, Paul, and Moses. Its purpose: to teach God's will and eternal truths. Includes many types of material such as stories of heroes, laws, songs of praise, etc. Intense, shiny colors and blocky, cartoon-style forms in pictures of a little boy playing and telling about the Bible and of people from Biblical history. Scriptural References. Preschool through second grade.

Reference

7. Coen, Rena Neumann. *The Old Testament in Art*. Minneapolis: Lerner, 1970. 71p.

   Knowledgeable, clearly worded text stresses the way each artist expresses his individual illumination of a Bible subject such as the Garden of Eden, David, Isaac and Jacob, Joseph, etc. The variety of artists represented includes Cranach, Michelangelo, Blake, Benjamin West, etc. Paintings, sculptures, and stained glass windows are reproduced with varying success, mostly in black and white. Upper elementary and up.

8. Daves, Michael. *Young Reader's Book of Christian Symbolism.* Illus. Gordon Laite. Nashville: Abingdon, 1967. 128p.

   Symbols of the Old Testament and Jewish worship, Holy Week, the Resurrection, Jesus Christ, the early church, the Trinity, the Bible, the Gospel writers, and more are handsomely illustrated in rose and blue over black and white. Various crosses are included. History and Biblical setting of each are given. Has an introduction and index. Upper elementary.

9. Coleman, William L. *Who What When Where Book about the Bible.* Illus. Dwight Walles. Elgin, Ill.: Cook, 1980. 121p.

   Nuggets of miscellaneous information about Bible personalities, ancient culture, heaven, theology, prayer, moral actions, history of the Bible, symbols, etc. are haphazardly arranged. The book has a large format, contains many bright pictures, and has quite a few puzzles and games. Informal treatment. Upper elementary.

10. Latham, Judy. *Women in the Bible: Helpful Friends.* Illus. Paul Karch. Nashville: Broadman, 1979. 48p.

    Interestingly written, concise accounts of Deborah, Esther, Mary and Martha, Dorcas, and Lydia, with enough imaginative detail to round out the stories without detracting from accuracy. The text uses short sentences. There are attractive color illustrations. First through fourth grades.

11. McElrath, William N. *A Bible Dictionary for Young Readers.* Illus. Don Fields. Nashville: Broadman, 1965. 126p.

    Bible verse references are given for the approximately 2000 simply written entries, as well as multiple definitions of a term, when needed. Pronunciation guides are limited to proper names, unfortunately. Needs more three-tone drawings to create interest and strengthen the explanations. Third to fifth grades.

12. Matthews, Velda. *Basic Bible Dictionary.* Illus. Richard Wahl and Romilda Dilley. Cincinnati: Standard, 1983. 128p.

    Has over 1000 entries, some pronouncing guides, but there are many important omissions. The definitions vary in length from a word or phrase to a long paragraph, and often are unclear or contain personal comment. Has a conservative tone. The illustrations often are not on the same page as the words they represent. Fourth to sixth grades.

13. Mickelsen, Beverly. *The Family Bible Encyclopedia.* 2 vols. Elgin, Ill.: Cook, 1978.

    Impressive coverage of more than 2000 items is understandable by middle elementary children but useful for older ages as well. It is clear and well-researched, contains a pronouncing guide, and has helpful Scriptural references. The conservative tone and reference to Jesus Christ in entries not associated with the New Testament make it appropriate for Christian use only. Has a well-defined format but its color illustrations are merely decorative. Fourth grade and up.

14. Moore, Joan Andre. *Astronomy in the Bible.* Nashville: Abingdon, 1981. 176p.

    How the sun, moon, constellations, and planets are treated in the Bible. Tells of stars known by Amos, Job, and Jesus. Has historical data, including those of Sumerian origin, discusses theories about the Star of Bethlehem. There are black-and-white drawings, diagrams, photographs, an index, and a bibliography. Fifth grade and up.

15. Potter, Charles Francis. *Is That in the Bible?.* New York: Ballantine, 1933. 272p.

    For dedicated list and trivia lovers and Bible students. Divided into topics such as children, athletics, angels and demons, music, medicine, sex, etc., the 1000 questions are answered by a Scripture citation and some explanatory comment. The style and language indicate the book is over fifty years old, but it is instructive and non-denominational. Upper elementary and up.

16. Shissler, Barbara Johnson. *The New Testament in Art.* Minneapolis: Lerner, 1970. 67p.

    Although the quality of the color and black-and-white reproductions of paintings, sculptures, and stained glass windows varies, it is adequate to demonstrate the techniques and emotions of each artist as explained in skillful, sensitive commentary. Includes works by Van Gogh, Raphael, El Greco, Giotto, Gislebertus, and others. The book has Scriptural references. Sixth grade and up.

17. Tarrant, Chris. *Life in Bible Times.* Illus. Kim Shaw. Nashville: Abingdon, 1985. 48p.

    Ten Biblical situations from Jacob through Paul introduce bits of information about the associated historical periods. The Moses section tells about pharaohs, papyrus, and mud bricks; Ruth's about agricultural methods; Jeremiah's about Babylonian warfare. Interesting but too cursory to be a real reference tool. Its best feature is the large, detailed, color artwork. Contains a time line and topical index. Third to sixth grades.

18. Tester, Sylvia Ruth. *The World into Which Jesus Came.* Illus. Mina Gow McLean. Elgin, Ill.: Child's World. 96p.

    Simply presented, useful information about daily living: plants and animals; Jerusalem and the Temple; laws about food, burial, illness, etc.; holidays; religious leaders and groups; principal geographic areas and cities; neighboring countries and occupying nations. Written as seen through the eyes of an imaginary family in Capernaum. Has well-done color pictures, maps, diagrams, and an index. Kindergarten and up.

19. Witter, Evelyn. *In Jesus' Day.* Illus. Wayne Sherwood. St. Louis: Concordia, 1980. 31p.

    Brief, interesting encyclopedic information about everyday life in New Testament times: how people cooked, slept, shopped, traveled, laundered, worked, celebrated holidays, and more. Low-key, rather vague black-white-taupe illustrations. Vocabulary level for fourth grade and up.

FLORA AND FAUNA

20. Lerner, Carol. *A Biblical Garden.* Illus. author. New York: Morrow, 1982. 48p.

    Twenty plants and trees known to be native to Biblical areas in Old Testament times are exquisitely illustrated in both color and black and white. Two short descriptive paragraphs, a citation from the Jewish Bible, and the Hebrew and scientific names are given for each. Fifth grade and up.

21. Mitchell, Vic, illus. *Animals of the Bible.* Belleville, Mich.: Lion, 1978. unp.

    Crisp, realistic depictions of domestic animals--sheep and goat, donkey and mule, horse, camel, cattle--and wild ones--fox and jackal, deer and gazelle, wolf, leopard, bear, lion. Contains short descriptions of their habitats, usage, and activities. Has Scripture citations. Kindergarten to third grade.

22. Mitchell, Vic, illus. *Birds of the Bible*. Belleville, Mich.: Lion, 1978. 45p.

    A variety of birds, such as the eagle, peacock, quail, dove, and raven, are illustrated with colorful clarity. Informative nuggets about their origins and habits are given in an easy-to-read text. Kindergarten through fourth grade.

23. Mitchell, Vic, illus. *Plants of the Bible*. Ann Arbor, Mich.: Lion, 1978. 40p.

    Eighteen flowers, food plants, weeds, gums, spices, and herbs are attractively illustrated, and their uses in Bible times described. Examples are hyssop, mustard, papyrus, flax, lentils, tares. An interesting text with short sentences. Kindergarten through fourth grade.

24. Mitchell, Vic, illus. *Trees of the Bible*. Belleville, Mich.: Lion, 1978. 45p.

    Fourteen trees and the grapevine are precisely pictured and their usage described. Included are those which provided wood such as the acacia and cedar of Lebanon, and fruit such as the fig, date, palm, and olive. Contains Scripture citations. Kindergarten through fourth grade.

25. Paterson, John, and Katherine Paterson. *Consider the Lilies: Plants of the Bible*. Illus. Anne Ophelia Dowdon. New York: Crowell, 1986. 96p.

    Meticulous, elegant botanical illustrations in luminous colors show Biblical flowers, fruits, shrubs, crops, trees, weeds. Each has a lengthy informative caption and Scripture passages or a Bible story which mentions it. Describes both symbolic meanings and practical uses of the plants. Has a list of Bible references and an index. Fourth grade and up.

Stories

26. Alexander, Pat. *The Nelson Children's Bible*. Illus. Lyndon Evans. Nashville: Nelson, 1981. 256p.

    Fast paced, well-integrated account of the Old and New Testaments. Short sentences and paragraphs for personal reading on third grade level. Gospels and Acts only from the New Testament. Good first Bible. Enlivened by three-tone and full-color action-filled pictures.

27. Allen, J.F. *Illustrated Bible for Children*. Illus. Carlo Tora. Nashville: Nelson, 1982. 416p.

    More than 185 Old Testament stories include the historical books, some of the kings, Elijah and Elisha, David and Saul, Daniel, Job (out of order). Principal events of the Gospels and Acts; section on Revelation. Good narrative flow. Generally straightforward tone, but Christian input such as the foretelling of Jesus in Genesis limits its usage. Large, too bright, realistic illustrations. Third to sixth grades.

28. Arch Books. St. Louis: Concordia.

    Extensive series of individual Bible stories usually retold in easy verse form with lively full- and two-color illustrations in simple cartoon style. Their greatest strengths are eye-appeal to children and the vast number of topics covered. Also includes some general Bible guides. Each book has Scripture references and use notes directed to adults. Old Testament titles include: Genesis, *The World God Made*, *A Garden and a Promise*, *Adam and His Family*, *Cain and Abel*, *Noah and God's Promise*, *Story of Noah's Ark*, *The Silly Skyscraper*, *Two Cities That Burned*, *Abraham, Sarah, and the Promised Son*, *Isaac's Chosen Wife*, *The Story of Jacob*, *Rachel and Leah*, *The Boy Who Saved His Family*; Exodus, *The Princess and the Baby*, *Moses and the Ten Plagues*, *Simon Was Safe*, *When God Laid Down the Law*; Numbers, *When God Made Balaam's Donkey Talk*; Joshua, *The Walls Came Tumbling Down*; Judges, *The Story of Deborah*, *The Man Who Won Without Fighting*, *Sampson's Secret*; Ruth, *Ruth and Naomi*; Samuel, *Samuel the Judge*, *The Boy with a Sling*, *The Secret of the Arrows*, *The Prince and the Promise*; Kings, *The Wise King and the Baby*, *The Temple King Solomon Built*, *Good Little King Josiah*, *The Story of Joash*, *The Water That Caught on Fire*, *Elijah and the Wicked Queen*, *A Ring of Fiery Horses*, *King Solomon's Dream*; Prophets, *The Story of Zerub-*

babel, The Day God Made It Rain, The Boy Who Came Back to Life, What's the Matter with Job?, The Man Caught by a Fish, Three Men Who Walked in Fire, Daniel in the Lion's Den, The Braggy King of Babylon; Esther, *The Queen Who Saved Her People*; Psalms, *Sing a Song of Gladness*; Proverbs, *Proverbs: Important Things to Know.*

New Testament titles include: Christmas, *Secret of the Star*; *Mary's Story*; *The Night the Angels Sang*; *The Baby God Promised*; *A Song for Joseph, Anna and the Christ Child*; *The Happiest Search*; *The Little Mouse's Wonderful Journey*; *Clem the Clumsy Camel*; *Armond and the First Christmas*; *Ben's Blanket and the Baby Jesus*; *The Little Shepherd and the First Christmas*; *Little Benjamin and the First Christmas*; *The Secret Journey*; *The Innkeeper's Daughter*; *Bethlehem's Brightest Star*; *A Christmas Lullaby*; *Simeon and the Baby Jesus*; *Simeon's Secret*; *The Baby Born in a Stable*; *Donkey Daniel in Bethlehem*; Parables, *The Good Samaritan, The Father Who Forgave, Jon and the Little Lost Lamb, The Son Who Said He Wouldn't, The Seed That Grew to Be a Hundred, No More Than a Mustard Seed, The Boy Who Ran Away, The House on the Rock, The King's Invitation, The Pearl That Changed a Life, The Rich Fool, The Parables of Jesus*; Miracles, *The Beggar's Greatest Wish, Captain Gaius Sees a Miracle, The Man Who Met Jesus at Bethesda, The Lame Man Who Walked Again, The Boy Who Gave His Lunch Away, The Little Boat That Almost Sank, He Remembered to Say Thank You, The Little Sleeping Beauty, Jesus and Bartemaeus*; Jesus' life and general teachings, *Young Jesus in the Temple, John the Baptist, The Temptation of Jesus, The Man Who Learned to Give, Through a Needle's Eye, A Penny Is Everything, Jesus' Second Family, The Day the Little Children Came, Zacchaeus Meets the Savior, The Stranger at Jacob's Well, Amrah and the Living Water, The Great Surprise, Two Men in the Temple, Sermon on the Mountain, The Lord's Prayer, Jesus' Twelve Disciples, The Greatest Gift Is Love*; Easter, *The Donkey Who Served the King, The Bread and the Wine, Jesus Forgives Peter, The Thief Who Was Sorry, Nicodemus Learns the Way, The Man Who Carried the Cross for Jesus, Kiri and the First Easter, Grandfather's Story, Doubting Thomas, The Fisherman's Surprise, The Most Wonderful King*; Acts, *O Happy Day, The Glory Story, Stephen the First Martyr, Dorcas Sews for Others, The Man Who Slept through a Sermon, The Prisoner Who Freed Others, He Didn't Mind Getting Wet.*

Bible guides include *Books of the Old Testament, Books of the New Testament, Events of the Bible, Places of the Bible.*

Preschool through third grade.

29. Bartlett, David, and Carol Bartlett. *Adam's New Friend: And Other Stories from the Bible.* Illus. Scott Stapleton. Valley Forge, Pa.: Judson, 1980. 95p.

    Witty retellings of twenty-two stories from the Old and New Testaments include Adam, Noah, Joseph, Daniel, the best known parables and miracles, Paul's conversion. Modern language, informal tone. Good for reading aloud and story telling. Some instructional comment. Amusing cartoon illustrations in blue, black, white. Index of Scripture passages. Kindergarten and up.

30. Batchelor, Mary. *The Children's Bible in 365 Stories.* Illus. John Haysom. Belleville, Mich.: Lion, 1985. 416p.

    Scope extensive for patriarchs, prophets, kings; life and teachings of Jesus. Good highlights of Paul's life and other events in Acts. Some material from Epistles and Revelation, tiny sample of Psalms and Proverbs. Some imaginative amplification and fictionalization. Skillful narrative in lively, comprehensible style retains dignity of original. Some Christian bias. Luminous, realistic, well-researched, expressive illustrations on almost every page. Index. 365 sections with Scripture citations. Reading level for fourth grade, interest level for kindergarten and up.

31. Batchelor, Mary. *The Lion Book of Bible Stories and Prayers.* Belleville, Mich.: Lion, 1980. unp.

    Thirty-four short, lively narratives followed by associated little prayers. Arranged by themes familiar to young children such as kindness, forgiveness, babies, parties, fear, holidays. Busy, cheerful format illustrated by twenty-four different artists, plus photographs in black and white and color for much eye appeal. Kindergarten to fourth grade.

32. Becker, Joyce. *Bible Crafts.* New York: Holiday, 1982. 114p.

    Crisp précis of the creation; Noah's ark; the tower of Babel; Abraham, Sarah, and Isaac; Jacob's ladder; Joseph's coat; Moses and the Hebrews in the wilderness; Ruth; Daniel and the lions; and Jonah are followed by instructions for inventive related crafts of varying difficulty. Stories and crafts are very well integrated. Has an index. Fourth to sixth grades.

33. Beers, V. Gilbert. *The Victor Family Story Bible*. Wheaton, Ill.: Victor, 1985. 640p.

    Main events of Genesis and Exodus, Balaam, Joshua, Gideon, Deborah, Samson, Ruth, Samuel, Saul, David, Solomon, the principal prophets, Job, Jesus' life and teachings, highlights of Acts, and Revelation presented in simplified and shortened form. Lively style, much dialogue, supportive detail, personal opinion. Summary paragraphs bridge gaps between stories. Thought-provoking questions applying to child's daily life, conduct, and relationship to Jesus after each chapter. Information sections compare Biblical and familiar things of today such as shoes, boats, laws, money. Uses large type. Bright, realistic pictures by various artists. Religious concept learning levels include children from preschool through age seventeen. Contains maps and topical and Scriptural indexes. Generally useful from kindergarten through fourth grade.

34. Buck, Pearl S. *The Story Bible*. Wheaton, Ill.: Tyndale, 1976. 526p.

    The most popular stories from Genesis through Pentecost are related in a smoothly written, easy-to-read, and straightforward narrative. For fourth grade and up.

35. Bull, Norman J. *One Hundred One Bible Stories*. Illus. Val Biro. Nashville: Abingdon, 1982. 175p.

    Much material is omitted, and the stories are very condensed, especially those of the Old Testament. No division between Daniel, Judas Maccabeus, and the Nativity to indicate Old Testament, Apocrypha, and New Testament sections of the Bible. No Scripture citations. Parables and miracles are best parts, being told in clear, lively language. Has vigorous color pictures on every page. Large type. Fourth to sixth grades.

36. Christie-Murray, David. *The Illustrated Children's Bible*. Illus. Ken Petts, John Berry, Neville Dear, Norma Burgin. New York: Grosset & Dunlap, 1982. 414p.

    Christian-oriented, well-drawn-together narrative in crisp British style includes good Old Testament selection of the usual creation, Noah, Joseph, Moses, David, plus Kings, and a summary of the return to Jerusalem and its restoration. Twenty-third Psalm. Details of tabernacle and Temple. No sex (concubines are wives, David does not see Bathsheba bathing, Rahab has no profession, etc.). New Testament includes life of Jesus, principles of his teaching, parables, miracles. Little on Acts, Paul's life, theology. Author's bias that Judaism prepares the way for the coming of Christ stressed in the Old Testament section. Large, authentic, realistic illustrations. Encyclopedic information illustrated in boxes on pages. Fifth grade up.

37. Demaree, Doris Clore. *Bible Boys and Girls*. *Bible Heroes*. *Exciting Adventures*. *Followers of God*. *Helping Others*. *Living for Jesus*. Illus. Clive Upton. Anderson, Ind.: Warner, 1970, 1974. 31p. each. Bible Stories for Children Series.

    Each book contains fourteen pared-down incidents from both the Old and New Testaments expressing a general theme but disjointed in effect. Some are told in rhyme, all in short sentences arranged on the pages to look like free verse. Often choppy. Large pictures show detailed but idealized figures in rich colors. Scripture citations. Needs adult input and knowledge of the complete Bible story to be intelligible. Kindergarten to third grade.

38. Dienert, Ruth Graham. *First Steps in the Bible*. Waco, Tex.: Word, 1980. 191p.

    Extensive modernization and revision of Charles Foster's *First Steps for Little Feet along Gospel Paths*. Conversational style, clear concepts, conservative tone. Understanding and positive attitude. Principal portion is Jesus' life, with the events told in short sections accompanied by personal comment, question lists, and notes to parents. Illustrated with fine color photographs, many of Israel, and paintings. Preschool through third grade.

39. Efron, Marshall, and Alfa-Betty Olsen. *Bible Stories You Can't Forget: No Matter How Hard You Try*. Illus. Ron Barrett. New York: Dell, 1979. 107p.

    Eight well-known stories from both Old and New Testaments include Noah, the tower of Babel, Joseph, David, Samson, Passover, the Wise Men, and the Prodigal Son. Amusingly modernized into contemporary, startling language and situations, giving the old tales new sparkle and child appeal. Third grade and up.

40. Egermeier, Elsie. *Egermeier's Bible Story Book*. 5th ed. Anderson, Ind.: Warner, 1969. 576p.

    Longtime favorite first published in 1923. Comprehensive in scope--twenty-four stories about Moses, sixty stories about Jesus, etc.--and well organized. Sprightly, pictorial narrative style helps overcome the defects of closely printed pages and uninspiring illustrations of muddy photographs, gaudy color plates, and dull black and white reproductions. Pronouncing guide to unfamiliar words. Third grade and up.

41. Ford, Lauren. *Little Book about God*. Illus. author. Garden City, N.Y.: Doubleday, 1934. unp.

Unusual format in which gemlike little pictures are interspersed throughout a handprinted black text picked out in blue and red. After the creation and the Garden of Eden, a long and imaginative bridge about the development of civilization, taming animals, learning agriculture, building homes, etc., leads to people becoming quarrelsome and lazy and the Noah story. Later God hears a hungry girl crying and sends Gabriel to bring her milk. She grows up to be Mary. The Nativity is told in a factual manner, but elsewhere the author includes personal and saccharine input. The stated theme is why there are B.C. and A.D. periods in history. Preschool to second grade.

42. Foster, Charles. *Bible Stories from the Old and New Testaments*. Illus. Huntley Brown. Racine, Wis.: Golden, 1966. 254p.

Undistinguished, uneven collection. Some stories are presented only partially (Isaac's sacrifice is ignored) or bowdlerized (Hagar's role unidentified). Jesus' ministry runs together confusingly. Intrusive, unhelpful little explanations. No Scripture references. Occasional three and full color, full page illustrations done from interesting angles are often cluttered. Well-bound, handsome format. Fourth to sixth grades.

43. Grant, Amy. *Amy Grant's Heart to Heart Bible Stories*. Illus. Jim Padgett. Fort Worth, Tex.: Sweet, 1985. 96p.

Thirty short, conversational versions of the most familiar Old and New Testament stories in chronological order but no attempt has been made for continuity. Many written as lively first-person narratives. Four incidents from Acts included. Large, sharply drawn illustrations full of action and character, in color. Preschool through fourth grade.

44. Hayes, Wanda. *A Child's First Book of Bible Stories*. Illus. Kathryn Hutton and Heidi Petach. Cincinnati: Standard, 1983. 127p.

    Limited coverage. Old Testament stories include only the better-known personalities. The New Testament has Jesus' birth and death, a few teachings and intermediate events, a bit of the early church, and a brief description of heaven from Revelation. Done in an easy style, with concepts on the level of young children. Big, simple pictures in color and black and white. Kindergarten to fourth grade.

45. Hodges, Turner. *The Bible Story Library*. 7 vols. Illus. Donald D. Wolf and Margot L. Wolf. Boston: Audel, 1963. 636p.

    Numerous Bible translations were used in preparing the text, and clergymen of all faiths have approved its faithfulness to Scripture. Serious, formal style. Murkily illustrated with poor quality reproductions of well-known paintings, Gustave Doré engravings, etc. Fifth grade and up.

46. Hoth, Iva. *The Picture Bible*. Illus. Andre Le Blanc. Elgin, Ill.: Cook, 1978. unp.

    Very colorful comic strip format presents the most popular events from the Old Testament and the Gospels plus some severely condensed versions of Hebrews, Jude, Revelation, and other New Testament books. Well-drawn figures. Appropriate explication and dialogue for interesting, easy reading. Less successful section on the history of the Bible itself. Fifth grade and up.

47. Hurlbut, Jesse Lyman. *Hurlbut's Story of the Bible: For Young and Old*. Illus. Ralph Pallen Coleman and Steele Savage. Grand Rapids: Zondervan, n.d. 821p.

    One hundred and sixty-eight stories from the Old Testament (Pentateuch, Joshua, Judges, Kings, the kingdoms of Israel and Judah) and the Gospels and Acts written in a didactic but sprightly style. Small, precise three-tone drawings decorate the text. Also contains groups of full-page, undistinguished color pictures situated far from their associated text. Thick and heavy. Pronouncing guide. Appendices include study questions, a history of each Biblical book, and maps. Fourth grade and up.

48. Lehn, Cornelia. *God Keeps His Promise: A Bible Story Book for Young Children*. Illus. Beatrice Darwin. Scottdale, Pa.: Herald, 1970. 192p.

Capsule versions of the most popular Old Testament stories run directly into selections from the Gospels and Acts, plus bits of Philippians and Revelation. Appealing, readable style. Small children can understand and appreciate the text, but it is very selective. Active, humorous, sketchy pictures in black and white and color. Preschool to third grade.

49. Lindvall, Ella K. *The Bible Illustrated for Little Children*. Illus. Paul Turnbaugh. Chicago: Moody, 1985. 191p.

Often confusing, incomplete, one-paragraph stories from the Old (89) and New (94) Testaments. Repetitive, condescending style; simplistic tone and language. Uses terms like "mommies and daddies" instead of "men and women." Inappropriate even for its intended audience of very young children. Strong, solid, color pictures are more mature than the text, but are sometimes careless. The same blind man is pictured with three different faces on three subsequent pages. Scripture references. Questions after each story. Preschool to first grade.

50. McCallen, A.J. *Listen! Themes from the Bible Retold for Children*. Illus. Ferelith Eccles Williams. Ann Arbor: Servant, 1976. 191p.

Bible stories and passages grouped by theme rather than being arranged chronologically. Some Apocrypha. Clear, easy language. Directed to children ten and under. Guide for parents and teachers, notes on the themes. Usefully indexed by people and places, topics, and words. Scripture citations (Jerusalem Bible). Appealing, often amusing, cartoon-type figures in both black and white and warmly colored pictures.

51. McCallen, A.J. *Praise! Songs and Poems from the Bible Retold for Children*. Illus. Ferelith Eccles Williams. Ann Arbor: Servant, 1979. 96p.

Modernized, freely translated selections from the Psalms are vigorous and easily understood. Material from Isaiah, Joel, Matthew, Luke, Ephesians, and Revelation is also included. Scripture citations, responses for worship. Jolly cartoon-style illustrations in warm colors and black and white show both Biblical and current situations. Kindergarten through fourth grade.

52. Maniscolo, Joe. *Bible Hero Stories*. Illus. author. Cincinnati: Standard, 1975. unp.

Joseph's story is told fairly completely, with an emphasis throughout on God's plan for him. Jesus' life is more condensed, with some highlights of his ministry and little about events after the Resurrection. Paul's career is outlined, and those who don't accept his teachings are called evil. Lucid, interesting style but personal bias. Many large, undistinguished illustrations in color and black and white. First to fourth grades.

53. Marshall, Catherine. *Catherine Marshall's Story Bible*. New York: Crossroad, 1982. 196p.

Perfect blend of big, brilliant illustrations by youthful artists from throughout the world and a colorful, easy-to-read text that covers a limited selection of the main Scriptural events smoothly and gracefully. Coffee table book format. Variety of artistic styles, some charmingly anachronistic. Personal Christian comment and interpretation by author. Kindergarten through adult.

54. Russell, Yvonne S. *My First Bible Word Book*. Illus. June Goldsborough. Chicago: Rand McNally, 1983. 60p.

Very short retellings of ten familiar Old Testament Bible stories and fifteen New Testament incidents from Jesus' life and teachings. Each is followed by a vocabulary list from the story. The words are to be matched with words identifying objects in the large accompanying color picture. Art-work has a lively, childlike quality. First to third grades.

55. Schoolland, Marian M. *Marian's Big Book of Bible Stories*. Illus. Dirk Gringhuis. Grand Rapids: Eerdmans, 1947. 351p.

Felicitous combination of good scope from creation through Acts, plus some of Revelation, a quick coverage of each story, short sentences, and lively writing. Occasional, very bright full page illustrations in pedestrian style. Perennial favorite. Indexed by Old and New Testament personalities. Guide to eleven of Jesus' parables. Kindergarten to fourth grade.

56. Stoddard, Sandol. *The Doubleday Illustrated Children's Bible*. Illus. Tony Chen. New York: Doubleday, 1983. 384p.

    Good basic collection in which both Testaments are successfully integrated into a dramatic narrative whole, with the stories flowing logically together. Puzzlingly, Moses' demotion from prince to shepherd is omitted, and the Song of Solomon is included. Text retains a dignified tone but is lightened enough for easy reading. Elegant, action-filled illustrations are not always keyed to the text. Scripture citations. Large, attractive format. Fifth grade and up.

57. Taylor, Kenneth N. *The Bible in Pictures for Little Eyes*. Chicago: Moody, 1956. 190p.

    Disjointed, sometimes confusing presentation of 183 one-paragraph stories written in a reading primer style. No transitions to connect the parts. Subjects are often introduced but never clarified, requiring adult explanation and input. No reason for the Flood is given until the end of the story. Satan tempts Eve directly; no snake is involved. Coverage ends with Paul's shipwreck. Language often mincing, as in "grape juice" instead of "wine." Illustrations resemble old Sunday school teaching pictures. Preschool to second grade.

58. Taylor, Kenneth N. *The Living Bible Story Book*. Illus. Richard Hook and Frances Hook. Wheaton, Ill.: Tyndale, 1979. 192p.

    Superficial, choppy collection with surprising omissions. Moses does not part the Red Sea, Jacob and Esau are not mentioned, David's career is limited to his defeat of Goliath, and so forth. Aggressively Christian tone. Jumps all the way from Esther to the Annunciation and ends with Jesus ascending into heaven. Discussion questions but no Scripture citations. Realistic illustrations show vigorous men, tender women, sweetfaced children, a gently powerful Jesus. They are not always associated with the text, however. Third to sixth grades.

59. Thompson, Jean Bernard. *Bible Stories in Rhyme*. Illus. Paul Turnbaugh. Chicago: Moody, 1986. 119p.

    Christian emphasis. Creation and the fall, Noah, Abraham, Joseph, and six more of the better known Old Testament stories and a précis of Jesus' life and teachings. Told in long poems firmly metered in iambic pentameter and trimeter. God's plan in history stressed. Competently written. Large type and numerous very brightly colored pictures. Scriptural references. Kindergarten to fourth grade.

60. Van Der Land, Sipke. *Stories from the Bible, Newly Retold*. Illus. Bert Bouman. Grand Rapids: Eerdmans, 1979. 205p.

    Stories are so freely reinterpreted that they are no longer truly Biblical. Burdened by gratuitous personal comment, destroying the succinct quality of the originals and adding an opinionated tone. Florid style. Illustrations portray Jesus as curly-haired and beardless. Handsome format. Middle elementary grades.

61. Van Ness, Bethann. *The Bible Story Book*. Illus. Harold Minton. Nashville: Broadman, 1963. 672p.

    Strong Christian tone dominates a simplified, cropped, and rearranged version of the Bible in a continuous narrative form. "Exploring the Bible" sections present interesting additional information on temples and synagogues, animals and plants, history, everyday life, etc. Story and person indexes. Sturdy illustrations. Third to sixth grades.

62. Wangerin, Walter. *The Bible: Its Story for Children*. Chicago: Rand McNally, 1981. 416p.

    Comprehensive, unbiased treatment of the Old and New Testaments as one extended story. Well integrated and written with vitality and imagination. Good coverage of Paul and the early Christian church. Ecumenical board of editorial consultants. Scripture references. Sweeping, brilliantly colored, expressive illustrations with captions. Maps, drawings, diagrams. Fifth grade and up.

63. Weed, Libby. *Read-n-Grow Picture Bible*. Illus. Jim Padgett. Ft. Worth, Tex.: Sweet, 1984. 319p.

    Introductory coverage includes Genesis and Exodus; Joshua, Deborah, Gideon, Ruth, Samson; Saul, David, and Solomon; Elijah, Joash, Jonah, Daniel, Esther, and Nehemiah; life of Jesus, best-known parables; life of Paul and other incidents from Acts. Comic strip format with brief, large print text. Each story is a separate, self-contained segment. Plain, straightforward presentation. Accurate, interesting pictures in deep colors. Scripture references. Suitable for adults of limited reading ability as well as children from fourth grade and up.

Miscellaneous

64. Adler, David A. *The Bible Fun Book*. New York: Bonim, 1979. 48p.

    Isaiah, Jonah, David, Jacob, Adam and Eve, Moses, Goliath, tower of Babel, Noah, Daniel, creation, and other Old Testament personalities and incidents are the themes of rebuses, mazes, riddles, scrambled words, arithmetic puzzles, magic tricks, identification quizzes and other learning entertainments. Drawings. Middle elementary grades and up.

65. Shofner, Myra. *The Ark Book of Riddles. The Second Ark Book of Riddles*. Illus. Dwight Walles. Elgin, Ill.: Cook, 1980, 1981. unp.

    Noah figures in many of these excruciating jokes, along with Abraham, Adam and Eve, Samson, Job, Paul, and others. Contains many plays on words with the various books of the Bible. Good child-level humor. Funny black-and-white drawings. Kindergarten to fourth grade.

OLD TESTAMENT

Story Collections

66. Bash, Ewald. *Legends from the Future*. Illus. Anne Gayler. New York: Friendship, 1972. 95p.

    Twentieth-century satiric updates of Adam and Eve, Cain and Abel, Noah, Abraham, Joseph, Exodus, and the tower of Babel indicate mankind hasn't improved over the centuries. Somewhat dated product of the 1960s but thought-provoking. Amusing, sketchy black-and-white pictures. Fifth grade and up.

67. Behnke, John. *10 + 1 Bible Stories from Creation to Samson: Retold in Everyday Language for Today's Children*. Illus. Gloria Claudia Ortiz. Ramsey, N.J.: Paulist, 1984. 60p.

    Modern, breezy, sometimes slangy retellings of creation, Adam and Eve, Cain and Abel, the flood, the tower of Babel, Abraham, Isaac, Jacob and Esau, Joseph, Moses, and Samson. Significant omissions and strange assumptions in some weaken their value: e.g., Rachel is called the mother of all of Jacob's children. Strong black-and-white drawings, not always associated with the accompanying text. Scripture references. Kindergarten and up.

68. Boone, Pat. *Pat Boone's Favorite Bible Stories for the Very Young*. Illus. Hans Wilhelm. New York: Random, 1984. 61p.

Creation, the garden of Eden, the flood, the tower of Babel, Joseph, Samson, David and Goliath, Daniel, and Jonah freely interpreted but reasonably faithful, told in a comfortable, conversational, lap-book style on a very young child's level of interest. Coy at times (Eve says, "Hi, Daddy" to God). Each story ends with a comment or question to reinforce a little lesson. Large watercolors in which the short, sturdy men look like children despite their beards. Winsome animals. Gentleness of pictures and text make possibly frightening stories non-threatening. Preschool to second grade.

69. De la Mare, Walter. *Stories from the Bible*. Illus. Edward Ardizzone. London: Faber, 1929. 418p.

Creatively embellished accounts of creation, the flood, Joseph, Moses, Samson, Samuel, and Saul. Personalities and Biblical backgrounds come to vivid life. Good reading skills required for musical, flowery style. Black-and-white cross-hatched drawings scattered throughout. Sixth grade and up.

70. Edwards, Anne. *A Child's Bible: The Old Testament*. Illus. Charles Front and David Christian. New York: Paulist, 1978. 374p.

Too many important portions of the Bible stories are omitted or overemphasized to make this an authoritative, accurate collection. Isaac's sacrifice and Hagar and Ishmael are completely left out of Abraham's account, while Lot's experiences are covered in detail, for example. Some quotations from Proverbs, Ecclesiastes, Psalms, the Song of Solomon are so superficial as to be superfluous. Smooth, readable style. Animated and bright pictures. Fourth grade and up.

71. Evslin, Bernard. *Signs and Wonders: Tales from the Old Testament*. Illus. Charles Mikolaycak. New York: Four Winds, 1981. 337p.

Impressive production in which text, illustrations, and

format harmonize in beauty and strength. Includes the creation, Adam and Eve, Cain and Abel, Noah, the tower of Babel, Abraham, Isaac, Jacob, Joseph, Moses, Deborah, Samson, portions of David, Solomon, Elijah, Jonah, Daniel, Esther, and Judith (from the Apocrypha). Elegant, dramatic, imaginative writing vivifies the familiar characters and events with rich detail yet retains authenticity. Muscular, sensuous, brooding black-and-white artwork. Sixth grade and up.

72. Gaines, M.C. *Picture Stories from the Bible: The Old Testament in Full-Color Comic Strip Form.* Illus. Don Cameron. New York: Scarf, 1979. 222p.

Poorly illustrated, brief versions of the main stories in comic strip panels. Formal, Biblical language. Scripture references. Approved by Catholic, Protestant, and Jewish clergymen. Third through sixth grades.

73. Hannon, Ruth. *Children's Bible Stories: From the Old Testament.* Illus. Joe Giordano. New York: Golden, 1978. 45p.

Delicate illustrations in soft colors are the best feature of the twenty-seven stories of Noah, Moses, Joseph, David, and other most popular topics. The text is so truncated that it often doesn't make much sense. Because so much is left out the collection is neither interesting nor useful. Kindergarten to fourth grade.

74. MacMaster, Eve. *God Comforts His People.* Illus. James Converse. Scottdale, Pa.: Herald, 1985. 181p. Story Bible Series.

Material from Kings, Chronicles, Jeremiah, Ezekiel, Lamentations, Isaiah, Ezra, Haggai, Zechariah, Obadiah, Malachi, Joel, and Nehemiah skillfully drawn together to picture the life of the Israelites in exile, the fall of Jerusalem, and the subsequent rebuilding of the Temple and the city, as well as the various prophets of the period and their messages. Also stories of Esther, Jonah, Job, Daniel, and a bit of Ecclesiastes. Fresh, accurate text. Black-and-white drawings. Fourth grade and up.

75. MacMaster, Eve. *God Gives the Land.* Illus. James Converse. Scottdale, Pa.: Herald, 1983. 175p. Story Bible Series.

Comprehensive story of Joshua from Rahab and the Israelite spies in Jericho through the division of Canaan among the twelve tribes. From Judges are included the worship of foreign gods and the Lord's punishments, Othniel, Ehud, Shamgar, Deborah and the defeat of Sisera, Gideon and the Midianites, Abimelech, Jephthah, Samson, the disgrace of the Benjamites, Ruth and Naomi. Very readable. Black-and-white drawings. Fourth grade and up.

76. MacMaster, Eve. *God's Chosen King*. Illus. James Converse. Scottdale, Pa.: Herald, 1983. 192p. Story Bible Series.

Stories of Samuel, Saul, and David are well amalgamated from I and II Samuel, I Chronicles. Translations of the 121st, 100th, 23rd, 127th, and 150th Psalms. Maps and line drawings. Informal but accurate style. Fourth grade and up.

77. MacMaster, Eve. *God's Family*. Illus. James Converse. Scottdale, Pa.: Herald, 1981. 166p. Story Bible Series.

Well-rounded accounts of the creation, the fall, Cain and Abel, Noah, the tower of Babel, Abraham and Isaac, Esau and Jacob, and Joseph. Flowing and cohesive narrative enriched with imaginative detail but faithful to the original. Associated Scripture cited. Plain black-and-white drawings. Fourth grade and up.

78. MacMaster, Eve. *God's Justice*. Illus. James Converse. Scottdale, Pa.: Herald, 1984. 167p. Story Bible Series.

Many elements well coordinated into a clear and logical narrative. Emphasizes the prophets and the various kings with whom they dealt. Biblical books include II Kings, II Chronicles, Amos, Hosea, Isaiah, Micah, Zepheniah, Jeremiah, Nahum, Habakkuk. Topics include the fall of Samaria, the defense of Jerusalem by the Lord, the visions of disaster, the last days of Judah, the fall of Jerusalem. Map. Has black-and-white drawings. Fourth grade and up.

79. MacMaster, Eve. *God's Wisdom and Power*. Illus. James Converse. Scottdale, Pa.: Herald, 1984. 168p. Story Bible Series.

Narrative drawn from I and II Kings, II Chronicles, Proverbs, and the Song of Songs. Includes the selection of Solomon as David's successor, the rebuilding of the Temple, prosperity, and the turning away from the Lord to idol worship; the division of the kingdom under Jeroboam and Rehoboam; the reign of Ahab and Jezebel and concomitant rulers (an unruly lot partial to idols and scornful of the prophets Elijah and Elisha). Very brief section from Proverbs. Occasional black-and-white drawings. Fourth grade and up.

80. Mitchell, Vic, illus. *Great Stories from the Bible.* Los Angeles: Intervisual Communications, 1985. unp.

Pared-down versions of Noah and the flood, the Israelites crossing the Red Sea, David fighting Goliath, Daniel and the lions, and Jonah in the fish are captions for full-page watercolors, large and serious, which change scenes when a tab is moved. Preschool to second grade.

81. O'Connor, Francine M. *Stories of God and His People from the Old Testament.* Illus. Kathryn Boswell. Liguori, Mo.: Liguori, 1984. 32p. The ABCs of Faith Series.

Comforting little poems about creation, God's promise to Abraham, Moses in the basket and with the burning bush, Joshua at Jericho, David and Goliath, a psalm of praise, Solomon's choice of wisdom, and Daniel and the lions. All have a message relating them to God's love and care for the reader. Decorated with cozy three-color drawings. Preschool to second grade.

82. Talec, Pierre. *In the Promised Land.* Minneapolis: Winston, 1983. unp. The Bible and Its Story Series.

Old Testament stories from the death of Moses through the death of David, from the books of Joshua, Judges, Samuel, and the beginning of I Kings. Matter-of-fact prose condensation of Scripture is accompanied by excellent study aids, giving historical, geographical, and cultural details and comments. Interpretation of text is symbolic rather than literal at times. Quotes from Today's English Version of the Bible. Large, varied format with text blocks broken up by splashy, action-filled illustrations by five artists. Imaginative maps. Fourth grade and up.

83. Wahl, Jan. *Runaway Jonah and Other Biblical Adventures.* Illus. Jane Conteh-Morgan. New York: Caedmon, 1985. unp.

Colorful, vivacious retellings of Jonah, David and Goliath, Joseph sold into slavery and reunited with his family (skips most of the middle part of his story), and Noah. Well-designed, one-dimensional pictures of naive figures done in poster paint shades and full of interesting movement. Preschool to third grade.

84. Whaley, Katherine L. *Bible Stories from Long Ago: Wisdom and Courage from the Old Testament for Life Today*. Illus. Edgar Blakeney. Englewood Cliffs, N.J.: Prentice-Hall, 1984. 262p.

Short, punchy narratives in storytelling style treat material from the creation through the reign of Solomon. Author's input on character and emotions of the people involved is sometimes condescending. Informal, colloquial text is usually successful but occasionally jars mood by being too slangy. Emphasizes the point that people haven't changed much over the centuries. Fifth grade and up.

Individual Stories

85. Brodsky, Beverly. *The Story of Job*. Illus. author. New York: Braziller, 1986. unp.

Concentrates on the ancient folktale of the man who remains steadfast under God's severe testing and is amply rewarded, rather than attempting to deal with the long debate about suffering. Job's painful feeling of separation from God is well brought out, as is the point that God's mystery and power are unknowable. Simplified and shortened text retains Biblical cadence and vocabulary. Mysterious watercolors filled with agitated black lines and flooded with lustrous color create a somber, awed mood. Kindergarten and up.

86. Chaikin, Miriam. *Joshua in the Promised Land*. Illus. David Frampton. New York: Clarion, 1982. 83p.

Carefully written narrative of Joshua's life as the leader of the Israelites into the Promised Land. Added dialogue and an imaginary family for Joshua add to the interest and believability of the biography without detracting from Biblical accuracy. Sturdy, suitable woodcuts. Fourth to sixth grades.

87. Cioni, Ray, and Sally Cioni. *The Droodles Storybook of Proverbs*. Elgin, Ill.: Cook, 1981. 63p.

In headache-bright colors the Droodles, squatty cartoon figures with big feet, romp through twelve proverbs dealing with discipline, pride, gentle answers, friendship, generosity, and other pertinent topics. Each is interpreted through a little story or poem featuring characters with jokey names and based on everyday experiences with family, friends, and schoolmates. Kindergarten to fourth grade.

88. Craig, Diana. *Jacob and Esau*. Illus. Leon Baxter. Morristown, N.J.: Silver Burdett, 1984. 22p.

Lively and creative retelling of the brothers' relationship from birth through Jacob's return with placatory gifts. Stresses the different personalities: hairy and tough versus smooth-skinned and clever. Funny color pictures of a skinny weak-eyed Isaac; ruddy, spaghetti-haired Esau; boyish, curly-topped Jacob. Bible reference. Kindergarten to second grade.

89. Fulbright, Robert G. *Old Testament Friends: Men of Courage*. Illus. Bill McPheeters. Nashville: Broadman, 1979. 48p. Biblearn Series.

Short, undistinguished, generally incomplete versions of Noah; Isaac, Rebecca, and King Abimilech; Jacob and Esau (nothing about Rachel, Leah, life in Haran); Joshua and Caleb (only their first sortie into Canaan and Moses' choice of Joshua as his successor); Nehemiah rebuilding Jerusalem; Ezra teaching God's law. Plain pictures in subdued colors. Thought-eliciting questions. No Bible references. Kindergarten to fourth grade.

90. Garfield, Leon. *The King in the Garden*. Illus. Michael Bragg. New York: Lothrop, 1984. unp.

Anachronistic, pretentious text tells of Nebuchadnezzar, who has been reduced by God to bestiality for seven years so that he will know the value of God's presence. Little girl finds the gross, unkempt king eating her flowers, trims and cleans him, and they return to his palace. Elaborate illustrations contrast the serene garden of bubbly pools and carefully tended plants with the vexed, tangle-haired, talon-nailed king, seen from interesting angles and perspectives. Kindergarten to fourth grade.

91. Heifner, Fred. *Isaiah: Messenger for God*. Illus. Cliff Johnston. Nashville: Broadman, 1978. 48p. Biblearn Series.

Some speculative details about Isaiah's youth and friendship with Jotham liven an otherwise basic, dryly factual account of his experiences with Uzziah, Ahaz, and Hezekiah, his call by the Lord to prophesy, and his foretelling of the Messiah (identified with Jesus). Skillful color pictures. First to fourth grades.

92. Holt, Pat. *Gideon--God's Warrior*. Illus. David Scott Brown. Nashville: Abingdon, 1986. unp.

    Basic retelling of the account of timid Gideon called by God to oppose the Midianites. After the proofs of the burnt offerings and the wet and dry fleece, he plucks up courage and attacks with torches, trumpets, and clay jars. Brisk, plain style. Nothing extra. Low key, crosshatched, full-page drawings in black, white, and coral. Kindergarten to fourth grade.

93. McElrath, William N. *Judges and Kings: God's Chosen Leaders*. Illus. Cliff Johnston. Nashville: Broadman, 1979. 48p. Biblearn Series.

    Condensed but faithful and interesting biographies of Gideon, Samson, Solomon, Joash, Hezekiah, and Josiah. Done in a readable, straightforward style, with discussion questions, Scripture citations, and brightly colored, appropriate pictures. First to fourth grades.

94. McMinn, Tom. *Prophets: Preachers for God*. Illus. H. Don Fields. Nashville: Broadman, 1970. 48p. Biblearn Series.

    Elisha, Amos, Jeremiah, Jonah, Micah have their lives and missions covered in factual manner. "Thinkback" sections at the end of each biography. Adequate summaries. Large type and colorful, active but rather flat artwork help enliven the text. Third to fourth grades.

95. Prokop, Phyllis. *The Sword and the Sundial*. Elgin, Ill.: Cook, 1981. 141p.

    King Hezekiah is presented in a dramatic, fictionalized biography. The incidents from his boyhood and early reign are climaxed by God's demolition of Sennacherib's troops. Stresses king's piety and respect for the prophecies of Isaiah. Somewhat overwritten but well researched. Fifth grade and up.

96. Round, Graham, illus. *Naaman and the Little Servant Girl*. Minneapolis: Winston, 1980. unp. Winston Windows to the Bible Series.

    A burly, curly Naaman, broken out in scary blotches (not called leprosy, however), seeks Elisha's help on the advice of his Hebrew slave girl and splashes vigorously in the River Jordan to be cured. Has an easy text. Hilarious cartoon pictures. Scripture citation. Kindergarten to third grade.

97. Round, Graham, illus. *Nehemiah Builds a City*. Minneapolis: Winston, 1980. unp. Winston Windows to the Bible Series.

Nehemiah, in exile in Babylon, is notified by scroll that Jerusalem is in ruins and is allowed to return home to rebuild the city with the help of God and his industrious friends, thus confounding Sanballat and Tobiah. Cartoon people, full of life and color, illustrate the story. Preschool to early elementary.

98. Singleton, Kathy. *Gideon the Brave*. Illus. Arthur Baker. St. Louis: Concordia, 1982. unp. Palm Tree Bible Stories Series.

Gideon, faithful to God while the other Israelites are worshiping idols, is commissioned to lead an army against the Midianites. To show God's glory the army is reduced drastically in size but still routs the enemy from Israel. Funny illustrations. Preschool to second grade.

Individual Stories

ABRAHAM AND ISAAC

99. Cohen, Barbara. *The Binding of Isaac*. Illus. Charles Mikolaycak. New York: Lothrop, 1978. unp.

Isaac, old and blind, tells his twelve grandsons and one granddaughter about the time when he, Abraham's pampered darling, accompanied his father on a strange and frightening trip to the top of Mt. Moriah and was saved from being sacrificed by the voice of God. Sober, thoughtful tone. Stresses obedience to God. Splendid, powerful illustrations of virile, nearly nude figures. Fourth grade and up.

100. Golann, Cecil P. *Mission on a Mountain: The Story of Abraham and Isaac*. Illus. H. Hechtkopf. Minneapolis: Lerner, 1974. unp.

Unusual version in which Abraham carelessly gives Isaac a magnificent birthday party without inviting any poor people. A delighted Satan accuses Abraham of disobedience and evil. Thus God is goaded into ordering Isaac's sacrifice as proof of Abraham's loyalty. Handsome, stylized color pictures. Limited usage. Kindergarten to third grade.

101. McKissack, Frederick, and Patricia McKissack. *Abram, Abram, Where Are We Going?* Illus. Joe Boddy. Elgin, Ill.: Chariot, 1984. 64p.

Abraham's principal experiences--the wanderings, stay in Egypt, division of territory with Lot, birth and sacrifice of Isaac, finding of Rebecca--told in humorous, lively style. Second grade reading level, with early elementary vocabulary, repetition, short sentences. Contains accurate information, Scripture citations, and black-and-white drawings. Preschool to second grade.

102. McMeekin, Barbara. *Abraham's Big Family*. Illus. Arthur Baker. St. Louis: Concordia, 1983. unp. Palm Tree Bible Stories Series.

Easy-to-read retelling in which Abraham and Sarah leave their big house in Ur in response to the true God, who promises to make a mighty nation of them. Twenty-four years later they are still without a baby, but three men visit them in their tent camp to renew God's promise. Sarah laughs, but Isaac is born a year later. Very amusing color pictures. Preschool to second grade.

103. Rives, Elsie. *Abraham: Man of Faith*. Illus. William N. McPheeters. Nashville: Broadman, 1976. 48p. Biblearn Series.

Limited but serviceable account of Abraham's wanderings, including the incident with Pharaoh in Egypt, Isaac's birth, and the bringing of Rebecca to be his wife. Among episodes eliminated are the rescue of Lot and his family, the sacrifice of Isaac, Hagar and Ishmael. Pedestrian style; rather garish pictures. Many discussion questions and practical applications for today. Third to sixth grades.

104. Schindler, Regine. *A Miracle for Sarah*. Illus. Eleonore Schmid. Nashville: Abingdon, 1984. unp.

In short sentences Abram and Sarai's wanderings, Abram's personal relationship with God, and Sarai's intense longing for a child are effectively described on a young child's level. Story ends with a feast to celebrate Isaac's third year of life. Nothing about Hagar and Ishmael nor the deception in Egypt. Illustrations in muted colors have a solid, still quality. Kindergarten to third grade.

105. Singer, Isaac Bashevis. *The Wicked City*. Illus. Leonard Everett Fisher. New York: Farrar, 1972. 40p.

Lot and his daughters are a selfish bunch who are humiliated by the fusty appearance of their uncle but anxious to inherit his wealth. They generously allow him to persuade them to leave Sodom. Vivid, imaginative, sharply written. Illustrated with monumental figures as solid as if they were carved from wood, yet full of expressive vigor, in mahogany brown and white. Third to sixth grades.

CREATION

106. Davidson, Alice Joyce. *The Story of Creation*. Illus. Victoria Marshall. Norwalk, Conn.: Gibson, 1984. unp. Alice in Bibleland Series.

Little pigtailed Alice steps through her magic Bible storybook to see God's creation of the world from the dark, swirling void. The seven stages are shown in delicate, pastel pictures and described in simple rhymes. Preschool to third grade.

107. Fisher, Leonard Everett. *The Seven Days of Creation*. Illus. author. New York: Holiday, 1981. unp.

Spare and dignified text covering the splendor of creation from the void to Adam is illumined by magnificent acrylic paintings boldly designed with simplified, strong forms, dynamic rhythms, glowing colors. Preschool and up.

108. Heine, Helme. *One Day in Paradise*. Illus. author. New York: Atheneum, 1986. unp.

Bearded God in broad-brimmed hat and artist's smock spends five days in hard work building the heavens, laying out gardens, sculpting animals, etc. On the sixth he retires to his studio to design his masterpieces, a little boy Adam and a little girl Eve. He gives them Paradise as their playground. Tender, simple text expresses God's love for and pleasure in his creations. Joyful, softly gleaming watercolors show wooly mammoths, polar bears on an iceberg in a tropical river, the children astride huge, leaping panthers, and other imaginative scenes. Preschool to third grade.

109. Kasuya, Masahiro, illus. *The Beginning of the World*. Nashville: Abingdon, 1982. unp.

Charmingly childlike and unusual evocation of the seven days of creation done with simple shapes and sweeps of luminous color. The Sabbath is simply a blaze of golden yellow. One or two short, appropriate lines of text per page. Preschool to second grade.

110. Miyoshi, Sekiya. *The Oldest Story in the World*. Illus. author. Valley Forge, Pa.: Judson, 1969. unp.

Deceptively primitive yet sophisticated illustrations resembling colored chalk drawings on a blackboard and poster paints on shiny paper picture creation with simple exuberance. The void is a solid black page. At the end Adam and Eve are created simultaneously, given the marvelous gift of speech and proceed to name the quarreling animals. Imaginative, poetic text. Preschool to third grade.

111. Noe, Tom. *The Sixth Day*. Illus. Vernon McKissack. Notre Dame, Ind.: Ave Maria, 1979. unp.

Gathered around a churning patch of dirt which eventually forms a man, the newly created animals are critical of his value until he sings a beautiful song of praise to God and draws all of creation together. Chatty style. Whimsical pictures in orange, brown, black, and white. Kindergarten to fourth grade.

112. Reed, Allison, illus. *Genesis*. New York: Schocken, 1981. unp.

The seven days of creation, King James version, illustrated in an explosion of color and beauty, from the roiling chaos of the void to the pale, monumental figures of Adam and Eve awakening in a lush Eden. Dense and filled with forms and movement. Coffee table book. Text, superimposed upon a busy background, can be hard to read. All ages.

113. Schindler, Regine. *God's Creation--My World*. Illus. Hilde Heyduck-Huth. Nashville: Abingdon, 1982. unp.

Text is like a long, fervent, poetic prayer praising God's creation in order: the blue ball of the earth; the sky, water, and land; plants and animals; and the most remarkable creatures of all, human beings with their marvelous hands, brains, accomplishments. But God's presence is needed badly now because they have polluted the earth and not cared for one another properly. Asks for love and understanding. Full-page, pensive pictures in subdued colors and flat patterns are appropriate to theme but not appealing to small children. Kindergarten to third grade.

114. Weil, Lisl. *The Very First Story Ever Told*. Illus. author. New York: Atheneum, 1976. unp.

The creation, the Garden of Eden, and the fall of little boy Adam and little girl Eve are described simply, on the level of very small children. Even the pictures, done in swoops of gray on a dull gold background, look like a happy kindergartener's daubs with a paintbrush. Preschool.

DANIEL

115. Daly, Kathleen N. *Daniel in the Lions' Den*. Illus. Jim Cummins. Chicago: Rand McNally, 1984. unp. My First Bible Board Book Series.

Neat presentation of the basic plot: King Darius makes Daniel his chief ruler, and jealous princes trick the king into proclaiming a new law which will automatically condemn Daniel to death in the jaws of the lions. God saves him, of course. Reassuring pictures in warm colors show a young, modest, pious Daniel; sly, hunched princes; and almond-eyed, affectionate lions (who do not get to eat the princes in this version). Preschool.

116. Garfield, Leon. *The Writing on the Wall*. Illus. Michael Bragg. New York: Lothrop, 1983. unp.

In this version of Belshazzar's feast, Samuel, a skinny kitchen-boy, is ordered rudely about by haughty guests who stuff themselves with goodies blasphemously served on holy vessels from the Temple. When a giant hand begins inscribing on the wall, a stern Daniel with a floor-length beard is summoned to interpret the dreadful message. Misses the point of the Bible story. Big, sweeping color pictures of dissolute courtiers and grotesque gods seen from unusual angles. Kindergarten to third grade.

117. Heath, Lou. *Daniel, Faithful Captive*. Illus. J. William Myers. Nashville: Broadman, 1977. 47p. Biblearn Series.

Simple biographical narrative of Daniel's experiences with Nebuchadnezzar, Belshazzar, and Darius. Discussion questions relate Daniel's actions to those of people in modern day situations. No Scripture references. Somber color pictures. Third to fifth grades.

118. Hollyer, Belinda. *Daniel in the Lions' Den*. Illus. Leon Baxter. Morristown, N.J.: Silver Burdett, 1983. 22p.

Straightforward, colorful narrative tells something of Daniel's early life as well as the lion portion. Amusing pictures in soft tones of fat and skinny princes, an ascetic Daniel, cranky lions changing to purring pets. Kindergarten to fourth grade.

119. Petach, Heidi. *Daniel and the Lions*. Illus. author. Cincinnati: Standard, 1984. unp.

Very simple but complete statement of Daniel's problem with King Darius's decree and the happy resolution. The evil courtiers are eaten in the end. Text well matched by saucy, cartoon-style color pictures showing nastily sneering courtiers, calm and cotton-haired Daniel, chop-licking lions. Scripture reference. Preschool to second grade.

DAVID

120. Bennett, Marian. *David, the Shepherd*. Illus. Dick Wahl. Cincinnati: Standard, 1984. unp.

David as a youth, caring for his sheep, saving them from a bear and a lion, singing songs to God with his harp under a tree. Includes text of Twenty-third Psalm. Short, easy sentences. Undistinguished color pictures of young boy in a yellow tunic with his flock in a grassy countryside. Preschool.

121. Brin, Ruth. *David and Goliath*. Illus. H. Hechtkopf. Minneapolis: Lerner, 1977. unp.

Well-done, convincing narrative of David's childhood includes his training as a shepherd, his love of music, his slaughter of the huge lion and is climaxed by the battle with Goliath. Handsome, rather flat and stylized illustrations in muted colors. Kindergarten to third grade.

122. De Paola, Tomie. *David and Goliath*. Illus. author. Minneapolis: Winston, 1984. unp.

Dignified, simple retelling of David's trip to Saul's

army camp, Goliath's insulting challenges, and the famed battle. Witty, well-balanced illustrations show a very young boy with dark brown curls and a spiritual face and a toothy giant dressed in pink and gold. Cutouts to be mounted for puppets included. Preschool to second grade.

123. Hollaway, Lee. *David: Shepherd, Musician, and King.* Illus. Paul Karch. Nashville: Broadman, 1977. 48p. Biblearn Series.

Plain text begins with Samuel anointing David. Includes fight with Goliath, friendship with Jonathan, pursuit by Saul, Bathsheba. Rest of life is severely telescoped. Discussion questions. Unpretentious color illustrations. Third to fifth grades.

124. Hollyer, Belinda. *David and Goliath.* Illus. Leon Baxter. Morristown, N.J.: Silver Burdett, 1984. 22p.

Lively narrative of young David's exploits includes killing the lion, entertaining King Saul with harp music, polishing off Goliath (a pin-headed giant). Funny, busy, caricature color pictures. Kindergarten to third grade.

125. Patterson, Lillie. *David: The Story of a King.* Illus. Charles Cox. Nashville: Abingdon, 1985. 96p.

Absorbing presentation of David's life, faithful to the Bible but enlivened by imaginative details. Lengthy and thorough coverage of most of the main events. Many Psalms integrated into the text as songs David composed for various occasions. Black-and-white drawings. No Scripture citations. Fifth and sixth grades.

126. Williams-Ellis, Virginia. *David the Shepherd Boy.* Illus. Anna Dzierzek. Milwaukee: Ideals, 1981. unp.

Sweetened version of David's boyhood, telling of his bravery protecting his flock from bears and lions, his anointment by Samuel, his summons to court to soothe King Saul with song. Garish illustrations. Preschool to kindergarten.

ELIJAH

127. Craig, Diana. *Elijah, Messenger of God.* Illus. Leon Baxter. Morristown, N.J.: Silver Burdett, 1984. 22p.

In entertaining prose Elijah cautions Ahab, eats from ravens' beaks, lodges with the widow and resurrects her son, and bests the Baal priests. Vigorous, amusing color pictures. Kindergarten to third grade.

128. Entz, Angeline J. *Elijah the Prophet*. Illus. H. Don Fields. Nashville: Broadman, 1978. 48p. Biblearn Series.

Begins with Elijah's prophecy to Ahab about the coming drought, includes his flight into the desert, his sojourn with the widow of Zarephata, the contest between the priests of Baal and Jahweh, the still small voice of God heard in the cave, and the choosing of Elisha as his successor. Interestingly written, with short sentences and passable color illustrations. Third and fourth grades

129. Round, Graham, illus. *Elijah and the Great Drought*. Minneapolis: Winston, 1980. unp.

Slovenly Ahab rejects God's message, via Elijah, to reform. The drought follows, and the prophet takes shelter with a poor widow. Consequently, her jars of oil and flour become inexhaustible. A tidy retelling, with funny, eye-appealing cartoon art. Kindergarten to second grade.

ESTHER

130. Brin, Ruth F. *The Story of Esther*. Illus. H. Hechtkopf. Minneapolis: Lerner, 1976. unp.

Purim story retold in fairy-tale fashion and enhanced with appealing details. Perfect blend of text and illustrations. Artistically balanced, decorative, lively pictures show a plump and spoiled Ahasuerus, dignified Mordecai, prune-faced Haman, dainty Esther, etc. Kindergarten to fourth grade.

131. Mitchell, Kurt, illus. *Esther*. Elgin, Ill.: Cook, 1983. unp.

Excerpts from the Book of Esther, New International Version of the Bible, give a full picture of Esther's heroism in saving the Jews in Persia. Brightly colored, full-page illustrations depict Xerxes as a St. Bernard dog, Haman as a wolf, Esther as a curly ewe, Mordecai as a solemn ram, and the Persians as various other anthropomorphic animals. Odd combination of serious text and lighthearted artwork. Kindergarten to fourth grade.

132. Weil, Lisl. *Esther*. Illus. author. New York: Atheneum, 1980. unp.

Amusing, bold illustrations in black and blue on white enliven an informally told version of the Purim tale, as Esther gathers her courage and wit to foil the evil Haman. Kindergarten to fourth grade.

JONAH

133. Briscoe, Jill. *Jonah and the Worm*. Illus. Tom Armstrong and Florence Davis. Nashville: Nelson, 1983. 143p.

Little Worm is chosen by God for a mysterious mission (eventually revealed as devouring Jonah's sheltering vine) and leaves his friends and relatives at the pond to journey to Nineveh. His sacrificial obedience to God's will is contrasted with Jonah's rebellious attitude. God is called the Wonder Worker, and everything else is personified, many with coy names. Effusive, sentimental style. Anachronistic details such as running shoes and contact lens. Talk Time and Prayer Time sections after each chapter. Appealing black-and-white drawings. Kindergarten to fourth grade.

134. Daly, Kathleen N. *Jonah and the Great Fish*. Illus. Jim Cummins. Chicago: Rand McNally, 1984. unp. My First Bible Board Book Series.

Bare facts of the story simply told and highlighted by brilliantly colored, spirited pictures of a ship with a red-striped sail pitching in turquoise waters and a giant shark speeding off with Jonah in its smiling mouth. Preschool.

135. Davidson, Alice Joyce. *The Story of Jonah*. Illus. Victoria Marshall. Norwalk, Conn.: Gibson, 1984. unp. Alice in Bibleland Series.

Stepping through a magic book into Bibleland, Alice watches as Jonah tries unsuccessfully to evade God's directive and continues to resent the Ninevites even after they repent. Both he and Alice learn that God sees everywhere, expects obedience, and forgives lovingly. The illustrations are done in muted shades. Preschool to second grade.

136. Haiz, Danah. *Jonah's Journey*. Illus. H. Hechtkopf. Minneapolis: Lerner, 1973. unp.

Imaginative but faithful narrative opens in Nineveh where well-fed citizens sneer at ragged beggars, then proceeds to a mournful Jonah, his disastrous sea voyage, disappointment at Nineveh, and final realization of God's power and wisdom. The people in the clever color illustrations are full of personality. Kindergarten to fourth grade.

137. Hollyer, Belinda. *Jonah and the Great Fish*. Illus. Leon Baxter. Morristown, N.J.: Silver Burdett, 1984. 22p.

Witty, colorfully written version does not include the end of the story in which the plant that shaded Jonah withers but includes God's message about the value of repentant people, even Ninevites. Hilarious pictures include a pale-faced Jonah amid reeking seaweed and entrails inside the fish's belly. Kindergarten to third grade.

138. Hutton, Warwick. *Jonah and the Great Fish*. Illus. author. New York: Atheneum, 1984. unp.

Simplified Biblical text follows the main events of Jonah's adventures but omits his hatred for the Ninevites, the withered vine, and God's explanation of why he spared the former sinners. Wonderfully foamy, windy, storm-tossed watercolors in sea greens and blues. Humorous touches, as when Jonah lies, depressed, on a heap of sea creatures inside the great fish's multi-ribbed belly. Preschool and up.

139. Lindvall, Ella K. *Jonah and the Great Fish*. Illus. Barry Wilkinson. Chicago: Moody, 1984. 32p.

Jonah's story from the time he takes ship for Tarshish through the repentant Ninevites donning sackcloth, in easy-to-read text. Exciting, carefully detailed illustrations of foam-beaded waves, a red-mawed whale, elegant Nineveh, etc. Kindergarten to third grade.

140. Miyoshi, Sekiya, illus. *Jonah and the Big Fish*. Nashville: Abingdon, 1982. unp.

Simple retelling of Jonah's tale is gaily illuminated by pictures done in a child-like abstract style and lit by blocks of vivid color and gentle humor. God's rainbow-colored great fish keeps an eye on Jonah from beginning to end. Preschool to second grade.

141. Spier, Peter. *The Book of Jonah*. Illus. author. Garden City, N.Y.: Doubleday, 1985. unp.

Clear, dignified language, translated from seventeenth-century Dutch text, the Statenbybel, tells Jonah's entire story. Translucent colors light the witty, meticulous paintings of Jonah bundling a bag of belongings to rush to Joppa, sloshing amid seaweed and squid in the fish's belly, shouting his warnings in a magnificently detailed Nineveh, etc. Afterword includes maps, diagrams, historical information. Preschool and up.

JOSEPH

142. Cohen, Barbara. *I Am Joseph*. Illus. Charles Mikolaycak. New York: Lothrop, 1980. unp.

Beautiful format presents serious, poetic, accurate text and exciting, well-researched, powerful illustrations of semi-nude, virile men and lush women. For skillful, mature readers. Sixth grade and up.

143. Daly, Kathleen N. *Joseph and His Brothers*. Illus. Jim Cummins. Chicago: Rand McNally, 1984. unp. My First Bible Board Book Series.

So much is left out that Joseph's story doesn't make much sense. Cheerful, bright pictures show Joseph's brothers in strange striped and patterned loin cloths and off-one-shoulder robes, Pharaoh with many jewels and an alley cat. Preschool.

144. Lindvall, Ella K. *Joseph and His Brothers*. Illus. Chris Molan. Chicago: Moody, 1983. 32p.

Identical in format and illustrations to *Joseph and His Brothers* by Catherine Storr (item 149), with a slight change in text. Preschool to second grade.

145. Lindvall, Ella K. *Joseph and the King*. Illus. Chris Molan. Chicago: Moody, 1984.

Identical in format and illustrations to *Joseph the Dream Teller* by Catherine Storr (item 150). Text is modified to emphasize God's plan for Joseph. Kindergarten to second grade.

146. McMeekin, Barbara. *Joseph the Dreamer*. Illus. Arthur Baker. St. Louis: Concordia, 1983. unp. Palm Tree Bible Stories Series.

Peppy, informal but accurate version of Joseph's early life through his sale to Potiphar. Funny, expressive pictures in earth tones of beak-nosed, bead-eyed people. Scripture reference. Preschool to second grade.

147. Steele, Philip. *Joseph and His Coat of Many Colors*. Illus. Leon Baxter. Morristown, N.J.: Silver Burdett, 1985. 22p.

Breezy, creative retelling from Jacob's gift to Joseph of the colorful coat through his appointment by Pharaoh as supervisor of the grain warehouses. Much dialogue. Humorous, clear-cut, cartoon-style full-page pictures in watercolor tones of beardless brothers with wildly curly hair and tubby, bald Egyptians. Scripture reference. Third and fourth grades.

148. Steele, Philip. *Joseph and His Brothers*. Illus. Leon Baxter. Morristown, N.J.: Silver Burdett, 1985. 22p.

Joseph as a powerful Egyptian official from the beginning of the drought through his reunion with Jacob. Basic facts told simply and vividly in effectively shortened form. Joseph stresses his slavery in Egypt as part of God's plan to save his family. Funny cartoon illustrations in clear colors entertain more than elucidate. Scripture references. Third and fourth grades.

149. Storr, Catherine. *Joseph and His Brothers*. Illus. Chris Molan. Milwaukee: Raintree, 1982. 32p. People of the Bible Series.

Concise, simple text tells the story through Joseph's sale into slavery. Handsome, realistic illustrations show the sullen brothers as beardless teenagers and Joseph as a young boy. Authentic backgrounds. Preschool to second grade.

150. Storr, Catherine. *Joseph the Dream Teller*. Illus. Chris Molan. Milwaukee: Raintree, 1983. 32p. People of the Bible Series.

Joseph's career in Egypt: as Potiphar's overseer, betrayed by Potiphar's wife, interpreting the butler's and baker's dreams in prison, summoned before Pharaoh to explain the dream of the cattle, promotion to governor. Simply expressed text. Powerful pictures in luminous colors. Kindergarten to third grade.

151. Sommers, Jester. *Joseph: The Forgiver*. Illus. Michael Sloan. Nashville: Broadman, 1976. 48p. Biblearn Series.

Facts well drawn together in basic, easy-to-read biography which begins with six-year-old Joseph returning with his family to Canaan and ends with Jacob's death. Crisp artwork in attractive but unrealistic colors. Second to fourth grades.

152. Webber, Andrew Lloyd. *Joseph and the Amazing Technicolor Dreamcoat*. Illus. Quentin Blake. New York: Holt, 1982. unp.

Joseph's brothers are a seedy bunch of hippies, Pharaoh is natty in a white suit and gold neckchain, and Potiphar resembles a Czarist general in the hilarious illustrations that accompany the jazzy libretto of the rock opera originally written for children. Fresh and funny while remaining true to the Bible story. No music. Kindergarten and up.

MOSES

153. Hall, Rachel. *Escape through the Sea*. Illus. Arthur Baker. St. Louis: Concordia, 1983. unp. Palm Tree Bible Stories Series.

Truncated. God loves the Israelites, decides to free them from brickmaking and other drudgery, sends a few plagues down on Egypt (no killing of the firstborn). Passover is only a time for special food and prayer. At length the Egyptian army becomes ripples on the Red Sea and the Hebrews give thanks. Amusing, cartoony pictures. Preschool to fourth grade.

154. Hutton, Warwick. *Moses in the Bulrushes*. Illus. author. New York: Atheneum, 1986. unp.

Stately, simple text describes Pharaoh's decree, Moses' birth and early babyhood, his rescue from the ark by Pharaoh's daughter, and his adoption. Large, tender, pensive watercolors in subdued tones capture the magnificence of the Egyptian palace and the elegant princess. the cool blue of the Nile with its boats, birds, and beasts, and the rude but loving Hebrew home where the baby is nurtured. Preschool to third grade.

155. McKissack, Fredrick, and Patricia McKissack. *Look What You've Done Now, Moses.* Illus. Joe Boddy. Elgin, Ill.: Chariot, 1984. 64p.

Using basic early elementary vocabulary, short sentences, repetition, and much lively dialogue, Moses' life from the basket in the reeds to the glimpse of the promised land from Mt. Nebo's peak is told well. Brisk and up to date in language, fast-moving, interesting. Scripture citations. Busy black-and-white drawings in cartoon style. Preschool to second grade.

156. Mahany, Patricia Shely. *Baby Moses in a Basket.* Illus. Helen Endres. Cincinnati: Standard, 1984. unp.

Seen through the eyes of sister Miriam and brother Aaron, Moses is born, concealed from Pharaoh's soldiers, set afloat in the river, and adored by the Egyptian princess. Sentimentalized pictures of plump children and sweetfaced maidens in bright colors. Scripture reference. Preschool to kindergarten.

157. Mee, Charles L. *Moses, Moses.* Illus. Ken Munowitz. New York: Harper, 1977. unp.

Witty black-and-white full-page pictures, fresh and sophisticated in design and balance, show squatty figures with big, expressive eyes. Emphasizes the experience of being tiny and alone in the bulrushes, seeing fascinating creatures by day and scary eyes at night. Very simple text details baby Moses' story from Pharaoh's fear of the growing numbers of Hebrews through the fortuitous engagement of Moses' very own mother by Pharaoh's daughter to be his nurse. Preschool to second grade.

158. Round, Graham, illus. *Miriam and the Princess of Egypt.* Minneapolis: Winston, 1980. unp.

Effective retelling shows the anxiety of the Hebrew family over the mischievous baby Moses' safety, the delight of the long-eyed Egyptian maidens when they find the basket, and the joy of Miriam when she produces the perfect nurse. All in bright and appealing cartoon form. Scripture cited. Kindergarten to second grade.

159. Williams-Ellis, Virginia. *Moses in the Bulrushes.* Illus. Anna Dzierzek. Milwaukee: Ideals, 1981. unp.

Moses is born into an elegantly dressed Hebrew family, tenderly tucked into his reed basket, and discovered by Pharaoh's daughter, who is attended to by a dazzling array of handmaidens. When he is old enough to join the princess in the palace, he is a beautiful blue-eyed blond lad. Simple, straightforward text and very colorful, busy format. Preschool.

160. Young, William E. *Moses: God's Helper*. Illus. J. William Myers. Nashville: Broadman, 1976. 48p. Biblearn Series.

Choppily written retelling of Moses' entire life. Aaron's role in Egypt is unclear. Plagues are glossed over quickly. Wanderings in the wilderness, the Ten Commandments, and construction of the tabernacle are better handled. Factual tone. Discussion questions. Dramatic, colorswept illustrations. No Scripture references. Kindergarten to fourth grade.

NOAH

161. Bolliger, Max. *Noah and the Rainbow: An Ancient Story*. Illus. Helga Aichinger. New York: Crowell, 1972. unp.

The flood story told in basic, rhythmic language. Exceptional, subtly colored illustrations show one-dimensional forms arranged with vigor and freshness on the large pages that extract the essence of each subject pictured. Preschool to second grade.

162. Burnford, Sheila. *Mr. Noah and the Second Flood*. Illus. Michael Foreman. New York: Praeger, 1973. 64p.

Mr. James Noah and his family, direct descendants of the original, live alone on a mountain top with a group of animals. When man's pollution causes the world to decay, and heavy rains begin, the Noahs make a new ark and gather the remnants of the animal kingdom within it. Cleverly written and sharply satirical. Sturdy black-and-white drawings. Fifth grade and up.

163. Cartwright, Ann. *Norah's Ark*. Illus. Reg Cartwright. New York: Messner, 1984. unp.

Based on the Noah story, Norah and her animals at Puddle Farm are frightened when the television news announces a coming flood. They use an old barn turned upside down for an ark, and the mischievous animals have adventures until the waters recede and leave them a fine big farm pond. Flat, handsome illustrations have primitive peasant charm, interesting patterns. Crowded, abundant text. Kindergarten to third grade.

164. Cohen, Barbara. *Unicorns in the Rain*. New York: Atheneum, 1980. 164p.

Sensitive teenaged girl encounters an attractive young man on a train and is persuaded to visit a country house where his mysterious family is collecting pairs of animals and building an ark. They have warned their neighbors of an impending deluge, but no one believes them. Skillfully written and suspenseful projection of the flood into a future setting of a dreary, amoral, violent world. Sixth grade and up.

165. Daly, Kathleen N. *Noah and the Ark*. Illus. Jim Cummins. Chicago: Rand McNally, 1984. unp. My First Bible Board Book Series.

Abridged version gives no reason for the flood, concentrates on the many types of birds, animals, insects, and reptiles going up and down the gangplank of a big red ark. Fun for very small children. Jolly, colorful pictures. Preschool to kindergarten.

166. Davidson, Alice Joyce. *The Story of Noah*. Illus. Victoria Marshall. Norwalk, Conn.: Gibson, 1984. unp. Alice in Bibleland Series.

After Alice studies about Noah in Bible school, one rainy day she steps through a magic screen and views the story of the flood, beginning with wicked people fighting and ending with the disembarkation of the ark passengers. Returning home, she sees the rainbow and gives thanks to God for his loving care. Dainty pictures in light colors. Rhymed text. Kindergarten to second grade.

167. De Paola, Tomie. *Noah and the Ark*. Illus. author. Minneapolis: Winston, 1983. unp.

Simple, accurate text, stressing the promise of the rainbow. The illustrations of elegant, still, one-dimensional figures in medieval dress are done in muted colors. Preschool through second grade.

168. Elborn, Andrew. *Noah and the Ark and the Animals*. Illus. Ivan Gantscher. Salzburg: Neugebauer, 1984 (distributed by Alphabet, Natick, Mass.). unp.

During a prolonged rain a mare tells her colt the story of the flood in a fairly simple, all-inclusive way, beginning with the bad people and good Noah and extending through the promise of the rainbow. Every time the colt sees a rainbow, he will remember it is the symbol of God's covenant never to overwhelm the world again.

Rainy feeling in washy watercolors of big-eyed animals. Text and pictures well laid out. Kindergarten to fourth grade.

169. Farber, Norma. *How the Left-behind Beasts Built Ararat*. Illus. Antonio Frasconi. New York: Walker, 1978. unp.

Clever verse describes an ingenious way to save all the animals from the flood. After forming a committee for Staying Alive, they build a tremendous mountain (Ararat) and crowd together on it until the rain stops and the earth renews. Sophisticated vocabulary. Big, bold, three-color woodcuts. Kindergarten to third grade.

170. Haubensak-Tellenbach, Margrit. *Noah's Ark*. Illus. Erna Emhardt. New York: Crown, 1983. 25p.

Forthright, generally faithful text, embellished with details of the animals and their feelings. Strong reading appeal. Eyefilling églomise paintings done in radiant colors and a primitive style are crowded with gorgeous pairs of birds, beasts, and insects, plus intricate flowery, leafy landscapes. Kindergarten to third grade.

171. Hewitt, Kathryn. *Two by Two: The Untold Story*. Illus. author. New York: Harcourt, 1984. unp.

Anachronistic version in which Noah is mowing his lawn when God's messenger, wearing a bellman's outfit, brings him blueprints for the ark. To lure the animals, anthropomorphic in dress and behavior, Noah offers a cruise ship. Cranky at first during the rain, the passengers learn from Noah how to be happy together both on and off the ship. Funny, busy, cleverly detailed watercolors. Preschool to second grade.

172. Hutton, Warwick. *Noah and the Great Flood*. Illus. author. New York: Atheneum, 1977. unp.

Vast size of the ark, destructiveness of the deluge (drownings and skeletons), and isolation of the survivors are stressed in big, handsome watercolor illustrations. Simplified version of King James text. Preschool to second grade.

173. Lenski, Lois. *Mr. and Mrs. Noah*. Illus. author. New York: Crowell, 1948. unp.

The Noahs, red-cheeked wooden dolls, gather the animals, birds, and insects into a cozy, red-roofed ark and look after them carefully until the dove returns with her green leaf. The Noahs' sons have no wives, but otherwise the simply told story is close enough to the original. Jolly pictures in primary colors. Preschool to first grade.

174. Lindvall, Ella K. *Noah and His Ark*. Illus. Jim Russell. Chicago: Moody Press, 1983. 32p.

Imaginative, simple text includes enlivening details such as Noah's assigning feeding, cleaning, and cooking chores to each member of his family. Animated watercolors include cutaway version of the multi-decked ark loaded with animals and a fine parade of beasts winding down Mt. Ararat. Preschool to second grade.

175. Lorimer, Lawrence T. *Noah's Ark*. Illus. Charles E. Martin. New York: Random House, 1978. unp.

Busy scenes of Noah and his sons getting the ark together, the paired creatures being loaded and tended, the choppy waves of the flood, and the joyful disembarkation under a broad rainbow have great charm and humor. Lively, accurate text. Preschool to second grade.

176. Lowndes, Rosemary, and Claude Kailer. *Make Your Own Noah's Ark*. Illus. authors. Boston: Little, Brown, 1983. 96p.

Biblical story literally translated from the Hebrew; facts and figures about the size of the ark and the number of species it contained; long, clever poem about the voyage filled with splendid lists of supplies, construction methods, varieties of animals, and such; three-dimensional, colorful cut-out of the ark and its passengers on heavy paper to be assembled with scissors and glue. First to fourth grades.

177. McKellar, Shona. *The Beginning of the Rainbow*. Illus. Masahiro Kasuya. Nashville: Abingdon, 1977. unp.

Tiny tortoise follows the line of animals into the ark, creeping slowly up the ramp as the rain begins, and serves as the focus of an appealing flood story. Flowing, stylized pictures of handsome beasts, rain falling like a beaded curtain, a huge rainbow, etc., in lambent colors. Preschool to second grade.

178. McKie, Roy. *Noah's Ark*. Illus. author. New York: Random House, 1984. unp.

Abbreviated, plain-spoken text gives basic events. Sweeping scenes of ark construction, animal-gathering, the boat's crowded interior, the tremendous rainbow, etc., done in bright, busy cartoon style provide life. Preschool to second grade.

179. Mee, Charles L. *Noah*. Illus. Ken Munowitz. New York: Harper & Row, 1978. unp.

Hilarious black-and-white drawings of winsome animals and blocky people with big eyes and noses sparkle a simple and matter-of-fact retelling of the Ark tale. Preschool.

180. Prescott, D.M. *Noah and His Ark*. Illus. Patricia and Andrew Skilleter. Anderson, Ind.: Warner, 1984. 42p. Very First Bible Stories Series.

Well told for small children, with neat pictures in soft colors of the ark construction, jeering neighbors, pretty animals, serene Noah family. Preschool to kindergarten.

181. Rounds, Glen. *Washday on Noah's Ark*. Illus. author. New York: Holiday, 1985. unp.

Updated, entertaining version in which farmer Noah hears heavy rains forecast on the radio and decides to build an ark for his family and farm animals. Hundreds of uninvited wild ones cram in, too. When the rain stops, a determined Mrs. Noah ties the snakes together in square knots to make herself a clothesline and hang out forty days' worth of laundry. Funny, active pictures in subtle colors. Kindergarten to third grade.

182. Singer, Isaac Bashevis. *Why Noah Chose the Dove*. Illus. Eric Carle. New York: Farrar, 1973. unp.

Hearing a rumor that Noah will take only the best of living creatures on the ark, each animal, from the hippopotamus down to the cricket, proclaims its special virtue. The dove, however, modestly keeps still. All are welcomed on board, but the unassuming dove earns the special honor of being Noah's messenger. Fine big animals done in decorative graphics style, spattered colors, intricate patterns. Clever, gently satirical text. Kindergarten to third grade.

183. Spier, Peter. *Noah's Ark*. Illus. author. New York: Doubleday, 1977. unp.

Introduced by a seventeenth-century poem which tersely tells about "the Flood." Joyfully creative wordless picture book of minutely detailed watercolors excels in every aspect, especially when showing the wonderfully varied creatures being loaded, the problems of caring for them, and their delighted escape from confinement. Humor and love of all life abound. Preschool and up.

184. Wildsmith, Brian. *Professor Noah's Spaceship*. Illus. author. New York: Oxford, 1980. unp.

All kinds of animals and birds living peacefully in a modern forest are threatened by pollution and seek refuge with Noah, who is building a rocket with robotic aid. They travel on the huge craft for forty days, supposedly toward the future, but a guidance malfunction sends them into the past at the time right after the flood. The animals have another chance. Vibrant, elegant illustrations. Second to fourth grades.

185. Williams-Ellis, Virginia. *Noah's Ark*. Illus. Anna Dzierzek. Milwaukee: Ideals, 1981. unp.

Short, sober text. Romanticized illustrations of a wrinkled, white-haired Noah in a brilliantly striped robe, his handsome young sons in purple, blue, and gold. The ark tosses in an artistic network of lightning bolts. Kindergarten and first grade.

186. Yeatman, Linda. *Noah's Ark*. Illus. Bob Gault. New York: Coward, 1984. unp.

Brief version in which the rain has already begun before the Noahs begin building the ark. The reason for it is never mentioned, but otherwise the basics are covered. Pert cartoon-style, brightly colored illustrations. Press-out ark and animals included. Kindergarten to third grade.

PSALMS

187. Anderson, Debby. *God Is with Me*. Illus. author. Cincinnati: Standard, 1984. unp. Happy Day Book Series.

Small child's version of Psalm 139 shows cartoon-style children with Smile Faces at night and in the morning, indoors and out, snorkeling deep in the ocean, standing on a snowy peak. Simple, appropriate text. Full New International Version of the psalm also included. Preschool to second grade.

188. Carwell, L'Ann. *The Good Shepherd Prayer.* Illus. Pam Erickson. St. Louis: Concordia, 1979. unp.

Freely interpreted version of the Twenty-third Psalm in which little children are told that God cares for, directs, forgives, protects, comforts, and provides for them. The shepherd image is completely lost, as is the Biblical language. The Lord does all these things whether we are rich or poor, large or small, laughing or crying, etc. Large, lively cartoons illustrate each idea. Preschool to second grade.

189. Keller, W. Phillip. *A Child's Look at the Twenty-Third Psalm.* Illus. Lauren Jarrett. Garden City, New York: Doubleday, 1985. 96p.

Exhaustive, knowledgeable comparison of Jesus' care for human beings with the shepherd's care for his sheep. Covers all aspects of the psalm and much more. Includes earmarking, shearing, insect infestation, pasturage, the rod and the staff, etc. All tied strongly to Christianity. Short sentences, exhortatory tone. Sketchy, unexciting black-and-white drawings. Fourth to sixth grades.

190. Murphy, Elspeth Campbell. *Everybody Shout Hallelujah! Verses from the Psalms on Praise.* Illus. Jane E. Nelson. Elgin, Ill.: Chariot, 1981. unp. David and I Talk to God Series.

Children appreciate being praised by parents and teachers and in turn they praise God for his careful plan of creation and his love. They sing, shout, clap, jump for joy. Ideas drawn from Psalms 9, 33, 50, 98, 104, 107. Cheerful color and black-and-white pictures of farms, homes, children blowing bubbles, etc. Preschool to second grade.

191. Murphy, Elspeth Campbell. *It's My Birthday, God: Psalm 90 for Children.* Illus. Jane E. Nelson. Elgin, Ill.: Chariot, 1983. 24p. David and I Talk to God Series.

Eternity of God expressed in the psalm is translated into a little girl's thoughts on her birthday. Mixed with happy party details are meditations on the infinite age of God and his inexhaustible love. Simple illustrations in pale colors and black and white. Preschool to second grade.

192. Murphy, Elspeth Campbell. *Sometimes I Get Scared: Psalm 23 for Children*. Illus. Jane E. Nelson. Elgin, Ill.: Chariot, 1980. unp. David and I Talk to God Series.

Shepherd image is explained and maintained as the sheep and a little boy undergo similar experiences of needing guidance and protection, the boy in familiar frightening situations such as thunderstorms and nightmares. Gentle pictures in color and black and white. Preschool to second grade.

193. Murphy, Elspeth Campbell. *Sometimes I Have to Cry: Verses from the Psalms on Tears*. Illus. Jane E. Nelson. Elgin, Ill.: Chariot, 1981. 24p. David and I Talk to God Series.

Taken from Psalms 6, 30, 38, 46, 103, and 119. A little boy is sad because his dog has been run over and muses that God understands his feelings, comforts him like a father, helps him through a dark night of sickness to joy in the morning. Pastel and black-and-white illustrations of familiar situations. Preschool to second grade.

194. Murphy, Elspeth Campbell. *Sometimes I Need to Be Hugged: Psalm 84 for Children*. Illus. Jane E. Nelson. Elgin, Ill.: Chariot, 1981. 24p. David and I Talk to God Series.

A little boy sees a nest of baby sparrows tenderly cared for by their mother. After a disappointing day, his own mother hugs and encourages him, and he feels God's tender loving care as well. Vaguely related to the psalm. Attractive pictures in color and black and white of everyday experiences. Preschool to second grade.

195. Tudor, Tasha, illus. *The Lord Is My Shepherd*. New York: Putnam, 1980. unp.

Each phrase of the King James version is illustrated with charming, old-fashioned New England country scenes: grazing cattle, quiet ponds, sun-barred forests, churchyard graves, small wild animals. A sunbonneted little girl and her Corgi dog wander through them. Artwork delicate in detail and color. Preschool and up.

196. Walters, Julie. *God Loves Me: Three Psalms for Little Children*. Illus. Kathryn Kelly. Notre Dame, Ind.: Ave Maria, 1977. unp.

Psalms 23, 91, and 139 are each summarized on an adult level, followed by little picture-story interpretations for small children showing experiences with which they can identify readily. A little girl enjoys a day of play (139), a little boy camps out and has imaginary adventures (91), another little boy imagines himself as a lamb cared for by Jesus (23). Cartoon-style pictures in bright blue, gold, green. Preschool to third grade.

RUTH

197. Barrett, Ethel. *Ruth.* Ventura, Calif.: Regal, 1980. 128p.

Brisk, easy-to-read fictionalization begins with Naomi's move to Moab and ends with the birth of Obed. Much dialogue, short sentences. Emphasis on Ruth's conversion to the Israelite God and her romance with Boaz. Fourth grade and up.

198. Parris, Paula Jordan. *Ruth: Woman of Courage.* Illus. Robert H. Cassell. Nashville: Broadman, 1977. 48p. Biblearn Series.

After a somewhat confusing summary of Naomi's experiences in Moab, the story of her return to Bethlehem with Ruth is told in a straightforward, simple way. Ruth is rewarded for her bravery and loyalty to her mother-in-law with a new marriage and a son. Thus they all become ancestors of Jesus. In the static illustrations Ruth and Naomi are glamorized with pale skin and red lips while the other figures look more appropriate to the place and period. Discussion questions. Third to fifth grades.

SAMUEL

199. Kendall, Joan. *The Story of Samuel.* Illus. Patricia Papps and Andrew Skilleter. Anderson, Ind.: Warner, 1984. 43p. Very First Bible Stories Series.

Simple, accurate version of Samuel's boyhood, from Anna's prayer at the Temple through the death of Eli and his sons. Neat, realistic pictures in pastel colors. Preschool to second grade.

200. Patterson, Yvonne. *Happy Hannah.* Illus. Kathryn Hutton. Cincinnati: Standard, 1984. unp.

Saccharine, basic pictures of a girl robed in blue praying

in the Temple, talking to white-bearded Eli, and caring for a pretty little boy. Easy, rhymed version of Hannah's sorrow over her infertility and her promise to God that her son, if given to her, will serve in the Temple. Preschool to kindergarten.

201. Whaley, Richie. *Samuel: Prophet and Judge*. Illus. Dean Shelton. Nashville: Broadman, 1978. 48p. Biblearn Series.

Although a few areas are omitted, Samuel's career is well traced from Hannah's prayer at the Temple onward. His devotion and obedience to God are stressed, and the facts of his life are clearly given. Effective, large, color illustrations. Second to fifth grades.

TOWER OF BABEL

202. Garfield, Leon. *King Nimrod's Tower*. Illus. Michael Bragg. New York: Lothrop, 1982. unp.

In a vaguely medieval setting a boy who has found a rough, recalcitrant dog and is trying to train it talks to the animal about the workmen building a huge tower that will put the King on a level with God. Instead of pulverizing the tower and running the risk of hurting the boy, God confounds the workmen by having them each speak a different language. Too many plot details obscure the story's meaning. The pictures are done in warm tones. Kindergarten to third grade.

203. Hirsh, Marilyn. *The Tower of Babel*. Illus. author. New York: Holiday, 1981. unp.

Noah's descendants emigrate to the plain of Shinar, build a village, then an impressive city, then a grand tower to make them greater than anyone else. They neglect their homes and crops, and finally the Lord chastises them by changing their one language into a babble of many. Embellished story is true to the Biblical Tower of Babel and appealingly illustrated with industrious people in black and white. Preschool to third grade.

204. Schell, Mildred. *A Tower Too Tall*. Illus. Masahiro Kasuya. Valley Forge, Pa.: Judson, 1979. unp.

When a king sees two little boys making a tower of stones, he decides to glorify himself by building a tower of his own to reach heaven, thus making himself greater even than God. It is dashed down. The workers, now all speaking different languages, flee the city. The little boys rebuild their tower, but just for their own amusement. Vigorous pictures in deep colors show grimly determined, muscular men raising the tower into the clouds, then stunned and bewildered, milling at its broken base. Preschool to second grade.

NEW TESTAMENT AND JESUS

205. Martin, Wayne W. *The Gospel of Mark: A New Translation for Children*. Illus. C.F. Payne. Nashville: Upper Room, 1984. 127p.

Translated directly from the Koine Greek manuscripts into clear modern language but not simplified in meaning or impact. Well-executed style. Introductory information. Glossary gives interpretive notes for terms such as faith, Holy Spirit, parable, Pharisee, etc. Marginal notes include pronouncing guides, word definitions, references to associated Scripture verses, explanatory personal comments, general information. Has full-page, photographically realistic color illustrations and maps. Fourth grade and up.

Story Collections

206. Gaines, M.C. *Picture Stories from the Bible: The New Testament in Full-Color Comic Strip Form*. Illus. Don Cameron. New York: Scarf, 1980. 143p.

Pedestrian artwork lessens the impact of selections from the lives of Jesus, Paul, and the disciples. Includes work of the early church. Biblically flavored dialogue with Jesus' words in red. Scripture references. Approved by Protestant, Jewish, and Catholic clergy. Fourth grade and up.

207. Steen, Shirley. *A Child's Bible: The New Testament*. Illus. Charles Front. New York: Paulist, 1978. 274p.

Main events of Gospels and Acts in an abbreviated overview and brief section of Revelation. Plain, consistent British style, with events fairly well integrated and simplified concepts. Jesus' teachings highlighted. Text arranged around eyecatching, stylized illustrations in vibrant colors on almost every page. Scriptural references. Fourth grade and up.

Personalities

208. Barrett, Marsha. *Early Christians: Workers for Jesus*. Illus. Ron Hester. Nashville: Broadman, 1979. 48p. Biblearn Series.

Biblically factual biographical chapters on Ananias, Barnabas, John Mark, and Priscilla and Aquila include portions of Paul's life as well. Material is drawn together successfully and uses dialogue for interest. Big pictures of handsome people in gaudy color. Thought-eliciting questions. No Scripture references. Kindergarten to fourth grade.

209. Blackwell, Muriel F. *Peter: The Prince of Apostles*. Illus. Paul Karch. Nashville: Broadman, 1976. 48p. Biblearn Series.

Imaginary account of Peter and Andrew as boys followed by their becoming disciples of Jesus, the full fishing nets miracle, the Last Supper, Peter's denial of Jesus at Caiaphas' house, and Peter's later ministry and imprisonment. Thought-provoking questions at end of each chapter. Clear, interesting style. Adequate color pictures. First to fourth grades.

210. Brown, Robert. *Luke: Doctor-Writer*. Illus. Ron Hester. Nashville: Broadman, 1977. 48p. Biblearn Series.

Speculative version of Luke's life and his role as companion and doctor to Paul and writer of a gospel and the Book of Acts. Assumes Luke was with Paul when he was imprisoned in Caesarea, during the shipwreck on Malta, and in Rome. Suggests methods he might have used in gathering information for his writings and lists special themes and material found in Luke's gospel. Well-written reconstruction. Garishly colored, sturdy pictures. First to fourth grades.

211. Caldwell, Louise. *Timothy: Young Pastor*. Illus. Paul Karch. Nashville: Broadman, 1978. 48p. Biblearn Series.

Supposition concerning Timothy's childhood and first introduction to Paul's preaching in Lystra is smoothly incorporated into the Biblical accounts of Timothy's missionary career, traveling with Paul and Silas, leading the church at Ephesus, and doing missionary work on his own. Crisp, attractive illustrations show him as a red-haired young man. Thought-provoking questions. No Scripture references. First to fourth grades.

212. Landorf, Joyce. *I Came to Love You Late*. Old Tappan, N.J.: Revell, 1977. 192p.

Martha, a bustling and hardworking person, complains loudly when Jesus doesn't hurry to heal Lazarus' illness nor rebuke Mary for sitting at his feet instead of helping with the housework. After the Crucifixion her attitude changes, and she devotes herself to abandoned and handicapped children. Overwritten and sentimental but contains good historical detail. Martha has a well-delineated personality. Sixth grade and up.

213. Laux, Dorothy. *John: Beloved Apostle*. Illus. William N. McPheeters. Nashville: Broadman, 1977. 48p. Biblearn Series.

Somewhat fictionalized narrative includes probable details of daily life, childhood, calling by Jesus, general activities of Jesus and the disciples, specific incidents referring to John, his later ministry with Peter, and writings. Clear, easy style. Appropriate illustrations in warm colors in which a red-haired John is easily identifiable. Kindergarten to fourth grade.

214. Naish, Jack. *Philip: Traveling Preacher*. Illus. Ron Hester. Nashville: Broadman, 1978. 48p. Biblearn Series.

Imagined but fact-based details fill out the non-Biblical areas of Philip's life. Considered to be a Hellenic Jew, Philip related well to a variety of people. After his conversion by Peter in Jerusalem, Philip's fruitful career as deacon and preacher is followed. Straightforward, readable style. Bright pictures full of strong, handsome people. Third to sixth grades.

DISCIPLES

215. De Kort, Kees, illus. *Jesus Goes Away*. Minneapolis: Augsburg, 1978. unp. What the Bible Tells Us Series.

The disciples at the Ascension, in the Upper Room, and

touched by the Holy Spirit at Pentecost are arrestingly pictured in stocky forms and glowing color. Lucid, brief text. Preschool and kindergarten.

216. Rowell, Edmon L. *Apostles: Jesus' Special Helpers*. Illus. James Padgett. Nashville: Broadman, 1979. 48p. Biblearn Series.

Meager facts available in the Bible about the disciples are gathered into chapters for each one and presented in a crisp, absorbing way, with little personal input by the author. Historic facts of the period flesh out the accounts. Not much variety in the color pictures of robed men with black beards. Third to sixth grades.

MARY

217. Hintze, Barbara. *Mary: Mother of Jesus*. Illus. James Padgett. Nashville: Broadman, 1977. 48p. Biblearn Series.

Little is added to the Biblical account, and Mary remains a vague figure. Includes probable details of daily life in Mary's childhood, her engagement to Joseph, the annunciation, the visit to Elizabeth, the birth of Jesus, and the presentation of the baby at the Temple. The Magis and the flight into Egypt are eliminated. Also describes the visit to Jerusalem when Jesus is twelve, news of Jesus' ministry reaching Mary in Nazareth, her witness of the Crucifixion, and her joy at the Resurrection. Sturdy pictures with strong, vertical lines and rich, muted colors. Kindergarten to fourth grade.

218. Holmes, Marjorie. *Two from Galilee*. Old Tappan, N.J.: Revell, 1972. 224p.

Mary, beautiful and loved by all in Nazareth, is happily awaiting her marriage to Joseph when God intrudes abruptly into their lives. Serenely, Mary accepts the humiliation of unwed pregnancy, and finally her unwavering faith convinces Joseph and her parents that she will indeed bear the Messiah. Richly descriptive and imaginative. Good reading skills required. Sixth grade and up.

JOHN THE BAPTIST

219. Human, Johnnie. *John the Baptist: Forerunner of Jesus.* Illus. James Padgett. Nashville: Broadman, 1978. 48p. Biblearn Series.

Straightforward narrative of John's life with only a small amount of imagined detail. Essence of his preachings included. Importance of his role to prepare people for Jesus' coming as the Messiah is emphasized. Discussion questions for each chapter and personal reflections for daily living at the end. Contains color illustrations. Third to sixth grades.

220. Klug, Ronald. *John the Baptist.* Illus. Betty Wind. St. Louis: Concordia, 1984. unp.

John's adult career in verse form includes his days in the desert, preaching and baptizing; his baptism of Jesus; his conflict with Herod; his assurance that Jesus is the Messiah; his decapitation. Bold, colorful pictures. Preschool to third grade.

PAUL

221. Arbuckle, Gwendolyne. *Paul: Adventurer for Christ.* Illus. Tom Armstrong. Nashville: Abingdon, 1984. 94p.

Matter-of-fact, easy-to-read survey of Paul's life and preachings. Just enough imaginary detail to draw the material together. Main theological ideas extracted from the Epistles. Two-tone drawings are dark and strong. Fourth to sixth grades.

222. Barrett, Ethel. *Paul: One Man's Extraordinary Adventures.* Ventura, Calif.: Regal, 1981. 127p.

Short, simplified, colloquial account loosely based on Acts and Galatians in which Paul is known as "egghead" in his childhood, grows up short and self-satisfied, and then is transformed by Jesus. Highlights of his missionary career. Much dialogue, exclamatory phrases, personal comment. Quick and easy reading for fourth grade and up.

223. Ready, Dolores. *The Man Who Learned About Jesus.* Illus. Kathryn Shoemaker. Minneapolis: Winston, 1978. unp. Christian Heroes Series

A portion of Saul's life: his encounter with Jesus on the road to Damascus, his first actions as a Christian missionary which put him in danger, his escape from the city in a basket lowered down the wall by his friends. Simple, lively style with matching pictures in color and black and white. Kindergarten to third grade.

224. Tucker, Iva Jewel. *Paul: The Missionary*. Illus. Ron Hester. Nashville: Broadman, 1976. 48p. Biblearn Series.

Readable, basic biography with a minimum of extraneous detail. Paul shown as a caring, cheerful person with rock-like faith: in Damascus, traveling with Barnabas, jailed in Philippi, shipwrecked on Malta, interceding for Onesimus. Thought-provoking questions. No specific Scriptural references. Third to sixth grades.

ZACCHAEUS

225. De Kort, Kees, illus. *Zacchaeus*. Minneapolis: Augsburg, 1970. unp. What the Bible Tells Us Series.

Rich, unscrupulous little man climbs up a tree to see Jesus better. To everyone's surprise, Jesus dines with him and changes his life. Told in simplest terms. Richly colored pictures of bright-eyed people. Preschool and kindergarten.

226. Maier-F., Emil. *Jesus Befriends Zacchaeus*. Illus. author. Nashville: Abingdon, 1983. unp.

Brief but accurate retelling, greatly enhanced by vibrant color pictures in which foreshortened, simplified figures with large, dark eyes enact the story against a stylized desert setting. Jesus' love for the sinner and Zacchaeus' whole-hearted repentance are very well expressed. Useful adult guide for usage and interpretation. Preschool to second grade.

227. Stortz, Diane. *Zacchaeus Meets Jesus*. Illus. Vera Gohman. Cincinnati: Standard, 1984. unp.

Lively account of the short, unpopular, dishonest tax collector's encounter with Jesus and the subsequent transformation of his life. Repetitive and rhythmic text. Neat illustrations in clear, bright colors. Preschool to second grade.

Jesus' Life and Teachings

OVERALL BIOGRAPHIES

228. Bull, Norman J. *The Story of Jesus*. Illus. Mike Codd. Nashville: Abingdon, 1982. 157p.

With imagined names for various New Testament characters and details of daily life in Jesus' time added to the Gospel accounts, an absorbing narrative from the betrothal of Mary and Joseph through the descent of the Holy Spirit at Pentecost is created. Many parables and other teachings are incorporated logically into the story and their meanings clarified. Free-flowing style, well-knit construction. Authoritative. Extensive section with encyclopedic information on houses, occupations, travel, religion, food, dress, etc., in first-century Palestine. Realistic color pictures, endpaper maps. Subject and parable (with Gospel references) indexes. Fifth grade and up.

229. Coleman, William. *Jesus, My Forever Friend*. Illus. Wayne A. Hanna. Elgin, Ill.: Cook, 1981. 125p. Wonderful World of the Bible Series.

Most of the facts, Biblical episodes, Scriptural quotations, geographical and cultural information, little stories of how children today can lead Christian lives, identification games, etc., in this volume are in some way associated with Jesus. The arrangement is random, the language informal, the tone and theology conservative. Illustrated with color photographs, comic strips, cartoons, paintings, and drawings. Third to sixth grades.

230. Coleman, William. *The Palestine Herald*. Vols. 1-4. Illus. Paul Turnbaugh. Elgin, Ill.: Chariot, 1985. unp.

Events of Jesus' life presented in chatty newspaper format with articles about Bible events mingled with Dear Esther columns, public opinion polls, quizzes, news stories about current events. Advertisements for camel milk, rent-a-cheetah, mint leaf deodorant, phylactery sale, etc. Has an instructive, lively style and is humorous. Illustrated with two-color drawings. Scriptural references. Volume One includes birth of Jesus, John the Baptist, calling of the disciples, etc. Volume Two includes miracles such as the calming of the storm, Gadarene swine, feeding of 10,000, walking on water, etc. Volume Three includes more miracles such as the healing of the blind and the raising of Lazarus, parables, and other teachings. Volume

Four includes the Last Supper, Crucifixion, Resurrection. Fourth grade and up.

231. Daly, Kathleen. *Jesus Our Friend*. Illus. Jim Cummins. Chicago: Rand McNally, 1984. unp.

Sketchy and incomplete. Omits birth, divinity. Cites some of the miracles, love of children, role of service to others. Easy-to-read text, but overall message is confusing. Sparkling color pictures will appeal to young children, but stories will need a lot of amplification. Preschool.

232. Dickens, Charles. *The Life of Our Lord*. Philadelphia: Westminster, 1934. 127p.

Jesus' life is cohesively organized, drawn directly from the Bible, written with typical Dickensian grace. But the work is prejudiced, didactic, and occasionally inaccurate. Appropriately illustrated with nineteenth-century style engravings. Sixth grade and up.

233. Dudley-Smith, Timothy. *The Lion Book of Stories of Jesus*. Illus. Terry Gabbey. Belleville, Mich.: Lion, 1986. 93p.

Jesus' life and teachings skillfully gathered in forty-four two-page segments. Best known parables. Vivid, unbiased, clear, faithful to Gospel accounts. Very readable. Low-key, carefully detailed, serious watercolors. Scripture citations. Kindergarten and up.

234. Egermeier, Elsie E. *Egermeier's Picture-Story Life of Jesus*. Anderson, Ind.: Warner, 1965. 128p.

Adaptation of portions of *Egermeier's Bible Story Book* contains eighty-three stories. Begins with the journey to Bethlehem and ends with the Ascension. Gospel accounts well assembled. Occasional valuable explanatory material. New Testament citations. Unpretentious, easily understood style. Realistic, brightly colored pictures. Fourth to sixth grades.

235. Griffin, William. *Jesus for Children*. Illus. Elizabeth Swisher. Minneapolis: Winston, 1985. 117p.

A contemporary interpretation of Jesus' life using a modern idiom and punchy style that is inappropriate, too updated, and personalized to have much Scriptural feeling. It oversimplifies and confuses at times. The beatitudes are especially startling. For example, it says that for those who mourn, "God will make jokes and do cartwheels to cheer you up." Good Samaritan parable is well done. Conversational style promotes easy reading and story-telling. Full-page, expressive, sturdy black-and-white drawings. Kindergarten to fourth grade.

236. Hayes, Wanda. *My Jesus Book*. Illus. Frances Hook. Cincinnati: Standard, 1958. unp.

Poorly organized incidents from Jesus' life lack effective continuity, are often confusingly incomplete, and need much additional explanation. Very brief stories include Jesus' birth and childhood, the Samaritan woman at the well, the healing of the ten lepers, washing the disciples' feet and more. Does not include the Crucifixion. It is easy to read and has Bible references. The idealized pictures include rosy-cheeked children; pink-nosed, bouncy lambs; manly but gentle Jesus. Soft-toned colors. Preschool to second grade.

237. Henderson, Felicity. *Learning about Jesus*. Illus. Michael Grimsdale. Belleville, Mich.: Lion, 1983. unp.

A quick look at Jesus' life, stressing his sonship to God, his love of all kinds of people, the importance of his sacrifice. Gentle, conversational tone especially suited to young children. Scripture references. Glossary of Biblical words. Appealing, precise watercolors in warm shades. Preschool to third grade.

238. Hook, Richard, and Frances Hook, illus. *Jesus: The Friend of Children: The Life of Christ for Younger Children*. Elgin, Ill.: Cook, 1977. 110p.

Powerful, authoritative full-page color illustrations show Jesus as both virile and gentle. Scripturally based, expressively written account of Jesus' life from the Annunciation through the Ascension. Short sentences, simple dialogue. Kindergarten to fourth grade.

239. Johnstone, Janet, and Anne Grahame, illus. *Bible Stories for Children*. Milwaukee: Ideals, 1981. unp.

The Nativity and some of the better-known parables and miracles are told briefly. Also includes Jesus' visit to the Temple at age twelve. Overall effect is sometimes disjointed. Unusual artwork with tall, thin figures set against decorative, elegant backgrounds. Kindergarten to second grade.

240. Lindvall, Ella K. *Jesus Begins His Work*. Illus. Chris Molan. Chicago: Moody, 1983. 32p.

Jesus' visit to Jerusalem at age twelve, the calling of the disciples, the marriage at Cana told in simple, effective language suitable for early elementary reading skills. Strong, realistic, well-executed color pictures. Preschool to fourth grade.

241. Lindvall, Ella K. *Read-aloud Bible Stories*. Vol. 1. Illus. H. Kent Packett. Chicago: Moody, 1982. 158p.

Very simple, homey versions of Jesus with Zacchaeus, Bartimaeus, the children, calming the storm, healing the ten lepers. Huge type, repetition, short sentences, clear message. Very large, humorous pictures in basic strong colors. Preschool to second grade.

242. Lindvall, Ella K. *Read-aloud Bible Stories*. Vol. 2. Illus. Ken Renczenski. Chicago: Moody, 1982. 158p.

Brief, plain retellings of Jesus calling Peter as a disciple, the prodigal son parable, the miracle of the loaves and fishes, the good Samaritan parable, and the Resurrection. Preschool level of comprehension. Text suitable for beginning readers. Giant type. Very simple but clever, appealing illustrations. Preschool to second grade.

243. Lloyd, Jeremy. *The Woodland Gospels: According to Captain Beaky and His Band*. Illus. Graham Percy. London: Faber, 1984. 63p.

Led by Captain Beaky, an owl, bat, toad, and rat decide they should spread the Gospel to all the forest creatures but get sidetracked by a rainstorm and shelter under an overturned boat. There the owl reviews briefly the life of Jesus from the Bible, with explanatory comments. The Winnie-the-Pooh-type characters are gentle and quirky and are illustrated by large, peaceful pictures of the plump, ingenuous animals. Second grade and up.

244. Melang, Karen. *Jesus, the Servant*. Illus. Keith Neely. St. Louis: Concordia, 1986. unp.

Jesus demonstrates servanthood by not choosing to be a king on a throne but someone entirely devoted to others, even to the sacrifice of his own life. The concept well expressed and explained for young children. The strong, realistic illustrations are done alternatively in black and white and ruddy color. Kindergarten to fourth grade.

245. Moncure, Jane Belk. *I Learn to Read about Jesus*. Cincinnati: Standard, 1983. 128p.

Primer for first grade with 196-word basic vocabulary and 84 additional Bible words such as Bethlehem, shepherd, blessed, temple, etc. Simple stories include Jesus' birth, visit of the Wise Men, Jesus at twelve in the Temple, miracle of the loaves and fishes, raising of Jairus' daughter, the lost sheep parable, Jesus and the children. Big, clear illustrations in color and black and white by various artists. Word lists. Preschool to first grade.

246. Murphy, Elspeth Campbell. *Jesus Does Good Things*. *Jesus Is God's Son*. *Jesus Loves Children*. *Jesus Tells Us about God*. Illus. Wayne Hanna. Elgin, Ill.: Cook, 1980. unp. My First Books About Jesus series.

Lively, simple illustrations and basic Christian concepts of Jesus' life, God's care and love, prayer and right living are expressed in a few short sentences in each little book. Preschool.

247. Nystrom, Carolyn. *Who Is Jesus?* Illus. Wayne Hanna. Chicago: Moody, 1980. unp. Children's Bible Basics Series.

Jesus, present always as part of the triune God, enters the world as a human being at the Nativity, experiences childhood, preaches and heals, dies for our sins. Adam and Eve story included. Emphasizes Jesus' perfection, mission to teach about God and to be a sacrifice. Believers will live with him forever in heaven. Mixture of Gospels and later New Testament theology. Simple language but too much information. Difficult concepts need additional explanation. Scripture references throughout. Cartoon-style figures enlivened by sweeps of brilliant color. Kindergarten to third grade.

248. Ramsay, DeVere. *God's People: Our Story: Bible Stories from the New Testament*. Illus. Francis Huffman. Nashville: Upper Room, 1984. 128p.

Twelve stories of Jesus, very condensed and somewhat fictionalized to make them more interesting to young children. Includes the Nativity, the visit to the Temple at age twelve, baptism by John, some parables and miracles, Holy Week, appearances of the risen Jesus, and Pentecost. Simple style in both text and rather stiff watercolors. No Scripture citations. Glossary and maps. Kindergarten to fourth grade.

249. Rawson, Christopher, and R.H. Lloyd. *The Story of Jesus*. Illus. Victor Ambrus. London: Usborne, 1981. 128p.

Well-researched presentation of parts of Jesus' life with details of everyday living and customs, holidays Jesus would have celebrated, foods and occupations. Includes Jesus' birth and boyhood, six well-known parables, seven miracles, Holy Week and the Resurrection. Concise, readable style. Finely detailed, vibrant illustrations. Some arranged in panels like comic strips. No Scripture references. Third grade and up.

250. Royer, Katherine. *Nursery Stories of Jesus*. Illus. Norma Hostetler. Scottdale, Pa.: Herald, 1957. 49p.

Excessively sweet snippets from Jesus' life include birth, boyhood, parables and other teachings, miracles, Zacchaeus, Mary and Martha, Easter. Anachronistic pictures show men in short haircuts, children in romper suits and puff-sleeved dresses, the Magi offering gifts in gay wrappings tied with ribbons. Preschool.

251. Schraff, Francis and Anne Schraff. *Learning about Jesus: Stories, Plays, Activities for Children*. Rev. Ed. Liguori, Mo.: Liguori, 1980. 80p.

Mary and Elizabeth, Jesus' birth and boyhood, the marriage at Cana and several other miracles, the Crucifixion, and the Resurrection retold briefly. Each accompanied by a very short playlet and a meaningful craft, game, or other activity. Kindergarten to fourth grade.

252. Schrage, Alice. *Birth of the King*. Ventura, Calif.: Regal, 1981. 118p.

The young Jesus with his family, his baptism by John, the gathering of the disciples, and other events and teachings of Jesus' early ministry combined into a unified narrative whole. Scriptural references. Dictionary of terms. Simple footnotes. Fourth grade and up.

253. Schrage, Alice. *The King Who Lives Forever*. Ventura, Calif.: Regal, 1981. 123p.

Short episodes from the latter part of Jesus' life told in an interesting, dialogue-filled narrative style. Includes the healing of a blind man, the resurrection of Lazarus, the meeting with Zacchaeus, some parables and teachings, the events from Holy Week through the Ascension. Dictionary of terms and footnotes. Scripture references. Fourth grade and up.

254. Storr, Catherine. *Jesus Begins His Work.* Illus. Chris Molan. Milwaukee: Raintree, 1982. 32p.

Somewhat different but equally simple, clear text as *Jesus Begins His Work* by Ella Lindvall (item 240). Identical illustrations and format. Kindergarten to fourth grade.

255. Van Vechten, Schuyler. *The Bethlehem Star: Children's Newspaper Reports of the Life of Jesus.* New York: Walker, 1972. unp.

News stories, notices, Dear Abby columns, features, want ads, etc., from the pages of an imaginary newspaper present highlights of Jesus' life in a memorable, clever way. Written by eleven-year-olds in a Sunday School class to accompany each week's lesson. Fourth to sixth grades.

256. Villiers, Marjorie. *Jesus Has Come.* Illus. Philippe Joudiou. Valley Forge, Pa.: Judson, 1978. unp.

Unique, decorative, abstract illustrations use blocks of rich color against intricately patterned and textured backgrounds. Brief text recounts Jesus' birth, childhood, and some events from his ministry. Ends with his teaching his friends the Lord's Prayer. Preschool to second grade.

257. Wangerin, Walter. *My First Book about Jesus.* Illus. Jim Cummins. Chicago: Rand McNally, 1983. unp.

Highlights of Jesus' childhood, baptism by John, temptations, calling of the disciples, healing of the paralyzed man and Jairus' daughter, good Samaritan parable, events of Holy Week and the Resurrection. Embellished, poetic language and storyteller's dramatic tone more suited to older children than the picture book format. Action-filled and carefully detailed watercolors in warm tones. Second to fourth grades.

Fiction

258. Holmes, Marjorie. *Three from Galilee.* New York: Harper & Row, 1985. 230p.

Idealized portrait of Jesus from toddler stage until he is ready to begin his ministry. Hannah and Joachim are depicted as adoring grandparents, Mary and Joseph as lifelong lovers, Jesus' brothers and sisters both loving and envious of him. Jesus has intimations of his future and of his past as part of God. He is gentle, strong, introspective, tender. Ends with his temptation by Satan in the guise of a rich, handsome youth. Carefully researched details give realism to setting but characters are type-cast. Fervent style verges on sentimental, yet story is absorbing and suspenseful, even though the outcome is well known. Good upper elementary readers.

259. L'Engle, Madeleine. *Dance in the Desert*. Illus. Symeon Shimin. New York: Farrar, 1969. unp.

Because of the dangers of wild beasts and bandits, a man, his wife, and their small son join a caravan as they flee to Egypt. In the desert night the little boy dances with a lion, an adder, eagles, mice, and other creatures, all of whom pay loving homage to him. Poetic, mystical text with harmonizing dramatic, firelit pictures. Third grade and up.

260. Speare, Elizabeth George. *The Bronze Bow*. Boston: Houghton Mifflin, 1961. 255p.

Daniel, a young Galilean who detests the Roman conquerors of his homeland, joins a band of rebels and robbers who oppose them. But a close friendship which develops with a boy and his sister who are followers of Jesus eventually leads Daniel to overcome his hatred and begin a new life of love. Strong characterization; fast, exciting pace. Fifth grade and up.

BIRTH

261. Allen, Dorothy. *Baby Jesus*. Illus. Patricia Papps and Andrew Skilleter. Anderson, Ind.: Warner, 1984. 43p.

Very simple version from the Annunciation by the angel Gabriel through the visit of the Magi. Baby is not identified as a savior. Delicate pictures in soft colors show fair-skinned Mary and baby amid dark-skinned men. Preschool.

262. Bierhorst, John. *Spirit Child: A Story of the Nativity*. Illus. Barbara Cooney. New York: Morrow, 1984. unp.

Exquisitely written and illustrated. Gospels of Matthew and Luke blended into Aztec story-telling traditions and European folklore to form poetic, musical, fresh, moving retelling of Christ's birth. Translated from Fray Bernardino de Sahagun's *Psalmodia Christiana* published in 1583 in Mexico. Events are seen through the eyes of the Aztec listeners in illustrations suffused with glowing colors and painstakingly detailed with birds, butterflies, flowers, and volcanic peaks. Kindergarten and up.

263. Brown, Margaret Wise. *Christmas in the Barn*. Illus. Barbara Cooney. New York: Crowell, 1952. unp.

The Nativity is shown in a nineteenth-century barn, with illustrations in strong, primary colors that capture the gentle strength of the horses and cattle and the furry delicacy of the mice as they watch the birth. Simple, poetic text. Preschool to second grade.

264. Daly, Kathleen N. *Baby Jesus*. Illus. Jim Cummins. Chicago: Rand McNally, 1984. unp.

Quickly told in simple terms. Vague and incomplete in certain areas such as the significance of Jesus' birth. Pictures in warm, shining colors are touched with wit and tenderness. Preschool.

265. De Kort, Kees, illus. *Jesus Is Born*. Minneapolis: Augsburg, 1967. unp.

Creatively simple illustrations in deep-toned colors distinguish a basic, brief account that includes the Wise Men's visit. Jesus is referred to as the Lord. Preschool to kindergarten.

266. De Paola, Tomie. *The Christmas Pageant*. Illus. author. Minneapolis: Winston, 1978. unp.

Reverent and touching depiction of solemn, sturdy small children in medieval clothes performing a Nativity play with large pull-toys of a donkey and sheep, done in muted colors. Text is simple, clear, dignified. Small cutouts of the characters for children to color and manipulate for their own pageants are included. Preschool to second grade.

267. De Paola, Tomie. *The Story of the Three Wise Kings*. Illus. author. New York: Putnam, 1983. unp.

In three Eastern countries Gaspar, Melchior, and Balthazar each observe the appearance of a new star and follow it to the birthplace of the infant king to worship and bring gifts. Warned by an angel not to reveal the baby's whereabouts to Herod, they return home secretly. Stately but easy-to-read text. Beautifully balanced, flat, decorative illustrations in warm, subtle colors. Medieval background. Preschool to third grade.

268. Dotts, Maryann J. *When Jesus Was Born*. Illus. Paul Zepelinsky. Nashville: Abingdon, 1979. 30p.

Designed for very small children, using repetitions of

words and familiar concepts. The Christ Child is referred to as a "special baby," with no further explanation. Story ends with shepherds' visit. Usage notes for adults. Two-tone, bland, sketchy drawings. Preschool.

269. Hautzig, Deborah. *The Christmas Story: Based on the Gospels According to St. Matthew and St. Luke.* Illus. Sheilah Beckett. New York: Random House, 1981. unp.

In this superficial and sentimentalized version Mary and Joseph are already married before the Annunciation. Although smoothly written, the text is weak and has gaps. Graceful illustrations in lush colors. Kindergarten to third grade.

270. Hoffman, Felix. *The Story of Christmas.* Illus. author. New York: Atheneum, 1975. unp.

Joseph is a roughly dressed countryman and Mary a farm girl who looks as though she may actually have delivered a baby as she rests in the stable. The angels are sweeping, extraterrestrial figures in blue and gold. Simple text is strongly flavored by the King James Version and extends from the Annunciation through the flight into Egypt. Preschool to third grade.

271. Kageyama, Akiko. *Journey to Bethlehem.* Illus. Taro Semba. Valley Forge, Pa.: Judson, 1983. unp.

Brief version of the angelic summoning of the shepherds to the stable and the visit of the Magi, drawn by a huge star, to the holy family. Gently witty color illustrations of sturdy little men and sheep making their way to the birthplace, baby angels tumbling in the sky, solemn kings, and a long file of peasants lining up to worship. Conversational text. Preschool to third grade.

272. Kurelek, William. *A Northern Nativity: Christmas Dreams of a Prairie Boy.* Illus. author. Montreal: Tundra, 1976. unp.

In the dreams of a twelve-year-old boy living in the 1930s the holy family is pictured in Depression settings: in a cattle feed lot, a garage, a grain elevator, a lumber camp, an igloo, a Salvation Army hostel, and other moving and imaginative situations. Themes are the universality of Christianity, obedience to God, the importance of simple faith. Illuminated by paintings in sharp colors, snapping with the crisp chill of the Canadian winter. Fifth grade and up.

273. Laurence, Margaret. *The Christmas Birthday Story*. Illus. Helen Lucas. New York: Knopf, 1980. unp.

Suitable for non-Christians in that Jesus is portrayed as wise and wonderful but not divine. Informal, imaginative text. Illustrations are stunning in coloration and design, with a sophisticated, Picasso-like simplicity. Preschool to second grade.

274. Lemoine, Georges, illus. *The Christmas Story: According to Luke and Matthew*. Mankato, Minn.: Creative Education, 1984. 32p.

Peculiar experiment in which the text, in two parts--the birth of Jesus and the shepherds and the angels--is repeated over and over, with new sections added until the entire story, taken from the New International Version, is told. Odd, incomprehensible pictures done in white and tones of gray are vague and mysterious. Angels look like seagulls, and a tree grows steadily and symbolically (but of what?) throughout. Third and fourth grades.

275. Lindgren, Astrid. *Christmas in the Stable*. Illus. Harald Wibery. New York: Coward, 1962. unp.

As a little girl sits on her mother's lap hearing the Christmas story, she pictures Mary and Joseph wandering through a snowy night and finding a snug barn much like the one on her farm for their shelter. Familiar, gentle-eyed animals welcome them. Bearded shepherds wearing overcoats are drawn to the barn by a huge star. No divinity is mentioned. Text and paintings pervaded by peace and beauty. Preschool and kindergarten.

276. Lloyd, Mary Edna. *Jesus, the Little New Baby*. Illus. Grace Paull. Nashville: Abingdon, 1951. unp.

Surrounded by gleaming light and joyous song, Jesus is born in the stable. Cow, donkey, and dove watch gravely. Very simple text. Gentle pictures in soft colors and black and white. Preschool.

277. Marshall, Martha. *What Child Is This?* Illus. James Conway. Wheaton, Ill.: Dandelion, 1982. 30p.

Enthusiastic presentation of the basic facts, stressing the roles of the few who know who the child really is: Mary and Joseph, the shepherds, Simeon and Anna, the Wise Men. Asks children today to follow their examples and love, worship, proclaim, and thank God for Jesus. Repetition, simple language, clear concepts for very young children and early readers. Large, bright, realistic pictures. Preschool to second grade.

278. Mee, Charles L. *Happy Birthday, Baby Jesus*. Illus. Ken Munowitz. New York: Harper & Row, 1976. unp.

Overly simplified, Biblically incorrect version in which Jesus has no special relationship to God, except that all people are God's children. Big-eyed, big-footed, blocky figures in the illustrations have a strong, crude charm. God is a giant, and the Magi are triplets jammed on one camel. Preschool and kindergarten.

279. Petersham, Maude, and Miska Petersham. *The Christ Child: As Told by Matthew and Luke*. Illus. authors. Garden City, N.Y.: Doubleday, 1931. 63p.

Serene beauty and graceful motion fill the black-and-white and softly tinted color illustrations. King James text includes the Nativity, the visit of the Wise Men, the flight into Egypt, and Jesus' visit to the Temple when he is twelve. Elegant typeface. Kindergarten and up.

280. Pienkowski, Jan, illus. *Christmas*. New York: Knopf, 1984. unp.

Visually stunning, creative illustrations show Jesus' story from the Annunciation through the return from Egypt. Dramatic black silhouettes on backgrounds glowing with color. Text illuminated with sweeping designs in brilliant shades and gold. Busy, exciting effect. Anachronistic medieval settings. Truncated King James text. Preschool and up.

281. Storr, Catherine. *The Birth of Jesus*. Illus. Gavin Rowe. Milwaukee: Raintree, 1982. 32p.

Straightforward, accurate coverage of material from the Annunciation through the return from Egypt. Omits the presentation at the Temple. Mature, meticulous illustrations in mellow colors. Preschool to third grade.

282. Trimby, Elisa, illus. *The Christmas Story*. New York: Lothrop, 1983. unp.

Excerpts from the King James Version of Mark and Luke and the portion of Isaiah that describes the messianic child to come illustrated in refreshingly distinctive down-to-earth style. Multicolored, crayoned look. Figures verge on caricature and have an unglamorized strength. Mary is unmistakably pregnant; Jesus is an anatomically correct, plump newborn; the shepherds are gap-toothed and knobbly handed; Herod is squat and coarse. Accurate backgrounds, with a cave for the stable. Kindergarten and up.

283. Weil, Lisl. *The Story of the Wise Men and the Child.* Illus. author. New York: Atheneum, 1981. unp.

Short but stately retelling of the Wise Men's arrival in Jerusalem seeking the king of the Jews, drawn from the Gospel of Matthew. Includes Herod's consternation and cruelties, the flight to Egypt, and the return to Nazareth. Unique, simplified, graceful black-and-white drawings with splashes of blue and gold. Preschool to third grade.

284. Williams-Ellis, Virginia. *The Baby Jesus.* Illus. Anna Dzierzek. Milwaukee: Ideals, 1981. unp.

Skillful retelling from the Annunciation through the visit of the Magi. Overwhelmingly busy, brightly colored pictures. Text is above the level of the preschool book format and more suited to kindergarten and early elementary ages.

285. Winthrop, Elizabeth. *A Child Is Born: The Christmas Story.* Illus. Charles Mikolaycak. New York: Holiday, 1983. unp.

Spectacular illustrations with male figures of powerful grace and vitality, dramatic skies filled with the rainbow streamers of angel wings, a tender Mary cherishing her haloed infant. Succinct, slightly simplified version of the King James text begins with the birth in Bethlehem and ends with the naming of the child. All ages.

CHILDHOOD

286. Cassandre. *Life When Jesus Was a Boy.* Illus author. Valley Forge, Pa.: Judson, 1981. unp.

Thorough, well-written narrative filled with information about Jesus' environment--geography, houses, toys, tools, money, birds, religious practices, education, flowers and plants, the city of Jerusalem, etc.--takes him from birth through the visit to the temple at age twelve. Full-page, static pictures in color reinforce the facts. Third grade and up.

287. Eberling, Georgia Moore. *When Jesus Was a Little Boy.* Illus. Katherine Evans. Milwaukee: Ideals, 1954. unp.

Intense blues, reds, and golds spark the simple pictures of a little boy in a long robe exploring his world of lambs, sunbirds, pomegranates, bread-baking, busy marketplaces, and other pleasures. Rhymed text. Preschool to second grade.

288. Morris, Susan, illus. *Jesus Was a Child like You.* Los Angeles: Intervisual Communications, 1981. unp.

Contrasts life as Jesus would have known it as a child with the life of a modern, middle-class American child. Includes cooking methods, school, clothing, games, housing, helping at home. Succinct text illustrated with moveable picture wheels which change scenes from one era to the other. Brightly colored, cheerful artwork. Kindergarten to third grade.

289. Rawson, Christopher, and R.H. Lloyd. *The Childhood of Jesus.* Illus. Victor Ambrus. London: Usborne, 1981. 32p. The Children's Picture Bible Series.

Jesus' life from birth through the visit to the Temple when he is twelve includes the Annunciation, the marriage of Mary and Joseph, the journey to Bethlehem, the visit of the Wise Men, Jesus' circumcision, the flight into Egypt, and life in Nazareth, with details of house and furnishings, religious customs, occupations, feasts, holidays, education, foods. Presented in panels similar to a comic strip, but the artwork is richly colored and meticulous. Lucid text. Third grade and up.

290. Yano, Shigeko, illus. *As Jesus Grew.* Valley Forge, Pa.: Judson, 1972. unp.

Stiffly written but useful account of daily life as Jesus would have known it as a little boy in Nazareth. Shows family activities with which young children can easily identify. Big oil paintings in brilliant colors depict Jesus against a beautiful background of land and sky. Preschool to second grade.

HOLY WEEK AND RESURRECTION

291. Beckmann, Beverly Ann. *From: Understanding the Resurrection*. Illus. Kathy Counts. St. Louis: Concordia, 1980. 40p.

New life arising from seeming death is illustrated by two gray double pages followed by a spread in warm color, as a blazing sunrise overtakes the darkness, spring leaves cover the once-bare branch, the Easter lily grows from the brown bulb, the fuzzy baby bird bursts from the silent egg, the butterfly emerges from the dry cocoon, and the risen Christ leaves the stone-blocked tomb. Helpful concepts. Preschool to fourth grade.

292. De Kort, Kees, illus. *Jesus Is Risen*. Minneapolis: Augsburg, 1969. unp.

Brief sentences tell events from Jesus' prayer in the garden of Gethsemane through the Crucifixion and his resurrected appearance to the disciples in the Upper Room. Impressive pictures of strong, squat figures against dark backgrounds and lit with glowing stained glass colors. Preschool to first grade.

293. Marshall, Martha. *The Wonderful Surprise*. Illus. James Conaway. Wheaton, Ill.: Dandelion, 1983. 31p.

Simple version of the Resurrection. Jesus surprises his friends after his crucifixion by appearing first to the women, then to the men on the Emmaus road, and later to Peter and other disciples. Short sentences, limited vocabulary. Adequate pictures in basic, bright colors. Preschool to early elementary.

294. Odor, Ruth Shannon. *The Happiest Day*. Illus. Helen Endres. Elgin, Ill.: Child's World, 1979. 30p.

Easy text begins with the sorrow of Jesus' friends after his death and continues with the joy of the women who discover the empty tomb and the risen Christ's comforting appearance to his disciples. Sentimentalized, simple pictures. Preschool to kindergarten.

295. Rawson, Christopher. *The Easter Story*. Illus. Victor Ambrus. Tulsa: Hayes, 1981. 33p. The Children's Picture Bible Series.

Crisp retelling of Holy Week, the Resurrection, and Pentecost complements the vigorous color artwork. Strong, intense Jesus lives his last days among carefully detailed disciples, soldiers, Pharisees, common people. All are full of life and individuality. Third to sixth grades, although it is in picture book format.

296. Storr, Catherine. *The First Easter*. Illus. Chris Molan. Milwaukee: Raintree, 1984. 32p.

Bare story from the Last Supper through Jesus' appearance to Mary Magdalene. Loses coherence and clarity by skipping supportive Scriptural details. Needs much additional explanation for intended audience. Forceful, expressive pictures reflect the mood of each scene. Preschool to second grade.

297. Villiers, Marjorie. *Jesus with Us*. Illus. Philip Joudiou. Valley Forge, Pa.: Judson, 1978. unp.

Abrupt, sometimes disjointed account of Holy Week, and some general, quick comments on the Resurrection, the spread of Christianity, and Christian love. Unusual illustrations with flat, almost featureless, figures lit by gleaming colors. Preschool to second grade.

298. Winthrop, Elizabeth. *He Is Risen: The Easter Story*. Illus. Charles Mikolaycak. New York: Holiday, 1985. unp.

Elegantly poetic, slightly modified version of the King James text. Strong, rhythmic artwork with rich, quiet colors, somber mood, careful attention to detail. Christ's bloody, crucified body is overwhelming. Each page has many more events than the picture shows, creating confusion. The resurrection promised in the book title is never shown truly, as the risen Jesus is depicted as a strange, white column with a golden stain. Would need interpretation for younger children. All ages.

Fiction

299. Procter, Marjorie. *The Little Grey Donkey*. Illus. Patricia Papps and Andrew Skilleter. Anderson, Ind.: Warner, 1984. 43p.

Spoiled, nervous donkey colt who would never help others is chosen to carry Jesus into Jerusalem. Filled with new love and trust, he quietly allows Jesus to mount and walks unafraid through the streets. Afterward he is willing to serve others. Sugary tone. Precise, delicately colored illustrations. Kindergarten and first grade.

300. Roche, Luane. *The Proud Tree*. Illus. Jim Corbett. Liguori, Mo.: Liguori, 1981. 64p.

Self-centered tree is cut down and used as the cross for the Crucifixion. Both the tree and Jesus suffer and die together, and it learns humility as they mingle sap and blood. Because the tree repents of its arrogance, it is resurrected as a new green shoot. Black-and-white drawings. First to fourth grades.

MIRACLES

301. De Kort, Kees, illus. *Jesus and a Little Girl*. Minneapolis: Augsburg, 1978. unp. What the Bible Tells Us Series.

Jairus begs Jesus to heal his daughter. Along with James, John, and Peter, Jesus goes to Jairus' house where the child has died and quietly brings her back to life. Text expresses perfectly the basic story. Strong, colorful illustrations. Preschool and kindergarten.

302. De Kort, Kees, illus. *Jesus at the Wedding*. Minneapolis: Augsburg, 1969. unp. What the Bible Tells Us Series.

Marriage at Cana portrayed with primitive, winning charm, aglow with color and good humor. Smiling, bright-eyed people reflect the joy of the wedding and Jesus' first miracle. Brief sentences. Preschool and kindergarten.

303. De Kort, Kees, illus. *Jesus Heals the Blind Man*. Minneapolis: Augsburg, 1968. unp. What the Bible Tells Us Series.

Miserable Bartimaeus, with bandaged eyes, begging bowl, and anachronistic white cane, wails for help from Jesus and is cured. Now wide-eyed with joy, he joins Jesus' followers. Pared-down text retains the impact of the miraculous. Vital, witty illustrations with simplified forms and luminous colors. Preschool and kindergarten.

304. De Kort, Kees, illus. *Jesus Stills the Storm*. Minneapolis: Augsburg, 1968. unp. What the Bible Tells Us Series.

Exciting pictures of the agitated disciples tempest-tossed in foaming indigo waters while Jesus sleeps and the contrasting flat calm after he has stilled the waves. Clearly told text. Preschool and kindergarten.

305. Erickson, Mary E. *Don't Cry for Anna.* Illus. Roger Whitney. Elgin, Ill.: Chariot, 1985. 45p.

Healing of blind Bartimaeus as seen through the eyes of his young son; casting out of demons from the madman into the Gadarene swine as witnessed by Roman centurions and an annoyed pig farmer; the raising of Jairus' daughter. Characters fleshed out, appropriate dialogue added to bring miracle stories to life. Easily readable. Strong drawings, some highlighted with crayon colors. Fourth to sixth grades.

306. Erickson, Mary E. *Survival at Sea.* Illus. Roger Whitney. Elgin, Ill.: Chariot, 1985. 45p.

Three miracles--the feeding of the five thousand, the curing of the leper, the calming of the storm. Gospel account for each is followed by well-dramatized version of the story with lively dialogue and pace. Effective, interesting treatment. Thought-provoking questions and prayer follow each episode. Two- and three-color realistic drawings. Fourth to sixth grades.

307. Hall, Rachel. *Jesus Goes to a Wedding.* Illus. Arthur Baker. St. Louis: Concordia, 1983. unp. Palm Tree Bible Stories Series.

Jesus gets a wedding invitation from Rufus and Judith and dresses carefully for the occasion. Good details of ceremony and celebration. Concludes that Jesus' first miracle is a sign of his greatness and God's glory. Cartoon-style illustrations. Preschool to third grade.

308. Hall, Rachel. *One Leper Says Thank You.* Illus. Arthur Baker. St. Louis: Concordia, 1983. unp. Palm Tree Bible Stories Series.

Chipper retelling of the time Jesus heals ten lepers from their "nasty skin disease," but only one returns to thank and worship him. The other nine think only about planning a celebratory party. Amusing pictures of black-eyed, bearded cartoon figures. Text divided into short, emphatic phrases. Scripture citation. Preschool to second grade.

309. Lindvall, Ella K. *Miracles by the Sea.* Illus. Chris Molan. Chicago: Moody, 1984. 32p.

Very simple presentation of the miracles of the full fishing net, the loaves and fishes, and Jesus walking on water. Emphasizes Jesus' divinity. Sweeping waterscapes and panoramas of attentive crowds skillfully painted in vivid colors. Preschool to third grade.

310. McKenna, Una. *The Man Born Blind*. Illus. Arthur Baker. St. Louis: Concordia, 1983. unp. Palm Tree Bible Stories Series.

Lively retelling with named characters and dialogue covers all the important points, including the Pharisees' anger when Abner testifies that Jesus has been sent by God. Winning pictures of cartoon-style people with personality, in earth-tone colors. Scripture reference. Preschool to second grade.

311. Maier-F., Emil. *Jesus and the Fishermen*. Illus. author. Nashville: Abingdon, 1983. unp.

Jesus calls Peter as a disciple, first telling him to cast his nets where there had been no fish before. After pulling in a huge catch, Peter worships Jesus and leaves all behind to follow him. Very simple text. Expressive illustrations use large, basic figures, strong lines, and rich, luminous colors. Excellent guide for parents and educators. Preschool to second grade.

312. Mitchell, Vic, illus. *Great Miracles of Jesus*. Los Angeles: Intervisual Communications, 1985. unp.

Brief, generally accurate accounts of the miracles of the loaves and fishes, the blind man and the pool at Siloam, the raising of Lazarus, calming the storm, and Jesus' resurrection (too condensed to be successful). Nicely detailed picture wheel illustrations show before and after scenes for each story. Preschool to third grade.

313. Rawson, Christopher, and R.H. Lloyd. *The Miracles of Jesus*. Illus. Victor Ambrus. London: Usborne, 1981. 32p. The Children's Picture Bible Series.

The wedding at Cana, feeding of the five thousand, curing of the leper, healing of blind Bartimaeus and the paralyzed man, calming of the storm on Lake Galilee, and raising of Jairus' daughter described in lively, accurate text and plentiful, expressive, and vigorous color pictures. Third grade and up.

314. Richards, Jean. *Jesus Went about Doing Good*. Illus. Paul Karch. Nashville: Broadman, 1982. 31p.

Healing of the blind, the centurion's servant, the ten

lepers; calming of the storm; feeding of the five thousand. Told in straightforward prose. Stresses the love and power of God as shown through Jesus' miracles. Crisp, two-color drawings. Third to fifth grades.

315. Singleton, Kathy. *Five Loaves and Two Fish*. Illus. Arthur Baker. St. Louis: Concordia, 1982. unp. Palm Tree Bible Stories Series.

Cousins Simon and Joel take a picnic lunch to the lake. Boat lands and crowds gather to hear Jesus tell wise stories and see him heal the sick. At suppertime boys offer Jesus their lunch and he uses it to feed thousands of people, with twelve big baskets of leftovers remaining. Jolly cartoon illustrations. Preschool to third grade.

316. Singleton, Kathy. *Levi, the Lame Man*. Illus. Arthur Baker. St. Louis: Concordia, 1981. unp. Palm Tree Bible Stories Series.

When Jesus sails into Capernaum, everyone rushes to see him. Crippled Levi's friends lower him through a hole in the roof of the house where Jesus is speaking, and Jesus forgives his sins and tells him to get up and walk. To the astonishment of the onlookers and delight of his friends, he does. Lively text. Amusing cartoon illustrations. Preschool to third grade.

PARABLES

317. Butterworth, Nick. *The House on the Rock*. Illus. Mick Inkpen. Portland, Ore.: Multnomah, 1986. unp.

A man chooses a big gray rock for a building site and erects his hut with sweat and strain. It stands firm through a thunderstorm. Another man quickly puts up a shack on sand, and it collapses with the first rain, illustrating Jesus' message in basic text. The color cartoon pictures are lively. Preschool and kindergarten.

318. Butterworth, Nick. *The Lost Sheep*. Illus. Mick Inkpen. Portland, Ore.: Multnomah, 1986. unp.

Farmer in striped, Biblical-style robe counts his sheep with modern calculator, misses one, and searches for it in the henhouse, up hills, through brambles. At last he rescues it from a river. He and the other sheep have a party to celebrate its return. Anachronistic but fun. Amusing color cartoon pictures. Preschool and kindergarten.

319. Butterworth, Nick. *The Precious Pearl.* Illus. Mick Inkpen. Portland, Ore: Multnomah, 1986. unp.

Merchant in fur coat and feathered hat lives in marble mansion with seven refrigerators and a money-stuffed mattress but sells all gladly to buy the perfect pearl. Simple, very updated version of parable. Clever illustrations in soft colors. Preschool to kindergarten.

320. Butterworth, Nick. *The Two Sons.* Illus. Mick Inkpen. Portland, Ore.: Multnomah, 1986. unp.

Parable of the two sons who are asked by their father to pick apples, in this version. The first grumbles but sets to work. The second agrees readily but procrastinates until his brother has finished the job. Jesus' message told in basic manner. Cheery cartoon pictures. Preschool and kindergarten.

321. De Kort, Kees, illus. *The Good Samaritan.* Minneapolis: Augsburg, 1970. unp. What the Bible Tells Us Series.

Answering the question, "Who is my neighbor?" Jesus tells the parable of a man beaten by thieves, ignored by fellow Jews, and cared for tenderly by a stranger. Easy-to-understand message. Vigorous and colorful artwork. Preschool and kindergarten.

322. De Kort, Kees, illus. *The Son Who Left Home.* Minneapolis: Augsburg, 1975. unp. What the Bible Tells Us Series.

The message of joyful forgiveness is not entirely clear in this brief version of the Prodigal Son. Illustrations, though clever and appealing to adults, have a coarse, Breughel-like quality, especially when the prodigal is carousing in the far country. Not suited to the very young audience of preschool to kindergarten children.

323. Doney, Meryl. *The Kind Stranger.* Illus. Graham Round. Minneapolis: Winston, 1979. unp. Winston Windows to Parables Series.

Appealing presentation of the tale of the elderly traveler felled by robbers' clubs in the desert and rescued by the kindly foreigner. Colorful cartoon art. Unfortunately, the question of "Who is my neighbor?" is not even asked, and the message is lost. Scriptural reference. Kindergarten to second grade.

324. Doney, Meryl. *The Lost Sheep*. Illus. Graham Round. Minneapolis: Winston, 1979. unp. Winston Windows to Parables Series.

Curly bearded shepherd searches through thorny bushes and snake-infested rocks until he finds his one hundredth sheep and returns her to the smiling flock of ninety-nine. He and his friends rejoice just as God rejoices when he reclaims a sinner who has strayed. Clear text. Amusing, shiny cartoons. Scriptural reference. Kindergarten to third grade.

325. Doney, Meryl. *The Loving Father*. Illus. Graham Round. Minneapolis: Winston, 1979. unp. Winston Windows to Parables Series.

The resentment of the elder brother is omitted from an otherwise appropriate retelling of the Prodigal Son. Jesus explains his meaning at the end. Bright and lively cartoon pictures enliven the story. Scriptural reference. Kindergarten to second grade.

326. Doney, Meryl. *The Two Houses*. Illus. Graham Round. Minneapolis: Winston, 1979. unp. Winston Windows to Parables Series.

In a straightforward manner the parable of the house built on sand and the one built on rock is told by Jesus to tubby, wide-eyed cartoon people in colorfully striped robes. Scripture reference. Kindergarten to second grade.

327. Dyer, Heather. *The Great Feast*. Illus. Bernard Brett. Elgin, Ill.: Cook, 1980. 29p. The Stories Jesus Told Series.

The great lord invites all the poor and handicapped in the city to his home for a banquet after all of the original guests have made excuses for not attending. Anachronistic in some details but readily understandable and interestingly written. Skillful illustrations in glowing colors. Third and fourth grades.

328. Fletcher, Jane. *The Lost Sheep*. Illus. Arthur Baker. St. Louis: Concordia, 1983. unp. Palm Tree Bible Stories Series.

Ezra, the shepherd, tends his flock of beloved sheep conscientiously. When fluffy little Henry strays, Ezra searches everywhere, finds him, and celebrates with a jolly party. Humorous text. Explanation of parable. Scripture citation. Lively cartoon-style pictures. Preschool to third grade.

329. Fletcher, Jane. *Weeds in the Wheat*. Illus. Arthur Baker. St. Louis: Concordia, 1983. unp. Palm Tree Bible Stories Series.

Jesus, preaching from a boat to a crowd gathered on the shore of the Sea of Galilee, tells about the evil man who stealthily puts weed seeds into a field of wheat. The farmer decides to let the two plants grow together and destroy the weeds at maturity, just as God will eventually separate the good people from the bad. Clear, informal style. Funny, beady-eyed men enliven the color cartoon illustrations. Bible references. Kindergarten to second grade.

330. Lindvall, Ella K. *The Lost Son and Other Stories*. Illus. Gavin Rowe. Chicago: Moody, 1984. 32p.

Short versions of the lost sheep and the lost coin. Main focus is on the prodigal son. God's joy at reclaiming repentant sinners is pointed out in each story. Easy to read. Large, precisely executed, carefully researched, panoramic illustrations in desert tones. Much interesting detail. Kindergarten to third grade.

331. Maier-F., Emil. *The Loving Father*. Illus. author. Nashville: Abingdon, 1983. unp.

Straightforward, short sentences tell parable well until the end, when the elder son's resentment should be made clearer. Strong, primitive-style figures in illustrations are sly, sorrowful, tender--surprisingly expressive despite their simplicity. Warm, clear colors. Helpful adult guide for usage. Preschool to second grade.

332. O'Connor, Francine M. *The Stories of Jesus*. Illus. Kathryn Boswell. Liguori, Mo.: Liguori, 1982. 32p. The ABCs of Faith Series.

The barren fig tree, the good Samaritan, the lost sheep, the wheat and the tares, the laborers in the vineyard, the mustard seed, and five more parables are retold in somewhat awkward but sincere verse form in terms related to young children's lives. Each explained simply and gently. Cheerful tone. Scripture citations. Small, winsome, two-color drawings. Preschool to second grade.

333. Petach, Heidi. *The Lost Sheep*. Illus. author. Cincinnati: Standard, 1984. unp.

Informal but accurate version teaches that God cares about what happens to everyone. Bright, humorous pictures show the shepherd in a sea of cheerful sheep, missing one, peering everywhere for the lost animal, and joyfully finding it. Excellent presentation for preschool to second grade children. Scriptural references.

334. Procter, Marjorie. *The Little Lost Lamb*. Illus. Patricia Papps and Andrew Skilleter. Anderson, Ind.: Warner, 1984. 43p.

Mischievous, talking lamb prances away from the flock in search of greener grass and adventure. Shepherd's love and forgiveness stressed. Plump, gray, black-legged hero stands out against softly colored, precisely detailed backgrounds. Scripture citation. Preschool to second grade.

335. Schindler, Regine. *The Lost Sheep*. Illus. Hilde Heyduck-Huth. Nashville: Abingdon, 1981. unp.

Hard life of the shepherd, constant care he lavishes on his flock, wholehearted search for the missing sheep are stressed in simple text. Pastel-colored, delicate illustrations. Kindergarten to second grade.

II
CHRISTIANITY

336. Baker, Paul. *Contemporary Christian Music: Where It Came From, What It Is, Where It's Going.* Westchester, Ill.: Crossway, 1985. 279p.

In-depth discussion of Christian music history from 1955 to 1984, emphasizing the gradual acceptance of rock and pop styles as valid means of spiritual expression, in spite of formidable opposition. Tells about well-known artists such as Amy Grant, Andrae Crouch, Pat Boone, and others known specifically in this field. Includes successful groups and albums, problems peculiar to Christian music promotion, secular crossovers, Christian music abroad, gospel songs. Discography, music comparison charts, bibliography, notes, index. Sixth grade and up.

337. Brown, Alan. *The Christian World.* Morristown, N.J.: Silver Burdett, 1984. 63p.

Diversity of Christian faith presents serious problems for an overview such as this. Unavoidably cursory and oversimplified. Includes basic beliefs common to all branches; brief section on Jesus and the early church; the Christian Bible; Orthodox, Roman Catholic, Protestant, Pentecostal faiths; a supposedly typical church; role of Mary; communion, baptism, and confirmation; holidays; ecumenism. Good color photographs, art reproductions, and drawings. Glossary, reading list, information centers in the United States, index. Fifth grade and up.

338. Flood, Robert G. *The Christian Kids Almanac.* Illus. Britt Taylor Collins. Elgin, Ill.: Chariot, 1983. 224p.

A collection of trivia. Personality sketches of Christian sports figures, missionaries, businessmen, inventors, entertainers, writers, etc. Information on Christian camps, magazines, organizations, films, music, architecture, and so on. Oddments about DNA, volcanoes, philately, photography, and more. Addresses of places to write for additional materials. Numerous black-and-white drawings and photographs. Index. Fourth grade and up.

DENOMINATIONS

339. Faber, Doris. *The Perfect Life: The Shakers in America*. New York: Farrar, 1974. 224p.

Factual, fair history of the early religious communal sect, founded by Mother Ann Lee, which arose in the eighteenth century and sought freedom of worship in America. Traces its progress to the present day. List of museums with displays of Shaker crafts, bibliography, index. Fifth grade and up.

340. Meara, Jane. *Growing Up Catholic: An Infinitely Funny Guide for the Faithful, the Fallen, and Everyone In-Between*. Illus. Bob Kiley. Garden City, N.Y.: Doubleday, 1985. 144p.

Amusing survey of the common experiences of American Catholic children includes much about parochial schools and attending mass, plus sidelights on priests, nuns, saints, retreats, heaven, hell, and more. Strong, unitive faith shines through the lovingly satirized mores. Illustrated in black and white with cartoons, photographs, lists, report cards, and so forth. Fifth grade and up.

341. Mitchell, Barbara. *Tomahawks and Trombones*. Illus. George Overlie. Minneapolis: Carolrhoda, 1982. 56p.

Spirited retelling of semi-legendary incident in which Moravians in eighteenth-century Bethlehem, Pennsylvania, frighten off Delaware Indian attackers with triumphant trombone blasts from a housetop on Christmas morning. Descriptions of Moravian customs and love of music. Easy reader level text. Lively two-color illustrations. Kindergarten to fourth grade.

Fiction

342. Arrick, Fran. *God's Radar*. Scarsdale, N.Y.: Bradbury, 1983. 224p.

When fifteen-year-old Roxie Cable and her family move

from New York State to a small Southern town, they are warmly received by their born-again Christian neighbors and become deeply drawn into the Fundamentalist group. Although Roxie is not completely won over to their way of thinking, she agrees to attend the church school and submits to her parents and Christian friends in the end. Slightly biased but generally straightforward picture of born-again groups. Taut, suspenseful writing. Sixth grade and up.

343. Hickman, Janet. *Zoar Blue*. New York: Macmillan, 1978. 140p.

A seventeen-year-old boy, a member of the German pacifist Society of Separatists of Zoar, Pennsylvania, feels morally compelled to abandon his religious precepts and join the Union Army in the Civil War. At the same time a young orphan girl who has been taken in by the Separatists runs away to look for her uncle. Both return to the community with a great appreciation of what it offers. Sober tone. Authentically and skillfully written. Fifth grade and up.

344. Hughes, Monica. *Beyond the Dark River*. New York: Atheneum, 1981. 152p.

Before a devastating atomic war an Indian tribe has withdrawn from civilization to live a pure, spiritual life in harmony with nature, and a group of Hutterites have isolated themselves to practice their strict religion unimpeded. When a child-killing illness sweeps the Hutterite community, a fifteen-year-old boy seeks the help of a young Indian medicine woman. Well written and absorbing. Fifth grade and up.

SOCIETY OF FRIENDS

345. Bacon, Margaret H. *The Quiet Rebels: The Story of Quakers in America*. New York: Basic, 1969. 229p.

The American Society of Friends is traced from the first arrivals in 1656 in Boston through its years of bitter persecution, its opposition to slavery, and its pioneering work for social change. Includes outstanding Quaker figures, the schisms and changes that have occurred over the centuries. Describes tenets of the faith. Sympathetic tone. Interestingly written. Fifth grade and up.

Fiction

346. West, Jessamyn. *The Friendly Persuasion.* New York: Harcourt, 1940. 214p.

The Birdwells are simple in their wants and staunch in their Quaker faith but adventurous enough to enjoy a horse race and courageous enough to shelter runaway slaves. They meet life on an eighteenth-century Pennsylvania farm with wisdom, humor, and love. Winning portrayals. Fifth grade and up.

MENNONITES

347. Dyck, Cornelius. *Twelve Becoming: Biographies of Mennonite Disciples from the Sixteenth to the Twentieth Century.* Illus. Richard Loehle. Newton, Kans.: Faith and Life, 1973. 126p.

Chronological biographical sketches of Menno Simons, Christopher Dock, Johann Cornies, John Oberholtzer, David Toews, Cornelius Klassen, Lena Graber, Joe Walks Along, etc. All are Mennonite luminaries who worked in countries throughout the world. Laudatory tone. Anecdotes and dialogue add interest value. Fifth grade and up.

348. Meyer, Carolyn. *Amish People: Plain Living in a Complex World.* New York: Atheneum, 1976. 152p.

Uses a typical family to illustrate the dilemmas and satisfactions of the Amish people and describes their work, worship, and social customs. Absorbing, carefully researched, understandingly written. Photographs. Sixth grade and up.

Fiction

349. De Angeli, Marguerite. *Henner's Lydia.* Garden City, N.Y.: Doubleday, 1946. unp.

Life in an Amish family tenderly presented as they enjoy their rural, segregated existence of hard work, homecooked food, good friends, and one-room-school education. Slight plot in which Lydia finishes a rug she is hooking and is allowed to visit the city with her father. Warmly appreciative tone. Illustrated with scenes of farm activities. Fourth to sixth grades.

350. Lasky, Kathryn. *Beyond the Divide*. New York: Macmillan, 1983. 254p.

After her father has been shunned by their Pennsylvania Amish community for disobeying the church elders, fourteen-year-old Meribah joins him as he emigrates west by wagon train. Their decency and kindness contrast with the greed and selfishness of their fellow travelers. Portrays Amish family life and religious ideals. Vivid, pictorial writing style. Well-realized characters and settings. Sixth grade and up.

351. Smucker, Barbara. *Amish Adventure*. Scottdale, Pa.: Herald, 1983. 144p.

After the car in which he is riding smashes into an Amish buggy, seventh-grader Ian is taken in by the Amish family and quickly learns to admire their kindliness, strict faith, and simple way of life. Contrived plot is rescued by the interesting, carefully researched, warmly presented details of Amish life. Lively style, fast pace. Notes, bibliography. Fifth grade and up.

352. Sorensen, Virginia. *Plain Girl*. Illus. Charles Greer. New York: Harcourt, 1955. 151p.

Amish life with its stress on close family ties and strict rules for living is accurately depicted in story of ten-year-old Esther who must attend public school. There she learns to enjoy non-Amish friendship without jeopardizing her religious beliefs. Interesting details, sympathetic characterizations, satisfying plot. Fourth to sixth grades.

353. Weiman, Eiveen. *Which Way Courage*. New York: Atheneum, 1981. 132p.

Tenets of her Old Amish religion--limited education, early marriage, rural living, and passive acceptance of any setback as being God's will--disturb fourteen-year-old Courage. When her younger brother becomes seriously ill, and their father refuses to seek medical treatment for him, she has some hard decisions to make. Understanding and well written. Fifth grade and up.

MORMONS

Fiction

354. Wells, Marian. *The Wedding Dress*. Minneapolis: Bethany House, 1982. 263p.

Bitter indictment of Mormons dominates competently written, suspenseful but lurid story of orphan girl who joins a wagon train bound for Salt Lake City and is cruelly deceived into a plural marriage. She is too bright and independent to submit satisfactorily, and eventually her husband shoots her for disobedience. Improbable happy ending. Sixth grade and up.

355. Williams, Barbara. *Brigham Young and Me, Clarissa*. Garden City, N.Y.: Doubleday, 1978. 80p.

Slight story of Brigham Young's fifty-first child, a spoiled eight-year-old daughter, portrays the Church of Jesus Christ of Latter Day Saints as overbearing, exclusive, self-satisfied, and rich. Description of daily life among the polygamous Mormons is uninteresting. Third to fourth grades.

III
CHRISTIAN THEOLOGY

356. Fogle, Jeanne S. *Signs of God's Love: Baptism and Communion*. Illus. Bea Weidner. Philadelphia: Geneva, 1984. 32p.

Excellent presentation that can be interpreted in more detail by an adult to suit each denomination. Baptism is equated with belonging to God and to the worldwide family of Christians, with the gift of the Holy Spirit. Communion can be interpreted literally or figuratively but is always a sign that God in Jesus is with us. Handsome graphics in bright colors. Concepts interpreted clearly, in large type. Preschool to third grade.

357. Hill, Harold. *From Goo to You by Way of the Zoo*. Rev. ed. Old Tappan, N.J.: Revell, 1976. 223p.

Colloquial, anecdote-filled, declarative argument for Creationism over Evolution. Claims to refute Darwin, carbon-dating, and anything else indicating the earth is more than ten thousand years old as corny science fiction. Discusses DNA, laws of thermodynamics, hybridization, fossils, the Holy Spirit, Adam and Eve, God, and much more. Bible verses amply quoted. Bibliography. Fifth grade and up.

358. Holland, Isabelle. *Abbie's God Book*. Illus. James McLaughlin. Philadelphia: Westminster, 1982. 80p.

Preteen Abigail keeps a diary in which she applies her own intelligence to her personal daily experiences and continually expands her knowledge of God through her thoughts. Her parents guide her with helpful comments but never press her to adopt their beliefs. Crisply written and realistic. Fifth grade and up.

359. Jahsmann, Allan Hart. *I Wonder: Answers to Religious Questions Children Ask*. Illus. Dick Cosper. St. Louis: Concordia, 1979. 120p.

Fundamentalist answers to questions concerning God, Jesus, angels, devils, sin, forgiveness, Christianity, etc. Pithy, informal style. Large, realistic, black-and-white drawings of children playing have an attractive solidity. Kindergarten and up.

360. Kater, John. *Another Letter of John to James about Church and the Eucharist*. Illus. Nancy Willard. New York: Seabury, 1982. 58p.

Answers a child's questions about church, the Eucharist, and God. Every Sunday is like a birthday, a special day to remember Jesus' resurrection and gather as part of his family. The Eucharist is a thanksgiving for Jesus and all of God's gifts, celebrated with special foods in memory of the Last Supper. God is unseen, but like the wind he gives signs everywhere of his presence. Three-color handprinted text and simple, zestful drawings. Preschool to second grade.

361. Mueller, Virginia. *What Is Faith?* Illus. Kathryn Hutton. Cincinnati: Standard, 1980. unp.

Faith is believing in the future of a seed, a caterpillar, a bird's egg; believing that a birthday is coming and that you will grow up someday; looking for God and his love in nature and family. Apple-cheeked small children are shown indoors and outside in familiar settings. Preschool and kindergarten.

362. Nystrom, Carolyn. *Why Do I Do Things Wrong?* Illus. Wayne A. Hanna. Chicago: Moody, 1981. unp.

Simple explanation of the origin of sin through Adam and Eve, the operation of Satan in the world, the forgiveness of sin through Jesus, and examples of sin in the everyday life of a little boy in blue overalls. Appropriate Scriptural references. Cartoon illustrations with big blocks of color. Preschool to second grade.

363. Schoolland, Marian M. *Leading Little Ones to God*. 2nd rev. ed. Illus. Paul Stoub. Grand Rapids, Mich.: Eerdmans, 1981. 173p.

Enthusiastic, skillful presentation of basic theology for young children. Discusses God, Jesus, the Holy Spirit, sin, prayer, the sacraments, righteous living, and eschatology. Many Scripture citations, memory verses, Bible readings, discussion questions, hymns, and prayers. Eighty-six sections. Dull color pictures. Preschool to second grade.

364. Schulz, Charles M. *And the Beagles and the Bunnies Shall Lie Down Together: The Theology in Peanuts*. Illus. author. New York: Holt, 1984. unp.

Collection of comic strips from 1958 to 1983 in which the cartoonist incorporates a Scriptural quote or theological message with gentle wit. Some concepts will be unfamiliar to children, but the characters are always appealing. Topics include eschatology, the Great Pumpkin cult, a specious miracle, the real meanings of Christmas, etc. Fifth grade and up.

365. Speerstra, Karen. *I Believe: A Child's Guide to Understanding Basic Christian Beliefs*. Illus. Erin Leigh. St. Louis: Concordia, 1980. unp.

Brief and simple statement of basic Christian beliefs: God is trinitarian, all-powerful, loving; Jesus is divine and human, taught love, was crucified to save humankind, rose again. Also stresses the Bible, Ten Commandments, prophets, and sacraments. Sprightly black-and-white drawings. Kindergarten to fourth grade.

ANGELS

366. Hunt, Marigold. *A Book of Angels*. Rev. ed. Huntington, Ind.: Our Sunday Visitor, 1978. 143p.

Lively accounts of angels' activities throughout the Bible include the Garden of Eden, Abraham's visitors and the destruction of Sodom, Jacob's ladder, Balaam, Tobit, Belshazzar's feast, the Annunciation, the angel at the garden tomb, Peter's release from prison, Revelation, and more. Some Roman Catholic doctrine. Stylish black-and-white drawings. Fourth grade and up.

367. Nystrom, Carolyn. *Angels and Me*. Illus. Wayne A. Hanna. Chicago: Moody, 1984. unp.

Passages on angels from Psalms, Genesis, Matthew, Hebrews, etc. Freely interpreted for small children. Discusses angels' creation, purpose as messengers and protectors, strength, wisdom. Various types mentioned. God's primacy over them stressed. Bright cartoon illustrations of a little boy in overalls and human-looking angels. Preschool to second grade.

DEATH

Fiction

368. Alex, Marlee. *Grandpa and Me: We Learn about Death*. Minneapolis: Bethany House, 1982. 43p.

Useful and sensitive presentation of Christian thought about death. In Denmark little Maria visits her grandparents on their farm, experiences the death of a kitten, and discusses it with her grandfather. Later she visits him in the hospital when he is terminally ill. At his death the family's grief is deep but tempered by a firm belief in resurrection. Realistic but positive tone. Fine color photographs of a lively child enjoying happy times on the farm as well as sad moments of mourning. Kindergarten to fourth grade.

369. Barker, Peggy. *What Happened When Grandma Died*. Illus. Patricia Mattozzi. St. Louis: Concordia, 1984. unp.

At death grandma left her old body, house, and life and will receive new ones in Heaven. Gentle and reassuring. Scriptural references. Ethereal, softly colored pictures and black-and-white drawings of grandmother with grandchildren and the funeral. Kindergarten to third grade.

370. Bunting, Eve. *The Happy Funeral*. Illus. Vo-Dinh Mai. New York: Harper, 1982. 40p.

Little Chinese-American girls mourn the death of their grandfather and participate in his funeral. Although the service is in the Chinese Gospel Church, traditional non-Christian rituals involving the burning of symbolic objects are performed to assist him happily into the world of spirits. Tender, simple text understands children's grief. Delicate, expressive black-and-white drawings. Kindergarten to fourth grade.

371. Coburn, John B. *Anne and the Sand Dobbies*. New York: Seabury, 1964. 121p.

Eleven-year-old Danny's two-year-old sister and his pet

dog die close in time. The effect of these different losses on Danny and his family, who are sometimes quarrelsome and careless of one another, is to strengthen and enlarge their love in a believable way. Theological questions of why God allows the good and innocent to die and what death and heaven are like are faced, with no pat answers given. Although Jesus is mentioned, the emphasis is on a universal God, and the book could be used for other faiths. Third through sixth grades.

372. Hogan, Bernice. *My Grandmother Died, but I Won't Forget Her*. Illus. Nancy Munger. Nashville: Abingdon, 1983. unp.

A little boy experiences common events associated with a death in the family: neighbors and friends bringing food and flowers, offering consolation; out-of-town relatives gathering; and the funeral. He misses his grandmother deeply, but the special experiences they shared will keep her memory alive and beloved. Gentle, understanding text matched by expressive black-white-beige illustrations. Preschool to third grade.

373. Koch, Ron. *Goodbye Grandpa*. Illus. Don Wallerstedt. Minneapolis: Augsburg, 1975. 96p.

Frightened by his grandfather's impending death from cancer, eleven-year-old Joey refuses to visit him at the nursing home. When Joey becomes lost on Christmas Eve and receives love and concern from others, he realizes that he must overcome his own fear and think of his grandfather's welfare. Sympathetic treatment of Joey's reactions. Suggestions made through story to help children in similar situations. Christian faith of both family and grandfather help them accept death. Black-and-white drawings. Fifth grade and up.

374. Lee, Virginia. *The Magic Moth*. Boston: Houghton Mifflin, 1981. 64p.

Maryanne, ten-year-old middle child in the Foss family, is bedridden with an incurable heart defect. Mark-O, six, struggles with the knowledge that she will soon die, brings her daily gifts, asks questions about suffering and death. When Maryanne dies, a beautiful white moth emerges from its cocoon at her bedside. This symbol helps Mark-O realize that she has progressed to a new and better life after enriching her family, and will live forever in their hearts. Straightforward and well written. Fourth to sixth grades.

375. Nixon, Joan Lowery. *The Butterfly Tree*. Illus. James McIlrath. Huntington, Ind.: Our Sunday Visitor, 1979. unp.

Although Jennifer's great grandmother misses the blooming cherry trees after she moves from Washington to Texas to spend her final days, Jennifer shows her the special beauty of a tree covered with migrating Monarch butterflies. Depicts the loving care of the elderly, the sacrament of anointing the sick. Death treated as a normal part of the human journey toward unity with God. Bright pictures. Kindergarten to third grade.

376. Nystrom, Carolyn. *What Happens When We Die?* Illus. Wayne A. Hanna. Chicago: Moody, 1981. unp.

Cheerful, Fundamentalist view of life after death for little children. Small boy questions his mother after the death of a bird, and she discusses the Fall of Adam and Eve, Jesus' sacrifice, the soul, the resurrection of the body, and the beautiful wonders of heaven. Reassuring and comprehensible. Basic illustrations in brilliant colors. Scripture references. Preschool to second grade.

377. Sorenson, Jane. *Jennifer Says Good-bye*. Cincinnati: Standard, 1984. 128p.

Jennifer is a junior high student and new Christian who loses her beloved grandfather right after a joyful visit with her devout grandparents in Florida. Discusses grief, various aspects of a funeral, the consolations of the Christian faith. Emphatic, easy-to-read style. Poorly organized plot. Sixth grade and up.

378. Wangerin, Walter. *Potter, Come Fly to the First of the Earth*. Illus. Daniel San Souci. Elgin, Ill.: Cook, 1985. 52p.

Unusual fantasy dealing with death, resurrection, and the love of parents, friends, and God. While Potter is seriously ill, his best friend drowns. Fevered, angry, and grief-stricken, Potter has out-of-body experiences in which he becomes a dove and is guided by a mysterious oriole to learn the "holy things of God," such as sacrificial death and the promise of resurrection. Love, divine and human, is the core theme. Lush, poetic style. Realistic, full-page color illustrations. Fourth grade and up.

HEAVEN

379. Roberts, Evelyn. *Heaven Has a Floor*. Illus. Kees de Kiefte. Garden City, N.Y.: Dial, 1979. unp.

Heaven is a city with walls of jewel-like stones, pearl gates, gold streets, etc., all filled with the light of Jesus, according to the conservative Christian author. God has created it in the sky for angels and people. Designed to soothe a child's fear of death and written in simple, short sentences. Static, overly sweet, pastel pictures of children of various races and winged cherubs. Preschool to second grade.

380. Ziegler, Sandra. *Where Is Heaven?* Illus. Mina Gow McLean. Cincinnati: Standard, 1981. unp.

Mystery of heaven pondered by a young boy and his father as they sit in a boat, fishing. Disjointed text touches upon the manna in Exodus, Elijah and the fiery chariot, Jesus' promise of the many mansions, the heavenly host appearing to the shepherds, and the Second Coming. Undistinguished color artwork. Kindergarten to second grade.

Fiction

381. Zemach, Margot. *Jake and Honeybunch Go to Heaven*. Illus. author. New York: Farrar, 1982. unp.

Book's publication caused a furor in many areas because of its *Green Pastures* style. It depicts a rural black heaven as a place of barbecues, jazz bands, and a patriarchal God with a starry bow tie and appears to be set in the 1930s. The genial, folk-tale-type narrative tells of a fiercely contrary mule who kicks her way through the Pearly Gates, gaining admission to heaven for her master. Illustrations are splendid with flying forms and bursts of color. No racial slur seems intended in this warm and humorous depiction of a bygone culture. Kindergarten to fourth grade.

HOLY SPIRIT

382. Nystrom, Carolyn. *The Holy Spirit in Me*. Illus. Wayne A. Hanna. Chicago: Moody, 1980. unp.

Ways in which the Holy Spirit operates in the life of a little boy, helping him to avoid wrongdoing, care for himself properly, learn about Jesus, witness, pray, love others. Also discusses the inspiration of those who wrote the Bible, the disciples at Pentecost, the Fruits of the Spirit. Text and concepts on a young child's level. Simple pictures in vivid colors. Preschool to third grade.

383. Roberts, Sharon Lee. *Somebody Lives Inside: The Holy Spirit*. Illus. Lee W. Brubaker. St. Louis: Concordia, 1986. unp.

Although invisible like the wind, the Holy Spirit can be discerned by a child in various ways. It helps him understand Jesus, comforts him, leads him to right action, gives him strength, etc. Includes Fruits of the Spirit. Partially rhymed text is weak. Strange, mostly black-and-white pictures in which large, well-drawn heads of children appear to be growing from treetrunks. Kindergarten to third grade.

TEN COMMANDMENTS

384. Cioni, Ray, and Sally Cioni. *The Droodles Ten Commandments Storybook*. Illus. Jerry Tiritilli. Elgin, Ill.: Cook, 1983. 64p.

Short object lessons vaguely associated with the Commandments. Lenny makes television his god and has to be surgically cured; Marcia Branedrane uses her father's name to justify all kinds of mischief; angry Jenny dreams that she can destroy people she doesn't like, etc. Illustrations of gently grotesque, multicolored creatures cavorting through the various situations. Kindergarten to fourth grade.

385. Eller, Vernard. *The Mad Morality*. Nashville: Abingdon, 1970. 80p.

Typical Mad Magazine satirical comic strips, poems, and

cartoons illustrate each of the Commandments, and then a serious exposition follows. Modern applications include hypocritical churches, the generation gap, drunk driving, cheating on exams, etc. The bludgeoning wit of the 1950s and 1960s still makes valid points, even though the material is often dated. Sixth grade and up.

386. O'Connor, Francine M. *The Ten Commandments*. Illus. Kathryn Boswell. Liguori, Mo.: Liguori, 1980. 32p. ABCs of Faith Series.

Little stories told in verse deal with the importance of rules and then take each individual commandment and relate it to a small child's experiences. Those dealing with killing and adultery are modified and softened. Perky line drawings accented in red. Kindergarten to second grade.

GOD

387. Abrams, Connie. *God Is in the Night*. Illus. Kathryn Hutton. Cincinnati: Standard, 1984. unp.

A little girl and her mother talk about people such as firemen and hospital nurses who work at night, animals, and the moon and stars. Mother explains that God sees and cares for everything all over the world, in the dark as well as in the day. Reassuring, simple text and pictures. Preschool and first grade.

388. Anderson, Debby. *God Gives Me a Smile!* Illus. author. Elgin, Ill.: Cook, 1985. unp.

Wispy children of various races with Smile Face heads play outdoors, picnic, attend nursery school, snuggle in bed, etc., as text tells gently of God's eternity, creativity, love, protection, and understanding. Cheery pictures. Preschool.

389. Anderson, Debby. *God Is the Greatest!* Illus. author. Elgin, Ill.: Cook, 1985. unp.

Satisfying message is that although God is vast and powerful, he hears and loves little children and entrusts to them the care of earth's creatures. The appealing illustrations done in flat cartoon style with many colors and details show children feeding birds and pets, enjoying the farm, seashore, snowy woods, etc. Preschool.

390. Lo, Jim. *God Loves Everyone*. Illus. Carolyn Bowser. St. Louis: Concordia, 1984. unp.

Andy goes to church and hears his pastor explain that God loves Namibians, Ghanans, Nepalese, Indians, Chinese, Peruvians, Eskimos, etc., no matter what their age or color. Realistic black-and-white and color illustrations dominate simple text and show the peoples at their everyday activities. Strong Christian message of John 3:16. Preschool to second grade.

391. Marxhausen, Joanne. *3 in 1 (A Picture of God)*. Illus. Benjamin Marxhausen. St. Louis: Concordia, 1973. 47p.

Using the familiar skin, flesh, and seeds of an apple--three elements in one--as a comparison, the tripartite functions of God are explained. Additional themes include God's love, reconciliation, redemption, faith, and the Fruits of the Spirit. Bold, handsome design and poster bright colors add drama. Preschool to second grade.

392. Nystrom, Carolyn. *Who Is God?* Illus. Wayne A. Hanna. Chicago: Moody, 1980. unp.

Answers to a young child's questions about God's appearance, omnipotence, omnipresence, omniscience, perfection, holiness, justice are given in understandable terms with illustrations from familiar experiences. Gives an associated Scriptural reference. Text and simply drawn, colorful pictures center around a little boy and his family. Preschool to second grade.

393. Walters, Julie. *God Is Like: Three Parables for Little Children*. Notre Dame, Ind.: Ave Maria, 1974. unp.

Unaffected by weather and waves, a rock at the edge of a lake is a fine place for a little boy to play. As the child grows, the rock is unchanged like God the Father. As they light candles and a warm camp fire, the boy and his father are reminded that Jesus is the light of the world. When the wind blows over the woods and water with unseen force, it is like the Holy Spirit. Simple drawings of a child at imaginative play. Preschool to third grade.

394. Watson, Elizabeth Elaine. *Where Are You, God?* Illus. Ronald R. Hester. Nashville: Broadman, 1976. 32p.

Mop-haired little boy asks God if he lives up high and

can see the little boy sleeping, playing, misbehaving, praying, etc. Then, rather illogically, he answers his own questions by saying he knows God is everywhere. Splashy, big two-color pictures, brief text. Preschool to first grade.

395. Watson, Jane Werner. *My Little Golden Book about God*. Illus. Eloise Wilkin. New York: Simon, 1956. unp.

Greatness, goodness, lovingness of God described succinctly in musical language and illustrated with delicate beauty. Apple-cheeked tots enjoy flowers, insects, birds, starry nights, food, rain, bedtime prayers, adoring parents. Preschool to first grade.

396. Wells, Mick, illus. *God Loves Me*. Belleville, Mich.: Lion, 1981. unp.

Sharp color and simple cartoon figures enliven text about the caring love of parents, grandparents, and friends, who look after the child, comfort him when he is frightened, help him, and always have time for him. God, too, does these same things. Preschool.

397. Yano, Shigeko. *One Spring Day*. Illus. author. Valley Forge, Pa.: Judson, 1977. unp.

Although God is unseen, he exists in the same way as do the stars in the daytime sky, the bird hidden inside the egg, and the countryside over the crest of the hill. Full- and double-page spreads of misty, glowing pictures in an Impressionistic style. Preschool.

Creative Aspects

398. Andersen, Cay M. *Here Comes Jonathan!* Illus. Mary Lane. Orleans, Mass.: Paraclete, 1982. unp.

Fuzzy, impish white poodle barks, plays with his ball, and jumps about in sketchy, warm pictures. Text is in plaid, flowered, polka-dotted, multicolored large and small printing. Dog is shown being hugged by Jesus. Preschool.

399. Bennett, Marian. *God Made Chickens*. Illus. Heidi Petach. Cincinnati: Standard, 1985. unp.

Little girl on prosperous-looking farm tells how she and her brother feed and care for the chickens, how baby chicks develop within the egg, hatch, and are protected by their mothers, all according to God's plan. Many multicolored hens and a crested rooster in simple artwork. Preschool and kindergarten.

400. *Bright and Beautiful*. Belleville, Mich.: Lion, 1976. unp.

Bright things paired with beautiful ones: colors with flowers, water with fish, sun with butterflies, feathers with a pheasant, children's eyes with their smiles. Sparkling interpretation of the first line of the famous hymn. Preschool.

401. Caswell, Helen. *God's World Makes Me Feel So Little*. Illus. author. Nashville: Abingdon, 1985. unp.

Tousle-haired tot is overwhelmed by the size of the ocean, city, forest, and sky, and wonders if God cares about anything as small as he. Then he remembers God has created even tinier things--butterflies, kittens, flowers, mice--and knows God loves him. Quiet, thoughtful pictures emphasize beauties of Nature in soft colors. Preschool.

402. Doney, Meryl. *Discovering at the Zoo*. Belleville, Mich.: Lion, 1974. 28p.

Fine color photographs of plump and healthy seals, bears, elephants, giraffes, dolphins, tigers, etc., with interesting facts about each. Stresses the special shape, hue, and activity of each member of God's creation. Kindergarten to second grade.

403. Doney, Meryl. *Discovering Everyday Things*. Belleville, Mich.: Lion, 1974. 28p.

Closeups of objects such as finger whorls, tongue bumps, butterfly wings, insect eyes, microscopic pond animals, etc., are shown next to pictures of them in their normal, familiar sizes. Simple identifying text. Stresses beauty and variety of God's creation. Photographs in brilliant color and black and white. Preschool to second grade.

404. Doney, Meryl. *Discovering out of Doors*. Belleville, Mich: Lion, 1974. 28p.

Dew-spangled spider web, dandelion puffball, bright-eyed English robin, iridescent snail, and other common but fascinating objects from God's beautiful world are shown in excellent color photographs. Preschool to second grade.

405. Doney, Meryl. *Discovering the City*. Belleville, Mich.: Lion, 1980. 31p.

Lively, artistically photographed scenes of city life throughout the world. Buildings, skylines, parks, sporting events, happy crowds all show the excitement of the urban bustle and variety. Theme is God's role as creator and enabler of man's creativity. Simple text. Kindergarten to third grade.

406. Fitzgerald, Annie. *Dear God Kids Animal Friends*. Illus. author. New York: Simon, 1984. unp.

Red-cheeked, sketchy tots compliment God on plump kittens, tigers, fish, chickens, and other interesting animal creations. Preschool.

407. *God Made Me*. Norwalk, Conn.: Gibson, 1974. unp.

Chestnut-haired child tries out his eyes, nose, ears, arms, etc., doing satisfying things. Preschool.

408. *God Planned It So*. Norwalk, Conn.: Gibson, 1974. unp.

Round-faced toddlers see examples of God's plans being carried out in sweet-smelling flowers, happy play, night and day, growing up. Color pictures. Preschool.

409. Goddard, Carrie Lou. *God, You Are Always with Us*. Illus. Kozo Kakimoto. Nashville: Abingdon, 1983. unp.

Richly colored paintings in primitive style, one-dimensional, decorative patterns show the everyday beauties of God's creation to Mary and Jeremy on an early morning walk. They enjoy such wonders as a rooster, a rainbow, a radish, a cow, an ant, and a gorgeous flower garden. Preschool to kindergarten.

410. Goddard, Carrie Lou. *Isn't It a Wonder!* Illus. Leigh Grant. Nashville: Abingdon, 1976. unp.

God's wonderful creations include sun, wind, puppies, ponies, trees, eyes, arms, grandparents, and many other things meaningful to small children. All are good because God made them. Perky blue, gold, and white format shows children enjoying these pleasures. Preschool to second grade.

411. Johnston, Dorothy Grunbock. *Stop, Look, Listen*. Illus. Florence Masters. Cincinnati: Standard, 1977. unp.

Little girl appreciates all the familiar things she can

see, hear, taste, feel, and smell. She thinks of God and gives thanks for creation. Crisp, bright pictures of red-haired, freckled child with parents, pets, friends. Preschool and kindergarten.

412. Le Bar, Mary. *How God Gives Us Apples*. Illus. Kathryn Hutton. Cincinnati: Standard, 1979. unp.

Very simple explanation of the development of an apple tree. Seed inside fruit falls into the earth, responds to sun and rain, changes from seedling to tree, blooms, and bears fruit--all thanks to God's creation and nurture. Very colorful but pedestrian illustrations. Preschool to second grade.

413. Le Bar, Mary. *How God Gives Us Ice Cream*. Illus. Kathryn Hutton. Cincinnati: Standard, 1979. unp.

Simple verse text. Milk comes from the cow and is distributed to the grocery store; hens lay eggs; sugar canes are cut and processed. All are combined in an ice cream freezer by a happy family. God is thanked for his gifts. Basic, cheerful pictures. Preschool to second grade.

414. Le Bar, Mary. *How God Gives Us Peanut Butter*. Illus. Kathryn Hutton. Cincinnati: Standard, 1979. unp.

Farmers plant peanuts, and God gives them sun and rain to grow. Describes harvesting, drying, and processing of peanuts for eventual use on sandwich. Good details in plain, clear color pictures. Easy verse form. Preschool to second grade.

415. Linam, Gail. *God's Winter Gifts*. Illus. Ronald R. Hester. Nashville: Broadman, 1979. 32p.

Chubby little boy wakes up to a snowy world, dresses warmly, plays happily until he gets cold, and comes in for hot chocolate. His mother tells him snow is a beautiful winter gift from God. Adequate pictures. Preschool.

416. Meyer, Kathleen Allan. *God Sends the Seasons*. Illus. James McIlrath. Huntington, Ind.: Our Sunday Visitor, 1981. unp.

Special fun of each season sent by God is described in simple verses and big, colorful pictures of sturdy tots playing outdoors. All but city children can identify with them. Preschool.

417. Moncure, Jane Belk. *Thank You, God, for Fall*. Rev. ed. Illus. Frances Hook. Elgin, Ill.: Child's World, 1979. 24p.

Small, dark-haired boy enjoys autumn's treats--apples, football, pumpkins, colored leaves, crisp weather, family activities. His little prayers of thanksgiving are easily understood. Attractive illustrations in warm colors. Preschool and kindergarten.

418. Moncure, Jane Belk. *Thank You, God, for Winter*. Rev. ed. Illus. Frances Hook. Elgin, Ill.: Child's World, 1979. 24p.

Long-haired girl with rosy cheeks appreciates winter's joys--snowmen, icicles, skating ponds, snowbirds, Christmas, and Jesus--in idealized, softly colored settings. She thanks God for all these gifts in a simple text. Preschool and kindergarten.

419. Neeves, D'reen, illus. *God Made Them All*. Belleville, Mich.: Lion, 1981. unp.

Jolly, stylized insects, flowers, trees, sparrows, horse, pig, and children in brilliant colors. Three-word, repetitive rhymes tell how God made them all. Preschool.

420. Oda, Stephanie C. *Having Fun in God's World*. Illus. June Goldsborough. Norwalk, Conn.: Gibson, 1982. unp.

Pleasurable activities God provides for children--shopping, playing, going to church, having a birthday, visiting the zoo, etc.--are illustrated by a mop-haired little boy and his family and friends. Preschool.

421. Oda, Stephanie C. *We Celebrate God's Seasons*. Illus. Lynn Titleman. Norwalk, Conn.: Gibson, 1982. unp.

Daffodils, lambs, fledglings, and Easter for spring; summer fun in the park and Independence Day; autumn leaves, apple-picking, Thanksgiving; ice skating and Christmas for winter are shown in gay cartoon-like pictures. Short, rhymed text. Preschool.

422. Smart, Christopher. *For I Will Consider My Cat Jeoffry*. Illus. Emily Arnold McCully. New York: Atheneum, 1984. unp.

Hymn of praise to a cat is a portion of *Jubilate Agno* by the eighteenth-century eccentric but pious British poet. Everything Jeoffry is and does celebrates God, from his orison to the morning sun to his counteraction of the powers of darkness at night. Suitable, sketchy illustrations in black and white and clear color depict the cat in all his sinuous poses. Fourth to sixth grades.

HUMAN BODY

423. De Jonge, Joanne E. *A Beautiful Gift: Your Awakening Sexuality*. Illus. Pat Adamik. Grand Rapids: Baker, 1985. 95p.

Easily understood, thorough presentation of information on male and female sex organs, sexual intercourse, and puberty with explicit, well-done, two-color diagrammatic illustrations. Homosexuality, abortion, Caesarian-section, birth control, menopause, masturbation, vasectomy, and other terms are briefly defined. Little judgmental comment, except for condemning sex outside of marriage. Sexuality extolled as gift from a loving God. Glossary. Sixth grade and up.

424. De Jonge, Joanne E. *Skin and Bones: A Beginner's Guide to Your Great Insides*. Illus. Anne Thompson and Pat Adamik. Grand Rapids: Baker, 1985. 144p.

Stresses the miracle of God's creation as shown in the intricacies of the human body. Packed with facts about parts of the body and their operation, presented in a clear, interesting way. Reproductive system not included. Two-color, skillful drawings elucidate text. Fourth to sixth grades.

425. Dellinger, Annetta. *You Are Special to Jesus*. Illus. Jan Brett. St. Louis: Concordia, 1984. unp.

Three young children of different races are making fun of one another's looks when Jesus appears to them as a real person and explains how God created each one to be special and loved. They apologize and dance for joy. Cheerful pictures in black and white and color. Preschool to second grade.

426. Kehle, Mary. *You're Nearly There: Christian Sex Education for Preteens*. Rev. ed. Wheaton, Ill.: Harold Shaw, 1983. 80p.

All the clinical facts are presented clearly. Includes physical and emotional changes in puberty; sex within marriage; conception, pregnancy, and birth. The positive tone stresses God's constant supportive presence and the special value of each individual. Christian principles. Review questions for each chapter. Glossary. Black-and-white photographs and drawings. Fifth grade and up.

427. Macaulay, Susan Schaeffer. *Something Beautiful from God*. Westchester, Ill.: Crossway, 1980. 93p.

Development of the fetus chronicled from conception through birth and told in breathless, sentimental style. Babies born in difficult situations--African poverty, out of wedlock, physically and mentally handicapped--are also discussed. Original sin, redemption, heaven, and other Christian theology are strong themes throughout. Soft, expressive black-and-white photographs of children of several races and color section on the developing fetus. Kindergarten and up.

428. Neeves, D'reen, illus. *God Gave Me*. Belleville, Mich.: Lion, 1981. unp.

Unisex child in overalls states that God gave a mouth for eating a birthday cake, nose for smelling dinner cooking, ears to hear a car coming, eyes to see a picture book, and ten fingers and toes. All are good. Sketchy pictures in eye-catching colors. Preschool.

429. Nystrom, Carolyn. *Before I Was Born*. Illus. Dwight Walles. Westchester, Ill.: Crossway, 1984. unp.

Picture book of male and female sexual development from childhood through intercourse, pregnancy, and birth. Brief section on development of fetus. Strong underlying theme of God's plan for human beings including the joy of sex and reproduction within marriage. Simple and matter of fact. Soft-toned watercolors are both explicit and idealized, show nudes of Adam and Eve, boys skinny-dipping, little girl in her bedroom, married couple in bed, home birth. Kindergarten to third grade.

430. Townsend, Anne. *Marvelous Me: All about the Human Body*. Illus. Saroj Vaghela. Belleville, Mich.: Lion, 1984. 41p.

Emphasis on God's creativity and love of each individual. Brisk highlights and interesting oddments of circulation, respiration, digestion, nutrition, cell types, birth, the five senses, bones, etc. Admiring tone. Generously illustrated in color with cartoons, charts, diagrams, and excellent photographs. Index. Third to sixth grades.

IV
CHRISTIAN DEVOTIONAL MATERIALS

CONCEPTS

Alphabet

431. Egermeier, Elsie. *Picture Story Bible ABC Book*. Anderson, Ind.: Warner, 1963. unp.

Goes from Angels, who often do errands for God, Baby Jesus, Children, whom Jesus loves, etc., through Xodus, Young man raised from the dead, and Zacchaeus. Each letter has a page of text describing the Scripture cited for the person or object. Old-fashioned, sometimes saccharine tone. Simple children's prayers. Poor color lithographs. Kindergarten to second grade.

432. Fitzgerald, Annie. *Dear God Kids ABC*. Illus. author. New York: Simon, 1984. unp. Dear God Kids Series.

Red-cheeked cartoon children think about God through the alphabet. Objects such as dog, grass, valentine, and zebra are mixed with abstractions such as everything, joy, and love. Lacks the clarity of concept necessary for a good ABC book. Better as a discussion-starter about God's role in a child's life. Preschool and kindergarten.

433. Harrison, Marc. *The Alphabet Book*. Illus. author. Nashville: Nelson, 1985. unp. Bible Look-and-Learn Book Series.

Confusingly arranged items and upper case letters only make this a poor concept book. Knowledge of Bible stories such as Abraham, Eve, Lot's wife, Queen Esther, Xerxes, etc., essential for comprehension. Bright, whimsical pictures. Preschool.

434. Klug, Ron, and Lyn Klug. *My Christmas ABC Book*. Illus. Jim Roberts. Minneapolis: Augsburg, 1981. unp.

Brown and orange are peculiar color choices for Christmas,

but the cartoon figures in Nativity scenes and family celebrations are winning and artfully arranged around large alphabet letters. Basic little Bible story at end. Preschool and kindergarten.

435. Russell, Solveig Paulson. *Bible ABC Book*. Illus. Don Pallarito. St. Louis: Concordia, 1967. unp.

Two-line verses identify familiar characters and objects from the Old and New Testaments; e.g., Isaac, olive trees, Esther, vines. Upper case letters only. Staid illustrations in restrained colors. Preschool and kindergarten.

436. Stifle, J.M. *ABC Book about Jesus*. St. Louis: Concordia, 1981. unp.

Less a concept book than twenty-six highlights of Jesus' life: A for the angel's announcement to Mary, E for the flight into Egypt, P for parables, X for chi, the Greek sign for Christ, etc. Brightly illustrated by a variety of artists. Kindergarten to first grade.

Colors

437. Beckmann, Beverly. *Colors in God's World*. Illus. Bill Heuer. St. Louis: Concordia, 1983. unp.

Portly Noah examines the rainbow and sees in its colors the red of apples, roses, and roosters' combs; the yellow of sunflower, sunshine, and lemon; the blue of sky and water, etc. Indigo is omitted from the color spectrum. God's covenant is mentioned, but not accurately, in the end. Splashy pictures. Preschool.

438. Doney, Meryl. *Discovering Colors*. Belleville, Mich.: Lion, 1974. 28p.

Well-reproduced photographs show colors as they appear naturally rather than grouped by hue. Vegetables, old bricks, toys, kittens, chameleons, and children with various skin colors are among the subjects. Text emphasizes the pleasure we receive from God's colorful world. Preschool to second grade.

439. Evans, Lyndon, illus. *God Made All the Colors*. Ann Arbor: Lion, 1979. unp.

Knobbly caterpillar wanders through splashy red flowers over a golden yellow beach, under a blue sky, to a feast of green apples, and states that God created colors and the caterpillar himself as well. Preschool.

440. Fitzgerald, Annie. *Dear God Kids Rainbow*. Illus. author. New York: Simon, 1984. unp. Dear God Kids Series.

This is a poorly done concept book, because the colors to be identified are not clearly enough defined. Apple-cheeked cartoon children paint a rainbow and talk to God about appreciating things such as green vegetables, white snowmen, brown mud, black sheep. Rainbow includes inaccurate pink and brown stripes. Preschool.

441. Harrison, Marc. *The Color Book*. Illus. author. Nashville: Nelson, 1985. unp. Bible Look-and-Learn Book Series.

Floppy, rakish red fish, green frogs, orange tigers, pink pigs, etc., are examples of God's colorful creations. Some, however, are confusing: e.g., yellow giraffe has too many brown spots to be readily identified as yellow. Preschool.

Numbers

442. Beckmann, Beverly. *Numbers in God's World*. Illus. Jules Edler. St. Louis: Concordia, 1983. unp.

One to six in God's world are cheerfully colored and interesting, including one leaf on a fall maple tree, three turtles sinking down into the pond, six children building a snowman, etc. But seven twigs, eight weeds, nine ants, and ten carrots are dull and murky. Objects are repeated in ten columns at end. Preschool.

443. Fitzgerald, Annie. *Dear God: Kids Count Their Blessings*. Illus. author. New York: Simon, 1984. unp. Dear God Kids Series.

One through twelve illustrated in lively cartoon style. Large, clear numerals, but objects to be counted as in seven, the seventh day of the week, are not always easily identified. Friends, fun, fruit, and fingers are among the good things God gives. Preschool to kindergarten.

444. Harrison, Marc, illus. *The Counting Book*. Nashville: Nelson, 1985. unp. Bible Look-and-Learn Book Series.

Amusing, cartoon-style, jug-eared people and jaunty animals from Bible stories in vivid colors illustrate one through twelve. One Jesus pounds at his carpentry work; Jonah swims with seven fish; Jacob's twelve luxuriantly bearded sons pose as a family group, etc. Clear numerals and objects to be counted. Preschool and kindergarten.

445. Petach, Heidi, illus. *I Can Count*. Cincinnati: Standard, 1984. unp.

Numerals and objects to be counted are clearly shown. Nature subjects of apple, puppies, haystacks, snowflakes, bluebirds, children of several races, etc. God is thanked at end. One-dimensional, ordinary color artwork. Preschool.

446. Ward, Alton. *10 Pennies for Jesus*. Illus. Patricia Mattozzi. St. Louis: Concordia, 1986. unp.

Counting book in which ten pennies are placed in a church offering basket on the left-hand pages, and on the right-hand pages are shown the uses to which the money is put. It buys Bibles, choir music, Sunday school materials; builds churches; helps worldwide missions and relief services, etc. Very simple, rhymed text and neat color pictures. Preschool and kindergarten.

Shapes and Sizes

447. Beckmann, Beverly. *Shapes in God's World*. Illus. Kathy Mitter. St. Louis: Concordia, 1984. unp.

The shapes include circles in the sun, moon, grapefruit; squares on concrete blocks, edge of turtle's shell; triangular pine trees, spiderwebs, mountain peaks. God made all, as well as a child's varied shape. Some examples are confusing. Illustrated with simplified figures, clean-cut lines, dynamic symmetry, unusual color tones. Preschool and kindergarten.

448. Beckmann, Beverly. *Sizes in God's World*. Illus. Jules Edler. St. Louis: Concordia, 1984.

Whether it is a short twig or a tall tree, a little baby or a big mother elephant, a light feather or a heavy nest, God takes care of it. Includes concepts of relative size and alike and different, given in a cursory way. Undistinguished artwork in subdued colors. Preschool.

449. Boyer, Linda L. *God Made Me*. Illus. Lorraine Arthur. Cincinnati: Standard, 1981. unp.

Doll-like, rosy little children are glad they weren't made into circles, squares, rectangles, triangles, ovals, or stars, because they feel comfortable and right exactly as God shaped them. Preschool and kindergarten.

450. Doney, Meryl. *Discovering Shapes and Designs*. Belleville, Mich.: Lion, 1980. 31p.

Examples of straight lines, circles, and spirals are shown in a wheel, ball, honeycomb, shell, etc. Other designs include the aerodynamics of a gull, the Concorde airplane, and a hang glider; a spider's web and lace; the creeping action of caterpillar and farm tractor, etc. Indicates that all man's inventions are derived from God's patterns in the world. Simple text. Excellent color photographs. Preschool to second grade.

451. *Great and Small*. Belleville, Mich.: Lion, 1976. unp.

The terms "big" and "little" are indicated by tree and ladybug, sky and bird, field and lamb, dog and bee. Deceptively childlike artwork with gleaming colors and fascinating little details. Preschool.

OBJECT LESSONS AND STORIES

452. Aaseng, Nate. *I'm Learning, Lord, but I Still Need Help: Story Devotions for Boys*. Illus. Judy Swanson. Minneapolis: Augsburg, 1981. 110p.

Fifteen object lessons about bad days, sibling rivalry, envy, friendship, overprotective parents, and other problems and challenges portrayed concisely in short story form. Familiar settings, didactic plots smoothly handled. Reinforcing Bible verses and brief prayers. Simple drawings. Fourth to sixth grades.

453. Aaseng, Nate. *Which Way Are You Leading Me, Lord? Bible Devotions for Boys*. Minneapolis: Augsburg, 1984. 112p.

Down-to-earth discussions on putting others first, obeying rules, being honest, accepting disappointment, trusting God, etc., followed by very short stories based on experiences common to older boys to illustrate the points. Suggestions for putting the lessons into action and prayers. Some soft-focus black-and-white photographs of boys in home and sports activities. Fifth grade and up.

454. Anderson, Grace Fox. *The Hairy Brown Angel: And Other Animal Tails*. Illus. Darwin Dunham. Wheaton, Ill.: Victor, 1977. 132p. Animal Tails Series.

Mixture of true and fictional anecdotes about pet dogs, cats, birds, turtle. Some are ill, some heroic, some disobedient, some lost, etc. Prayer, God's love, and acceptance of God's will are themes in all. Writing quality varies, but they are believable as object lessons. Black-and-white drawings. Third to sixth grades.

455. Anderson, Grace Fox. *The Incompetent Cat: And Other Animal Tails*. Illus. Janice Skivington Wood. Wheaton, Ill.: Victor, 1985. 44p. Animal Tails Series.

Most of the material carries low-key message about Christian living and God's love and deals with wild and domestic animals and birds. Included are a missionary's horse, a loving cow, a wounded Canada goose, and twenty-eight more items in a variety of forms: short short stories, poems, cartoons, nature facts. Uneven quality. Black-and-white drawings. Third to sixth grades.

456. Anderson, Grace Fox. *The Peanut Butter Hamster: And Other Animal Tails*. Illus. Richard Johnson. Wheaton, Ill.: Victor, 1979. 132p. Animal Tails Series.

Story collection of short true and fictional incidents concerning family pets, farm animals, and a few wild creatures. Christian messages such as stewardship, responsibility, and accepting God's will are included in each. Some animal poems. Black-and-white drawings. Third to sixth grades.

457. Beers, V. Gilbert. *My Favorite Things to See and Share*. Wheaton, Ill.: Victor, 1984. 190p.

Daffodils, eyes, pancakes, new shoes, summer clouds are among the favorites mentioned. Also included are Bible story objects such as Joseph's coat, David's sling, Balaam's ass, Jesus' manger. There are 144 topics. Each has sharp, lively, modern picture, short commentary, and discussion questions. Middle-class, attractive families of various races are shown. The writing is didactic. Introduction and afterword explain purpose and usage to parents. Contains a subject index. Preschool to third grade.

458. Bly, Stephen, and Janet Bly. *Questions I'd Like to Ask*. Chicago: Moody Press, 1982. unp.

Preteens ask 120 questions of fathers, mothers, teachers, older siblings, the President, pastors, friends, God, etc., on matters of faith and conduct. Forthright tone. Each devotional gives specific dramatized example, explanation, Bible passages, and a one- or two-sentence prayer. Conservative theology. Firm yet understanding. Fifth grade and up.

459. Bove, Vincent. *And on the Eighth Day God Created the Yankees*. Plainfield, N.J.: Logos, 1981. 174p.

Baseball Yankees of today and yesterday (Tommy John, Reggie Jackson, Bobby Richardson, Phil Rizzuto, etc.) give the philosophy of their success on and off the playing field. Emphasizes straight life, high morals, concern for young people. Black-and-white photographs. Sixth grade and up.

460. Coleman, William L. *The Good Night Book*. Illus. Chris Wold. Minneapolis: Bethany Fellowship, 1979. 128p.

Variety of interesting nighttime thoughts, each with appropriate Scriptural verse. Embraces meteors, dew, phosphorescent fish, heaven, baths, nocturnal animals, parental love, and more. Both new and familiar situations. Instructive. Stresses God's love and care, sharing, peace. Attractive format of rust and white photographs, drawings, text. Kindergarten to second grade.

461. Coleman, William L. *Listen to the Animals: Devotionals for Families with Young Children*. Illus. Chris Wold. Minneapolis: Bethany House, 1979. 128p.

Facts about the panda, porcupine, cicada, giraffe, robin, octopus, lizard, and many others are integrated into object lessons for human beings. Each has a Biblical quotation and review questions. Lively but sometimes ungrammatical style. Black-and-white drawings. First to sixth grades.

462. Coleman, William L. *My Magnificent Machine*. Minneapolis: Bethany Fellowship, 1978. 134p.

Short, informative chapters about the human body include conception, brain, muscles, freckles, digestion, bedwetting, baldness, and much more. Extols God's creativity, belief in Christ, right living. Successfully geared to children's interests and understanding. Black-and-white photographs. First to sixth grades.

463. Coleman, William L. *Today I Feel Like a Warm Fuzzy*. Minneapolis: Bethany House, 1980. 126p.

Tender, understanding thoughts addressed to small children on their emotions and behavior and how to understand and cope with them. Scripture cited for each. Free verse form. Includes anger, fear, reverence, confusion, self-importance, and forty-six more. Expressive photographs. Kindergarten to third grade.

464. Everett, Betty Steele. *I Want to Be Like You, Lord: Bible Devotions for Girls*. Minneapolis: Augsburg, 1984. 110p.

Twenty devotions stressing positive qualities demonstrated by Jesus and important to Christian living. Includes forgiveness, evangelism, prayer, obedience, peacemaking, modesty, etc. Each has Bible verse, discussion of the associated Biblical situation, brief object lesson related to a child's everyday experiences with family and friends, suggestions for action, and a prayer. Appealing photographs of children of various races. Fourth to sixth grades.

465. Groten, Dallas. *Will the Real Winner Please Stand*. Minneapolis: Bethany House, 1985. 158p.

Directed to those interested in track and field sports. Theme of each of the thirty-eight short, easy-to-read object lessons is strength through weakness. If one's best efforts are made, there is spiritual growth even in defeat. Earnest, enthusiastic tone. Supportive Scriptural quotations. Self-examination questions designed to steer readers to a better Christian life. Clear black-and-white photographs of attractive youths. Sixth grade and up.

466. Hanny, Diane. *Closer than My Shadow*. Illus. Richard Henkel. Plainfield, N.J.: Logos, 1979. 207p.

Prophecy, speaking in tongues, faith healing, honesty, duty, conversion, and the Fruits of the Spirit form bases for typical object lessons about happenings at home and church. Thought-provoking questions and prayer for each. Emphasizes work of Holy Spirit. Easy reading. Small line drawings. Fourth to sixth grades.

467. Haywood, Carolyn. *Make a Joyful Noise! Bible Verses for Children*. Illus. Lane Yerkes. Philadelphia: Westminster, 1984. 96p.

A dozen didactic discussions about friendship, God's love, answers to prayer, truth, peacemaking, etc. Each is followed by eight to twelve Bible verses, many from the New Testament and Psalms. Crosshatched black-and-white drawings of children and pets. Third to sixth grades.

468. Hein, Lucille E. *Thank You, God*. Valley Forge, Pa.: Judson, 1981. unp.

Familiar experiences--learning to read, enjoying picnics, helping around the house, contemplating the variety of creation, and more--described thoughtfully. A one-sentence prayer of thanks follows each. Serious, informative tone. Sketchy, appealing drawings in black, white, and violet. Kindergarten to second grade.

469. Huxhold, Harry N. *Adventures with God*. Illus. Arthur Kirchhoff. St. Louis: Concordia, 1966. 230p.

One hundred fifty short devotions on great variety of topics: a mine explosion, General MacArthur, a rose window, an impatient boy with a broken leg, St. Luke, crabgrass, etc. All relate an easily grasped spiritual truth and have an associated Bible verse and brief prayer. A few black-and-white drawings. Index of Bible readings. Third to sixth grades.

470. Jahsmann, Allan Hart, and Martin P. Simon. *Little Visits with God*. Illus. Frances Hook. St. Louis: Concordia, 1957. 286p.

Two hundred simply written incidents illustrate virtues such as kindness, honesty, forgiveness, etc., and associate them with thoughts about God and the teachings of Jesus in gentle and familiar ways. Associated passages from Scripture for each. Meditation and discussion questions. Prayers. Small line drawings. Index. Kindergarten to fourth grade.

471. Jahsmann, Allan Hart. *More Little Visits with God*. Illus. Frances Hook. St. Louis: Concordia, 1961. 325p.

Brief anecdotes and familiar situations explain to children about God, the Bible, prayer, Christian principles, and so forth. Contains discussion questions, Bible readings, and prayers. Index includes Scripture references.

Clear, conversational style. Black-and-white drawings scattered throughout. Kindergarten to fourth grade.

472. Johnson, Lois Walfrid. *You're My Best Friend, Lord.* Minneapolis: Augsburg, 1976. 111p.

For white, middle-class girls from loving homes. Contains anecdotes about making friends, attracting boys, forgiveness, death, disappointment, and so on. Biblical comment follows each. Conservative attitude. Positive, gentle tone. Conversational style. Drawings. Fifth grade and up.

473. Jones, Larry. *Practice to Win.* Wheaton, Ill.: Tyndale, 1982. 102p.

Devotions associated with the forty-five preseason days of practice for the official basketball season. Illustrates the joy of the sport. Valid, not forced, comparisons of basketball situations with life's problems. Sixth grade and up.

474. Klug, Ron, and Lyn Klug. *Christian Family Bedtime Reading Book.* Illus. Koechel/Peterson Design. Minneapolis: Augsburg, 1982. 125p.

Collection of mild, reassuring little stories, poems, prayers, and lullabies. Many are lessons in proper, loving Christian behavior. Also contains verses about nature and animals, simple prayers of praise, thanksgiving, and supplication, soothing songs about God and Jesus. Plain, cartoon-style drawings. Kindergarten to fourth grade.

475. Koenig, Norma E. *The Runaway Heart.* Illus. Ruth Lull. New York: Friendship, 1981. unp.

Brother and sister meet children from various religious, ethnic, and economic backgrounds in school and learn to appreciate all kinds of friends. Discussion guides and activity suggestions. Practical, thought-provoking approach to teaching tolerance, love, and the joys of variety. Realistic black-and-white drawings. First to fourth grades.

476. Magagna, Anna Marie, illus. *Best-Loved Bible Verses for Children.* New York: Platt, 1983. unp.

Eighteen familiar, mostly short passages, many from Psalms. The Lord's Prayer and Twenty-Third Psalm are complete. Beauty and variety of nature and humankind are stressed in double-page illustrations of wispy children of various races and serene animals done in pastels and charcoal against seasonal outdoor backgrounds and inside a cozy home. Preschool to second grade.

477. O'Connor, Francine M. *God and You*. Illus. Kathryn Boswell. Liguori, Mo.: Liguori, 1979. 32p. ABCs of Faith Series.

Sweet, poetic thoughts for young children about being special and important and about love. Familiar topics celebrated include Christmas, Jesus' life, the seasons, the alphabet. Decorated with four-color drawings. Preschool to third grade.

478. Peifer, Jane Hoober. *Good Thoughts about Me*. Scottdale, Pa.: Herald, 1985. unp.

Illustrates small children's happy acceptance of themselves as individuals enjoying the things they can see, hear, taste, smell, and do. Simple captions make positive statements, ending with the fact that God loves them just as they are. Appealing photographs softly reproduced in brown tones. Preschool.

479. Peifer, Jane Hoober. *Good Thoughts about People*. Scottdale, Pa.: Herald, 1985. unp.

The fine variety of sizes, shapes, ages, moods, occupations, and activities of people winningly shown in brown-toned photographs. Simple text appreciates the fact that God made everyone different. Preschool.

480. Peifer, Jane Hoober. *Good Thoughts at Bedtime*. Scottdale, Pa.: Herald, 1985. unp.

Remembering all the day's satisfying activities, special animals, good friends, the beauty of the seasons, and so on helps chase away lonely feelings at night. Gentle photographs in soothing brown tones illustrate the good sleepytime thoughts. Preschool.

481. Richards, Jean. *We Can Share God's Love*. Illus. Joy Friedman. Valley Forge, Pa.: Judson, 1984. 79p.

Earnest little object lessons in story form tell about accepting and enjoying people of different races, backgrounds, ages; being helpful and understanding at home; caring for and appreciating the natural world; handling grief. Prayer and Bible quotation for each. Indexed by topic and Bible verse. Simple drawings. Third to sixth grades.

482. Royer, Katherine. *Nursery Happy Times Book*. Illus. Norma Hostetler. Scottdale, Pa.: Herald, 1957. 49p.

Thankful thoughts about Sunday school, good things to eat, sharing toys, grandparents, etc., mixed with short lessons for the Biblical experiences of Timothy, David, and Elisha. Text for very young children uses rhyme and repetition. Lecturing tone. Brightly colored pictures of neat white boys and girls enjoying comfortable living. Preschool.

483. Schmidt, J. David. *Graffiti: Devotions for Girls*. Old Tappan, N.J.: Revell, 1983. 132p.

Fifty-six Fundamentalist brief bits of advice on gossip, holiness, self-worth, submission, prayer, menstruation, purity, materialism, etc. God's will and support are stressed. Down-to-earth and up-to-date language. Fifth grade and up.

484. Schmidt, J. David. *Graffiti: Devotions for Guys*. Old Tappan, N.J.: Revell, 1983. 131p.

Fifty-five Fundamentalist nuggets written in breezy, informal style. Places responsibility on boys to conform to Christian principles. Each devotion is based on a Scripture passage. Topics include self-control, pornography, associations with non-Christian girls, Bible reading, sin, and salvation, but they are given superficial treatment. Black-and-white cartoon-type drawings. Sixth grade and up.

485. Skold, Betty Westrom. *Lord, I Have a Question: Story Devotions for Girls*. Minneapolis: Augsburg, 1979. 122p.

Familiar problems such as following the crowd, accepting divorce and remarriage, getting along with siblings, etc., are described and sensible suggestions for their solutions given. Each has an associated Bible quotation and very short prayer. Simple drawings. Fifth grade and up.

486. Sorensen, David Allen. *It's a Mystery to Me, Lord: Bible Devotions for Boys*. Minneapolis: Augsburg, 1985. 110p.

Four friends around age twelve begin a series of adventures by climbing a ladder to peer into the window of an old house. The wise owner, Mrs. Gratz, becomes their mentor by recommending Bible passages to help solve their problems. They encounter death, shoplifting, divorce, a flood, and other probable and improbable events. There are Bible clues to look up, action ideas, and prayer for each chapter. Relaxed, readable style. Blue-and-white format. Photographs. Fifth grade and up.

487. Sorenson, Jane. *Five Minutes with God*. Illus. Steve Hayes. Cincinnati: Standard, 1985. 62p.

Fifty-seven Fundamentalist thought-stimulating pieces incorporating Bible verse, an incident from a child's everyday experiences more or less related to the verse, questions, and suggested response. Subjects include choosing appropriate friends, sharing with siblings, avoiding astrology and cults, attending church, and so forth. Serious tone. Fourth to sixth grades.

488. Sorenson, Stephen. *Growing Up Isn't Easy, Lord: Story Devotions for Boys*. Illus. Mark Mathews. Minneapolis: Augsburg, 1979. 111p.

Short stories to stimulate thought about self-acceptance, taking foolish chances, caring about others, and similar problems and challenges. Applicable Scripture and prayer for each. Fast moving and up-to-date. Stylized black-and-white drawings. Fourth to sixth grade.

489. Sorenson, Stephen. *Lord Teach Me Your Ways*. Illus. Charles T. Cox. Nashville: Abingdon, 1982. 96p.

Brief, didactic stories in which the characters, usually misbehaving children, find out something helpful for the conduct of their lives. Scriptural passages with similar lessons are cited and followed by appropriate prayers. Black-and-white pictures. Fourth to sixth grades.

490. Tengbom, Mildred. *Does It Make Any Difference What I Do?* Minneapolis: Bethany House, 1984. 160p.

Conservative Christian tone in fifty-eight short story-prayers about current problems: fathers without jobs, Judy Blume's books, drugs, death, stepfathers, friendship, etc. Sympathetic, straightforward style. Appropriate, discussion-stimulating questions after each episode ask for well-thought-out value judgments. Scripture verses. Pleasant black-and-white photographs of wholesome young people. Fifth grade and up.

491. Warren, Mary Phraner. *Lord, I'm Back Again: Story Devotions for Girls*. Illus. Judy Swanson. Minneapolis: Augsburg, 1981. 111p.

Faith, self-awareness, friendship, family conflict, joy, and other universal childhood experiences in little object lessons are reinforced by Bible passages and informal prayers. Lively style. Monotone drawings. Fourth to sixth grades.

492. Webb, Barbara Owen. *Now What, Lord? Bible Devotions for Girls*. Minneapolis: Augsburg, 1985. 111p.

Twenty-four examples of older girls' problems with step-families, friendships, day dreams, sibling conflicts, and others. Scriptural quotation is followed by commentary on the Biblical event, a short incident from the life of a modern girl, with suggestions for action in such a situation, Bible reading, and prayer. Situations are contrived to fit the topics. Conservative, easily understood explications. Purple-and-white format with attractive photographs of pensive girls. Fourth grade and up.

493. Wyly, Louise B. *Fun Devotions for Kids*. Illus. Dave McCoy. Cincinnati: Standard, 1985. 64p.

Thirty easy-to-read, very condensed retellings of Old and New Testament stories show God uses little items--Adam's rib, the boy Samuel, Elijah's cloud, a lunch of five loaves and two fishes, etc.--to do his will in the world. Children are admonished to love, trust, witness, use their talents, and so forth. Related Bible verses and prayers for each. Small black-and-white drawings. Preschool to third grade.

Parables

494. Aurelio, John. *Story Sunday: Christian Fairy Tales for Young and Old Alike*. Illus. Lonnie Sue Johnson. New York: Paulist, 1978. 93p.

Imaginative parables in traditional fairy-tale forms with grand castles, handsome princes, poor children, amazing wizards. Meanings are often multi-layered and include discussion-provoking themes such as the excesses of selfishness, the way to salvation, overcoming the fear of death, the power of the Resurrection. Black-and-white drawings. Fourth grade and up.

495. Barlow, Geoffrey. *Young People's Parables*. London: Quartet, 1983. 108p.

English teenagers write about their deepest concerns--

freedom, love, honesty, hypocrisy, greed, peacemaking, responsibility, stewardship of the earth, etc.--in forty-four parables awarded prizes in a Church of England competition. Several retellings of the Good Samaritan. Quality varies, but all are sincere. Sixth grade and up.

496. Barrett, Ethel. *Cracker*. Illus. Jim Padgett. Glendale, Calif.: Regal, 1979. unp.

Lesson about obedience in which bad-tempered, self-centered quarter horse bucks off his beloved little mistress, is forgiven, and learns he is happier when he is gentle and biddable, just the way Jesus teaches children to be. Exclamatory style. Colorful, action-filled pictures. Preschool to third grade.

497. Barrett, Ethel. *Ice, Water, Snow*. Illus. Jim Padgett. Glendale, Calif.: Regal, 1979. unp.

Ice, Water, and Snow struggle conceitedly for supremacy. Ice squeezes down on Water, then disappears under Snow's blanket. When the weather warms, all three join and learn that each is equally valuable. Belabors the point. Sparkling color illustrations. Preschool to third grade.

498. Barrett, Ethel. *Quacky and Wacky*. Illus. Paul Taylor. Glendale, Calif.: Regal, 1978. unp.

Hen hatches two duck eggs along with her own and tries hard to raise the babies as proper chickens, but they love water and long for another kind of life. Eventually they are given to a delighted mother duck and learn that God made them correctly after all. Gaiety and humor in the text and color pictures. Preschool to third grade.

499. Clanton, Bruce. *In Season and Out*. Illus. Tom Shea. Saratoga, Calif.: Resource, 1981. 84p.

Christmas, reconciliation, creation, change, and resurrection are some of the topics in a poetically written story collection of spiritual allegories. Grouped according to the four seasons. Folk-tale quality. Elegant black-and-white drawings. Useful series of indexes to the stories by themes, images, associated Scriptures, religious rites, and church seasons. Fifth grade and up.

500. Hazard, David. *The Peaceable Kingdom*. Illus. Juan Ferrandiz Castells. Lincoln, Va.: Chosen, 1982. 48p.

Four short stories deal gently with good versus evil, appreciating those who are different, growth and forgiveness, the transforming power of the infant Jesus. Fairy-tale style, with characters named Prince Song, Applecheek, etc. Also has three inspirational poems. Illustrated with photographs of woodcarvings sentimentally depicting winsome children and animals. Kindergarten to fourth grade.

501. Juknialis, Joseph J. *When God Began in the Middle*. Illus. Tom Fait. Saratoga, Calif.: Resource, 1982. 101p.

Poetic forms, rich imagery in stories of the origin of the four seasons and their significance in human life, Advent, the reason for stars, elves and leprechauns hoping to trade wealth for love, and other moral fairy tales and parables. Effective spiritual messages. Clean-lined black-and-white drawings. Sixth grade and up.

502. Juknialis, Joseph J. *Winter Dreams: And Other Such Friendly Dragons*. Illus. Barbara A. Salvo. Saratoga, Calif.: Resource, 1979. 87p.

Unicorn, a man who would be king, a sand dollar, truths and untruths, a contest between land and sea, and more figure in short parables, memoirs, meditations, and fairy tales. Sharing bread is the pervasive image for human caring. Story-telling style is sometimes wordy. Gently didactic messages concern God's love and man's blend of imperfection and goodness. Impressionistic black-and-white ink wash drawings. Sixth grade and up.

503. Keidel, Eudene. *African Fables: That Teach about God*. Illus. Kathy Bartel. Scottdale, Pa.: Herald, 1978. 93p.

Talking-animal stories from Zaire are related with folk-telling finesse and sly humor. Christian object lessons drawn from African lore. Readable and entertaining. Simple black-and-white drawings. Kindergarten to fourth grade.

504. Keidel, Eudene. *African Fables Book II: That Teach about God*. Illus. Paul Zehr. Scottdale, Pa.: Herald, 1981. 111p.

Twenty-seven traditional fables from Zaire, some dealing with monkeys, crocodiles, bats, wasps, leopards, etc., and some with people, are told to demonstrate spiritual truths. Explanatory paragraph at the end of each. Plain black-and-white drawings. Kindergarten to fourth grade.

505. Mitchell, Kurt. *Poor Ralph*. Illus. author. Westchester, Ill.: Crossway, 1982. unp.

Elderly man in modest circumstances likes to read his Bible. One morning he finds a huge yellow jewel in his bed. It reflects scenes from Scripture depicting God's promises to man. It is invisible to unbelievers, but eventually he finds a friend who has one, too. Bold, bright pictures with caricatured figures. Kindergarten to third grade.

506. Reid, John Calvin. *Bird Life in Wington: Practical Parables for Young People*. Illus. Reynold H. Weidenaar. Grand Rapids, Mich.: Eerdmans, 1948. 122p.

Like human beings, members of the First Birderian Church in Wington demonstrate disobedience, procrastination, ill manners, pride, and other unpleasantness for which they must be kindly corrected. Brief, didactic stories. Black-and-white drawings. Kindergarten to fourth grade.

507. Reid, John Calvin. *Parables from Nature: Earthly Stories with a Heavenly Meaning*. Illus. Macy Schwarz. Grand Rapids, Mich.: Eerdmans, 1954. 88p.

Entertaining presentation of eleven of Jesus' parables done in two ways: first as a nature story about bees, fish, flowers, etc., and then as a summarized version of the actual Bible passage. Clear lessons. Readable style. Black-and-white drawings. First to fourth grades.

POETRY

508. Davidson, Alice Joyce. *Psalms and Proverbs*. Illus. Victoria Marshall. Norwalk, Conn.: Gibson, 1984. unp. Alice in Bibleland Series.

After a stint at Bible school little Alice decides to write her own rhymed versions of short quotations from Psalms and fifteen Proverbs, turning them into devotional thoughts about God's protection, love, guidance, gifts, etc., as experienced in everyday life. Pastel greeting card art. Kindergarten to third grade.

509. Decker, Marjorie Ainsborough. *The Christian Mother Goose.* Illus. author and Glenna Fae Hammond. Grand Junction, Colo.: Christian Mother Goose Book Co., 1977. 111p.

Traditional nursery rhymes are paraphrased to give them a Biblical message. "The house that Jack built" becomes "the ark that Noah built," Little Boy Blue is a shepherd at the Nativity, the spider sits down to hear Miss Muffet's prayers of thanksgiving, and so on. Some original religious poems in the same vein. Saccharine tone. Numerous undistinguished drawings in black and white and color. Preschool to first grade.

510. Duncan, Lois. *From Spring to Spring.* Philadelphia: Westminster, 1982. 96p.

Exuberant, affecting black-and-white photographs by the author illuminate simple, appealing poems celebrating God's creation, seasonal joys, a baby's birth, mud, little churches, Hanukkah and Christmas, etc. First-line index. All ages.

511. Hopkins, Lee Bennett. *And God Bless Me: Prayers, Lullabies and Dream Poems.* Illus. Patricia Henderson Lincoln. New York: Knopf, 1982. 23p.

Many of the short, gentle poems in the collection are about God. Realistic, attractive illustrations in subdued colors and black and white complement the poetry. Preschool to second grade.

512. Kenneally, Christy. *Strings and Things: Poems and Other Messages for Children.* Illus. Gloria Claudia Ortiz. Ramsey, N.J.: Paulist, 1984. 47p.

Biblical themes such as Moses, creation, the Good Samaritan, the woman at the well, and the lost sheep illustrate growth, creativity, friendship, and love. Each devotion has a simple explanatory passage followed by a poem further relating the message on a child's level. Bold black-and-white decorations. Kindergarten to fourth grade.

513. Knapp, John. *A Pillar of Pepper: And Other Bible Nursery Rhymes.* Illus. Dianne Turner Deckert. Elgin, Ill.: Chariot, 1982. 128p.

In roughly chronological order short and long poems treat thirty-nine Old Testament subjects from creation through the prophets, and thirty-five New Testament topics, including the early church. There are also verses about every book of the Bible. Breezy, modern style in which

King Jereboam is known as Jerry the Nerd, for example. Quality ranges from reasonably adequate to labored. Spirited, handsome illustrations in rich colors and black silhouettes. Kindergarten and up.

514. Larrick, Nancy. *Tambourines! Tambourines to Glory!* Illus. Geri Greinke. Philadelphia: Westminster, 1982. 117p.

Seventy-six short prayers and spiritual poems drawn from a variety of nationalities and religions deal with thanksgiving for God's beautiful world, blessings for all kinds of people and animals, personal petitions, declarations of faith. Some of the poets are well known; others, young children or anonymous. Delicate line drawings. Author, title, first-line indexes. Kindergarten and up.

515. Mason, Alice Leedy. *Christian Bedtime Rhymes*. Illus. Frances Hook. Milwaukee: Ideals, 1984. unp.

Two familiar poems, "Wynken, Blynken, and Nod" and "The Land of Counterpane," and many well-known nursery rhymes have added verses at their ends giving them a Christian message. Other anonymous or unattributed little spiritual poems are mixed in. Color illustrations of idealized children singing, playing, listening to a bedtime story, etc. Preschool to third grade.

516. Miller, Calvin. *When the Aardvark Parked on the Ark And Other Poems*. Illus. Marc Hamilton. New York: Harper, 1984. 185p.

Jonah prays for the fish to burp, proud preacher Dan tries to build a church steeple taller than God, eighty-year-old Sarah tells Abie "she's gonna have a baby," Daniel hopes the kitties will get lockjaw, and other Bible subjects and additional themes about children and animals in an uneven poetry collection. Some of it is funny, some cautionary, and some too contrived. Cartoon-style black-and-white drawings. Index. Kindergarten to fourth grade.

517. Nordtvedt, Matilda. *Ladybugs, Bees, and Butterfly Trees.* Minneapolis: Bethany House, 1985. 111p.

Short poems are intended to tell interesting facts about some animal, bird, insect, or event in nature and then tie them to a related Christian teaching, but most of the comparisons are unconvincingly forced. Poems are contrived and badly written, without any creative spark. The rhymes are frequently awful. Each poem is followed by a related Bible quotation, questions, and prayer. Illustrated with lively black-and-white drawings. Preschool to third grade.

PRAYER

518. Brooks, Sandra. *I Can Pray to God*. Illus. Lois Axeman. Cincinnati: Standard, 1982. unp.

A little girl marvels at the good things that hands can do in work and play. The fingers, taken one by one, help her to pray by reminding her of her family and friends, preacher and teachers, the President and government, the sick and unhappy, and herself. Contains color pictures of children of various races enjoying daily activities. Preschool and kindergarten.

519. Eckblad, Edith. *God Listens and Knows*. Illus. Jim Roberts. Minneapolis: Augsburg, 1974. unp.

Softness is the theme in little verses about a baby's cheek, a whisper, a snowbank, a kitten's paw, creamy pudding, and other soft things felt and heard by happy children in big, sketchy, lively three-color pictures. Interwoven is the idea that a prayer to God may be soft, but it is always heard. Preschool.

520. Fletcher, Mary. *My Very First Prayer-Time Book*. Illus. Patricia Papps and Andrew Skilleter. Anderson, Ind.: Warner, 1984. 44p.

Too many subjects--how and why we pray to Jesus, the Lord's Prayer, graces, hymn texts for Christmas, Easter, morning and evening--are all crammed into a tiny book for very young children. Didactic tone. Expressionless illustrations in pale colors. Preschool and kindergarten.

521. Groth, Jeanette L. *Prayer: Learning How to Talk to God*. Illus. Jan Brett. St. Louis: Concordia, 1983. 24p.

Suggestions for prayers for Christian children include praise, thanksgiving, guidance, supplication, etc. Also how and when prayers are said: alone, with family, in church, anywhere. Realistic, skillful three-color drawings of children from comfortable families. Preschool to second grade.

522. Henderson, Felicity. *Learning about Prayer.* Illus. Michael Grimsdale. Ann Arbor, Mich.: Lion, 1983. unp.

Prayer is talking to God and Jesus at any time in any place, from the breakfast table to the moon. Prayer is thanking God, asking his help and forgiveness. It is not always answered satisfactorily. Easily understood language and concepts. Explication of the Lord's Prayer. Bright, cheerful pictures of family life. Kindergarten to third grade.

523. Kelling, Fern. *Prayer Is....* Illus. Ronnie Hester. Nashville: Broadman, 1978. 32p.

Simple definitions of prayers of thanksgiving, for guidance in right living, on behalf of others, of worship are tied to the young child's familiar experiences with friends and family. Large, sketchy two-color illustrations. Preschool to second grade.

524. Nystrom, Carolyn. *What Is Prayer?* Illus. Wayne A. Hanna. Chicago: Moody, 1981. unp.

Scriptural references about many aspects of prayer interpreted on small child's level. Themes: God hears all prayers at all times; God answers many prayers but not all; God hears confessions of sin and forgives. Includes some rules for praying and the Lord's Prayer. Examples from daily life. Colorful, cartoon-style illustrations. Preschool to first grade.

525. Richards, Dorothy Fay. *Pray in This Way.* Illus. Jenny Williams. Wheaton, Ill.: Dandelion, 1983. 32p.

Reasons for prayer include thanksgiving, sorrow, forgiveness, help, need. Sincere prayers can be made any time, in all kinds of situations. Examples include modern children and people in the Bible. The Lord's Prayer is cited as the perfect illustration. Busy format of lively large and small pictures well keyed to ideas in text, which is simple and clear. Kindergarten to second grade.

526. Wimberly, Vera. *Please Listen, God!* Illus. Linda Slovic. St. Louis: Concordia, 1977. unp.

Brief prayers given are not to be used literally but as examples of how children pray for things, both rightly and wrongly. Conduct of life stressed. Asking God's help with fear, envy, death, racial understanding, etc. Discussion questions and Scriptural quotations. Usage notes for parents. Attention-getting pictures of perky children of various races in color and black and white. Preschool to second grade.

PRAYERS

527. Alexander, Martha. *Poems and Prayers for the Very Young*. Illus. author. New York: Random, 1973. unp.

Joyful mix of familiar poets such as Robert Louis Stevenson and Elizabeth Madox Roberts writing on stars, clouds, songs, kites, seagulls, etc., along with well-known prayers and blessings. All appreciate God's many gifts. Soft-toned pictures of children at play outdoors and enjoying their homes. Preschool and kindergarten.

528. Alleman, Herman C. *Prayers for Boys*. Nashville: Nelson, 1981. 128p.

Six sections in this stiff, conservative collection include prayers for Christlike virtues, for daily situations, of thanksgiving, for others, for special occasions, and by famous theologians. Negative tone stresses human shortcomings. Index. Fourth to sixth grades.

529. Alleman, Herman C. *Prayers for Girls*. Nashville: Nelson, 1981. 128p.

Didactic, formal, conservative collection stresses duty, sin, human weakness. Much of the material is the same as in *Prayers for Boys* (item 528). Index. Fourth to sixth grades.

530. Bennett, Marian. *Thank You, God*. Illus. Heidi Petach. Cincinnati: Standard, 1985. unp.

Toddlers and other preschool children can open cardboard doors to discover everyday things for which they can give thanks. Sandy-haired boy in very simple, flat, color pictures appreciates a chocolate cake hidden under a kitchen mixer, his teddy bear inside a camping tent, his teacher behind the play equipment in the Sunday school, etc. Preschool.

531. Bernos de Gasztold, Carmen. *Prayers from the Ark and the Creatures' Choir*. Illus. Jean Primrose. New York: Penguin, 1976. 127p.

Two separate collections of spare, poignant, lapidary poems about a variety of God's creatures that include cock, dog, dove, cricket, starfish, peacock, lizard, foal, flea, giraffe, and forty-two more. Each one's prayer reveals a truth--sometimes painful, sometimes beautiful, sometimes amusing--about its existence. Unsentimental tone. Illustrated with faint, impressionistic line drawings. Fifth grade and up.

532. Cook, Walter L. *Table Prayers for Children*. Illus. Joni Fredman. St. Louis: Bethany, 1976. 63p.

Home, parents, one's behavior, and the weather are some of the less conventional topics of morning and evening graces. Most, but not all, mention food. Deals with children's true everyday concerns. Holidays section. Informal and brief. Handsome type and lively pictures done in coral and brown on a cream background. Preschool to second grade.

533. Cooney, Barbara, illus. *A Little Prayer*. New York: Hastings House, 1967. unp.

Original, lovely prayer asks for old-fashioned virtues such as the patience of the spinner, the philosophy of the fisherman, the pride in workmanship of the knife grinder, the good humor of old wine, and will be appreciated more by adults than by children. Fine illustrations portray vividly the character of the people and animals. Kindergarten to second grade.

534. Field, Rachel. *Prayer for a Child*. Illus. Elizabeth Orton Jones. New York: Macmillan, 1944. unp.

Gentle poem of thanksgiving for everyday blessings: good food, a soft bed, toys, a loving family. Also a plea to keep other children safe. Each idea is portrayed in subdued colors as a winsome little girl enjoys her home and friends and prepares for sleep in her cozy bedroom. Kindergarten to second grade.

535. *God's in His Heaven*. New York: Random, 1984. unp.

Plump, appealing tots in overalls and quaint dresses enjoy seasonal activities amid sixteen familiar quotations from Browning, Wordsworth, Rossetti, the Bible, etc. Nature's beauty, right living, and prayer are stressed. Color pictures include many perky animals. Preschool.

536. Gompertz, Helen. *First Prayers*. Illus. Vic Mitchell. Valley Forge, Pa.: Judson, 1980. 32p.

Forty prayers of thanksgiving in five categories. First

category is about child's parts and sensations (legs, hands, taste, smell, gloom, joy, etc.); the second, about family members, including cousins and grandparents; the third, about homes and gardens; the fourth, about pets and their care; and the fifth, about city experiences (stores, trains, buses, etc.). Too many examples for each topic, but all are familiar to small children. Bright pictures of cartoon-style people with large heads and circle eyes. Preschool.

537. Hague, Michael, illus. *A Child's Book of Prayers*. New York: Holt, 1985. 28p.

Unusually handsome and artistic presentation of twenty-one familiar devotions such as Now I Lay Me Down to Sleep, the Lord's Prayer, I See the Moon, etc. Children of various races realistically portrayed with clarity and elegance in both modern and old-fashioned settings, as they pray, think, dream, read, contemplate nature. Still, meditative mood. Christian emphasis. First-line index. Kindergarten to fourth grade.

538. Hayes, Wanda. *My Thank You Book*. Illus. Frances Hook. Cincinnati: Standard, 1964. unp.

Very small children thank God for good food, clothing, flowers, birds, Bible school, day, night, and other familiar and beloved things. Beautiful, pink-cheeked boys and girls in large pictures. Preschool and kindergarten.

539. Hein, Lucille. *I Can Make My Own Prayers*. Illus. Joan Orfe. Valley Forge, Pa.: Judson, 1971. 31p.

Children are encouraged to talk to God in their own language about experiences such as birthdays, Sunday school, night, bedtime, play, etc. Simple verse prayers for each occasion. Has three-color drawings. Preschool to second grade.

540. Holmes, Marjorie. *Nobody Else Will Listen*. Garden City, N.Y.: Doubleday, 1973. 133p.

Records a girl's conversations with God as she asks for guidance, support, and forgiveness, and thanks him for life's joys. Topics include family conflicts, school problems, boys, resisting temptations, coping with organized religion, jealousy, and other common concerns. The book has an understanding tone and uses informal language. Sixth grade and up.

541. Jahsmann, Allan. *Little Folded Hands: Prayers for Children*. Rev. ed. Illus. Frances Hook. St. Louis: Concordia, 1959. 48p.

Prayers for nighttime, morning, forgiveness, school, church, birthdays, missionaries, etc., and of thanksgiving and praise are Scriptural in language and concept. Old-fashioned and rather formal. Some familiar classics such as portions of hymns and the doxology. Sentimental color pictures of children at prayer and with Jesus. Preschool and up.

542. Johnson, Lois Walfrid. *Hello, God! Prayers for Small Children*. Illus. Judy Swanson. Minneapolis: Augsburg, 1975. unp.

Crisp, handsome, two-color graphics distinguish this thirty-prayer collection that gives thanks for families, food, party fun, animals, weather, love, etc. Also asks for blessings, protection, and forgiveness. Depicts familiar childhood situations in a short, conversational, gentle style. Preschool to first grade.

543. Johnstone, Janet, and Anne Grahame, illus. *Prayers for Children*. Milwaukee: Ideals, 1981. unp.

Unusual prayers from a miller's children, an old woman in a cottage, a cowboy, and a fisherman, as well as familiar selections such as the Twenty-third Psalm and the doxology. Dramatically illustrated with elongated figures of modern and old-fashioned children in elegant, colorful settings. Kindergarten to second grade.

544. Jones, Chris. *Lord, I Want to Tell You Something: Prayers for Boys*. Illus. David Koechel. Minneapolis: Augsburg, 1973. 96p.

Simply expressed, brief prayers that ring true, as they appreciate Christmas, computers, bugs; regret misbehavior such as lying and anger; ask for help with sports, parents, self-control, caring for others, etc. Line drawings in brown. Third to sixth grades.

545. Klug, Ron, and Lyn Klug. *Please, God: Prayers for Young Children*. Illus. Sally Mathews. Minneapolis: Augsburg, 1980. unp.

Enthusiastic little prayers about all the things that concern children: family, friends, birthdays, illness, fears, etc. Perfectly illustrated with energetic two-color cartoon-style artwork. Preschool and kindergarten.

546. Klug, Ron, and Lyn Klug. *Thank You, God: Prayers for Young Children*. Illus. Sally Mathews. Minneapolis: Augsburg, 1980. unp.

Straightforward, first-person thanks to God for pets, toys, parents, a blanket, Jesus, seasons, and other beloved and important things in children's daily lives. Large, three-color, cartoon-style illustrations filled with action, details, humor. Preschool and kindergarten.

547. Magagna, Anna Marie, illus. *First Prayers*. New York: Macmillan, 1982. 60p.

Wispy, sentimentalized figures in warm pastels of children quietly and joyfully at prayer in flowery fields and cozy bedrooms. Text contains generally familiar table graces, Bible passages, hymns, bedtime prayers, the Lord's Prayer, the doxology, and selections from poets such as Browning, Christina Rossetti, and Rachel Field. First-line index. Kindergarten and up.

548. Mitchell, Cynthia. *Here a Little Child I Stand: Poems of Prayer and Praise for Children*. Illus. Satomi Ichikawa. New York: Philomel, 1985. unp.

Outstanding, unusually fresh collection of both short and simple and long and richly detailed selections from a variety of cultures that includes Eskimo, Guyanan, Tewa, Indian, Islamic, Hindu, East African, Japanese, European, and American. Quotes some popular poets such as Ogden Nash, Eleanor Farjeon, Langston Hughes. Themes are asking blessings, giving thanks, celebrating the beauty of creation. Meticulously detailed, beautiful watercolors of scenes from a country kitchen to an African hut reflect pensive, joyful, peaceful, reverent moods. Kindergarten and up.

549. Mock, Dorothy K. *Thank You, God, for Water*. Cincinnati: Standard, 1985. unp.

Fine, full-page color photographs of children of various races in activities concerned with water such as sprinkling flowers, drinking from a hose, playing in a pool, smiling in the rain. Also includes clouds, icicles, snow scenes. One-sentence captions describe the importance of water to all life and as one of God's greatest blessings. Preschool.

550. Popson, Martha. *I Need to Talk to You, God*. Illus. Nancy Hannons. Norwalk, Conn.: Gibson, 1983. unp.

Quiet, penetrating short prayers in which a young girl deals with self-doubt, questions about God, everyday problems and mistakes. Strong undercurrent of faith. Empathetic, unassuming, universal. Decorated with simple sketches. Sixth grade and up.

551. *Prayers for Everyone*. Minneapolis: Winston, 1981. unp.

Thanksgiving prayers for parents, grandparents, aunts, and uncles. Prayers asking blessings on friends, world leaders, poor children, people at work. Plain language. Good color photographs of attractive children hugging, bathing, celebrating a birthday, etc. Kindergarten to second grade.

552. *Prayers for Home and School*. Minneapolis: Winston, 1981. unp.

Color photographs of attractive boys and girls illustrate thoughts about caring for others, appreciating everyday things, learning correct behavior, and asking for God's blessings in all of life. Kindergarten to second grade.

553. Roberts, Donald S. *Prayers for the Very Young Child*. Illus. Patricia Mattozzi. St. Louis: Concordia, n.d. 72p.

Three sections of short, rhymed prayers to be used for every day, at the table, and at bedtime. Basic vocabulary for early readers. Pictures of button-eyed children of various races in light, clear colors and black and white. Preschool to second grade.

554. Schreivogel, Paul A. *Small Prayers for Small Children: About Big and Little Things*. Illus. George Ellen Holmgren. Minneapolis: Augsburg, 1971. 32p.

Big, simply designed graphics and line drawings hand printed in intense colors to catch little children's eyes. One- or two-sentence prayers about the four seasons, anger, night, parents, friends, sunshine, etc. Preschool and kindergarten.

555. Smeltzer, Patricia, and Victor Smeltzer. *Thank You for a Book to Read*. *Thank You for a Drink of Water*. *Thank You for a Loaf of Bread*. *Thank You for a Pair of Jeans*. Minneapolis: Winston, 1980. unp.

A series in which boys and girls trace each item back

through the stages in its production and delivery to its ultimate source, God. Everyone and everything in the long chain is thanked. Informative and interesting. Excellent color photographs of each step. Preschool to third grade.

556. *Thank You for the World*. Minneapolis: Winston, 1981. unp.

Seven little prayers thanking God for animals, weather, seasons, etc., by various authors are placed on brilliant color photographs of a child in a field of red poppies, a tot filling sand pails, and other boys and girls happily enjoying the outdoors. Kindergarten to third grade.

557. *Thank You, God*. Norwalk, Conn.: Gibson, 1973. unp.

Zestful pictures in gay colors show sun, moon, flowers, clouds, butterflies, birds, milk, fruit, toys, pets, as kneeling children say simple prayers of appreciation. Preschool.

558. *Thank You Prayers*. Minneapolis: Winston, 1981. unp.

Simply told, grateful thoughts about parents, teachers, toys, pets, friends, nature, forgiveness, and good people everywhere. Excellent color photographs of children of various races sliding, hugging, stamping in a mud puddle, etc. Kindergarten to second grade.

559. Tuckett, Guin Ream. *Day's End: Bedtime Prayers for Young Children*. Illus. Joni Fredman. St. Louis: Bethany, 1979. 64p.

Short prayers and poems give thanks for seasons, Sundays, zoos, and other lovely things in life and ask help for crossness, crying, misbehavior. Also prayers for special occasions such as birthdays, Mother's Day, July Fourth. Four-color drawings. Preschool and kindergarten.

560. Tudor, Tasha, illus. *First Prayers*. New York: Walck, 1952. 48p.

Lord's Prayer, St. Patrick's Prayer, Twenty-third Psalm, Gentle Jesus Meek and Mild, favorite table graces, morning prayers, and other traditional selections are illustrated with delicate, tiny pencil drawings and color paintings of little children at prayer and meditation indoors and out. Preschool to second grade.

561. Tudor, Tasha, illus. *More Prayers*. New York: Walck, 1967. 40p.

Pictures in soft colors illuminate familiar prayers and selections from the Psalms. Preschool to second grade.

562. Wilkin, Eloise, illus. *Prayers for a Small Child*. New York: Random House, 1984. unp.

Table graces, thank-you prayers for nature's gifts, nighttime thoughts, the Lord's Prayer. Most are well known. Illustrated with sentimental charm. Round-faced tots, perky birds, pretty animals, and such, in painstaking detail and light colors. Preschool to second grade.

563. Wilkin, Esther. *The Golden Treasury of Prayers for Boys and Girls*. Illus. Eloise Wilkin. New York: Golden, 1975. unp.

Large, handsome, ecumenical collection of sixty-eight selections from Hindu, Buddhist, Jewish, African, Native American, Muslim, and Christian faiths. Contains quotations from Confucius, Seneca, Aristotle, the Koran, the Bible, as well as St. Francis, Langston Hughes, Robert Herrick. Themes include morning, forgiveness, animals, thanksgiving, and protection. Beautifully illustrated with full-page scenes of children throughout the world. Notes. Preschool to third grade.

564. Wilkin, Esther. *Little Prayers*. Illus. Eloise Wilkin. New York: Golden, 1980. unp.

Thirty-five selections from *The Golden Treasury of Prayers for Boys and Girls* (item 563). Same illustrations and balanced, ecumenical selection.

SONGS

565. Bryan, Ashley. *I'm Going to Sing: Black American Spirituals*. Vol. 2. Illus. author. New York: Atheneum, 1982. 53p.

Words and music (melody line only) of twenty-five songs. Includes standards like "When the Saints Go Marching In" and "It's Me, O Lord," and others less familiar. Handsome format with black-and-white block print style illustrations. All ages.

566. Bryan, Ashley. *Walk Together Children: Black American Spirituals*. Illus. author. New York: Atheneum, 1974. 53p.

Melodies and words of twenty-four spirituals such as "Mary Had a Baby," "Free at Last," "In His Hands," and "Roll, Jordan, Roll." Bold black-and-white illustrations styled after African decorative art. Historical introduction. All ages.

567. Lenski, Lois. *Sing for Peace*. Illus. author. Scottdale, Pa.: Herald, 1985. unp.

Ten children's hymns dating from 1950 and 1952 reprinted from *We Are Thy Children*, with words by Lois Lenski and music by Clyde Robert Bulla. Subjects are peace, kindness, service, good will toward others. Decorated with cheerful little black-and-white drawings. Simple tunes. Preschool to second grade.

568. Royer, Katherine. *Nursery Songbook*. Illus. Norma Hostetler. Scottdale, Pa.: Herald, 1957. 48p.

Simple songs about moral living, giving thanks, nature's beauties, God's love and care, plus some familiar hymns such as "Jesus Loves Me" and "Silent Night." Each has a full-page color picture of tidy tots enjoying everyday activities or of scenes from the Bible. Preschool.

569. Shoemaker, Kathryn, illus. *Children, Go Where I Send Thee*. Minneapolis: Winston, 1980. unp.

The Black American spiritual in cumulative verses counts from "one itty bitty baby born in Bethlehem" to twelve disciples, using events from both the Old and New Testaments. Breathtaking pictures of strong, flowing figures in gorgeously colored calicoes and stripes glowing against a blue-black background. Music. Kindergarten to second grade.

V
CHRISTIAN LIFE

570. Alden, Laura. *Sorry*. Illus. Dan Siculan. Elgin, Ill.: Child's World, 1982. 31p.

A little boy discovers that saying you are sorry can rectify many unhappy situations. He is late to the dentist, makes noise in church, knocks down another's sand castle, hurts his brother's feelings, etc., and apologizes. He asks God to help him learn to be kind and forgive others. Full page color pictures of the various incidents. Preschool to first grade.

571. Aldridge, Melanie. *Paula's Feeling Angry*. Illus. Peg Roth Haag. Elgin, Ill.: Child's World, 1979. 32p.

Paula's baby brother takes up so much of her mother's time that Paula gives him a hard, jealous pinch, and he cries. Her understanding mother talks with her about Jesus' commandment for us to love one another, draws her into helping care for the baby, and encourages her to overcome her anger. Three-color pictures of attractive black family. Preschool and kindergarten.

572. Anderson, Debby. *Friends*. Illus. author. Elgin, Ill.: Chariot, n.d. unp.

Big-headed, button-eyed smiling tots of all races appreciate friends who trust, share, help, forgive, love, etc., as Jesus does. Simple text. Preschool.

573. Bachman, Mary. *Choosing Is Fun*. Illus. Steve Hayes. Cincinnati: Standard, 1982. unp.

A little black boy enjoys selecting ice cream and picking a puppy, and he makes choices involving obedience, truth-telling, following Jesus. Also included are choices God has made: e.g., Jonah's going to Nineveh, Mary being

Jesus' mother, the Bible teaching his word. Easy text. Bright cartoon pictures. Preschool to first grade.

574. Barsuhn, Rochelle Nielsen. *Angry*. Illus. Kathryn Hutton. Elgin, Ill.: Child's World, 1982. 31p.

Everyday situations in which a pouting little girl gets angry with her friends and family when they disappoint her or expect her to do things which displease her. At the end of her upsetting day she prays and feels better. Adequate color pictures. Preschool to first grade.

575. Barsuhn, Rochelle Nielsen. *Sometimes I Feel....* Illus. Gwen Connelly. Wheaton, Ill.: Dandelion, 1985. 31p.

Emotions, such as happiness, empathy, frustration, thankfulness, sorrow, confidence, anger, love, loneliness, boredom, jealousy, exclusion, fear, are expressed in everyday situations. Prayer is encouraged. Simple, vividly colored pictures. Preschool to second grade.

576. Buchanan, Jami Lyn. *Letters to My Little Sisters*. Illus. Wendy Talbot. Ventura, Calif.: Regal, 1984. 128p.

Wholesome advice to preteen girls about putting personal morality before popularity, resisting peer pressure, dating and other boy-girl relationships, appreciating parents and siblings, commitment to God, etc. Liberally supported by Bible quotations. Warm, informal tone. Delicate black-and-white decorations of birds, clouds, trees. Sixth grade and up.

577. Buerger, Jane. *Growing as Jesus Grew*. Illus. Frances Hook. Elgin, Ill.: Child's World, 1980. 30p.

Growth takes many forms: getting bigger, learning at church and school, assuming responsibilities at home, being a good friend, talking to God. Idealized children pictured in rich pastels. Clear text. Preschool and kindergarten.

578. Buerger, Jane. *Obedience*. Illus. Helen Endres. Elgin, Ill.: Child's World, 1980. 29p.

Red-haired little boy is tempted to misbehave (sneak the dog indoors, slip his milk to the cat, cross against the traffic light, push to the front of the bus line, etc.), but he doesn't. He follows the rules even when his parents aren't watching. When this is hard, he prays for help. Scriptural quotations. Basic, colorful pictures. Preschool to second grade.

579. Cachiaras, Dot. *Sharing Makes Me Happy*. Illus. Lorraine Arthur. Cincinnati: Standard, 1982. unp.

Short, singsong rhymes praise all kinds of sharing, from sharing secrets, flashlights, and sandboxes to sharing the blame, the work, and the load. Also sharing by giving love as God does. Simple, bright pictures of preschoolers playing, helping others, praying. Preschool.

580. Donahue, Bob. *Don't Be a Puppet on a String*. Wheaton, Ill.: Tyndale, 1983. 89p.

Theme of learning to take responsibility for your own behavior includes chapters on getting along in your family, choosing a social group sensibly, avoiding cults, being suspicious of advertising claims, setting goals, praying, and so on. Self-awareness quizzes. Short sentences. Cartoons. Fifth grade and up.

581. Donahue, Bob. *Getting Your Act Together*. Wheaton, Ill.: Tyndale, 1983. 108p.

Advice on getting along in your family through empathy and communication, understanding various types of friendships, practicing good manners, controlling your temper, time management techniques, success strategies for school, overcoming depression, seeking God. Informal, superficial. Cartoons. Fifth grade and up.

582. Donahue, Bob. *How to Make People Like You When You Know They Don't*. Wheaton, Ill.: Tyndale, 1982. 104p.

Being created in the image of God's love, everyone can improve with patience, determination, and discipline. Self-analysis quizzes, grooming tips, lists of bad personality traits that may need to be overcome, suggestions for development of caring, positive behavior. Nothing new, but the encouraging tone and lively style are appealing. Cartoons. Sixth grade and up.

583. Eberle, Sarah. *What Is Love?* Illus. Jan Brown. Cincinnati: Standard, 1980. unp.

Pictures filled with dots, checks, and floral patterns show jolly, cartoon-style children showing love to family, friends, and neighbors, by helping, caring, and sharing in daily life situations, all because God loves them. Preschool to kindergarten.

584. Fletcher, Sarah. *Stewardship: Taking Care of God's World.* Illus. author. St. Louis: Concordia, 1984. unp.

Teenage babysitter explains good stewardship to three middle-class children. It includes helping at home; caring for one's body; using time, talents, and money wisely; loving others; and evangelizing for Jesus. Simple comic strip format with cartoon figures and easily understood dialogue. Murky color. Score of stewardship song included. Kindergarten to second grade.

585. Gambill, Henrietta. *Are You Listening?* Illus. Lois Axeman. Wheaton, Ill.: Child's World, 1984. 32p.

Hearing and obeying God's word in everyday life. Little boy is cooperative at home, helps others, tells the truth, shares with friends, prays, and so forth, illustrating various Scripture verses. Contains a song about listening. Basic, cheerful pictures and easily understood concepts. Preschool to second grade.

586. Gambill, Henrietta. *Self-Control.* Illus. Kathryn Hutton. Elgin, Ill.: Child's World, 1982. 31p.

Appealing pictures of a little black boy who shows self control when he waits his turn, is considerate of family and friends, keeps his temper, is quiet in church and the library, asks God's help in deciding what to do. Preschool to second grade.

587. *The Goal and the Glory.* Old Tappan, N.J.: Revell, 1986. 160p.

Short personal testimonies from thirty-three athletes, mostly men, representing twelve sports, about overcoming adversity on the playing field and in their personal lives. Some are strongly religious while others do not emphasize the spiritual. All are caring, courageous, and determined. Brisk, buoyant, easy to read. First published in *Guideposts Magazine* from 1975 to 1984. Fifth grade and up.

588. Klug, Ron. *I'm A Good Helper.* Illus. Sally Mathews. Minneapolis: Augsburg, 1981. Unp.

Tousle-haired child thanks God for the many ways there are to help at home and school. Vacuuming, baby-sitting, washing the car, helping the teacher hand out papers, weeding Grandpa's garden are some of the jobs pictured in cartoons done in brilliant colors like cerise and purple. Preschool to first grade.

589. Lewis, C.S. *C.S. Lewis, His Letters to Children*. New York: Macmillan, 1985. 120p.

Selected collection of Lewis's replies to letters from readers of his Narnia books, science fiction, and several other works written from 1944 through 1963. Some discuss the Christian symbolism in the Narnia series and credit children, unlike adults, with understanding it at once. Other theological matters touched upon gently. Warm and unpretentious. Fourth grade and up.

590. Moncure, Jane Belk. *Caring*. Illus. Helen Endres. Elgin, Ill.: Child's World, 1980. 28p.

Little girl shows concern for family, friends, and nature in familiar ways such as cleaning up at home, feeding birds, making a new child in the neighborhood welcome. She thanks God for his care for her. Simple color pictures. Preschool to first grade.

591. Moncure, Jane Belk. *Courage*. Illus. Helen Endres. Elgin, Ill.: Child's World, 1980. 31p.

In comfortably middle-class surroundings a young girl faces frightening situations such as going to the doctor and dentist, diving into the pool, starting a new school. She tries to be brave, as Jesus was. Abstract concept explained. Attractive, realistic color illustrations. Preschool to first grade.

592. Moncure, Jane Belk. *Joy*. Illus. Pat Karch. Elgin, Ill.: Child's World, 1982. 31p.

Ponytailed little girl feels joy when she makes a snowman, plays an angel in the Christmas pageant, finds a lost kitten, knows that Jesus loves her, and so on. Sweet-faced people in mild colors illustrate simple text. Preschool to second grade.

593. Moncure, Jane Belk. *Kindness*. Illus. Linda Sommers Hohag. Elgin, Ill.: Child's World, 1980. 29p.

Shows tots demonstrating many types of kindness--sharing lunch, taking turns, being gentle with pets, etc.--that can be practiced in daily life. They pray for the ability to show even more. Warm pastel pictures of ingenuous little children at home, church, and school. Preschool to first grade.

594. Morris, Susan, illus. *Jesus Shows Us How to Live*. Los Angeles: Intervisual Communications, 1981. unp.

Jesus' examples for a moral life include loving kindness to others, helping the sick, attending worship services, praying. Each is told briefly and illustrated with a moveable picture showing scenes from Jesus' life alternating with those from a modern child's. Colorful artwork with merry children and animals, a smiling Jesus. Preschool.

595. Mueller, Virginia. *Who Is Your Neighbor?* Illus. Lorraine Arthur. Cincinnati: Standard, 1980. unp.

Clear little explication that your neighbors are not only next door but also worldwide and come in all colors and nationalities. They should be helped when in need. Emphasis on caring and sharing. Illustrated with robust children in bright colors. Preschool to second grade.

596. Murphy, Elspeth Campbell. *God Cares When I Do Something Stupid*. Illus. Jane E. Nelson. Elgin, Ill.: Cook, 1984. 24p. God's Word in My Heart Series.

Although repeatedly warned to be careful in their play, two boys at a family reunion continue rough-housing until one is pushed down and hurt. The other, crying and feeling guilty, is comforted by his father, who reminds him that God understands and forgives. Pleasant illustrations in black and white and color. Kindergarten to third grade.

597. Murphy, Elspeth Campbell. *God Cares When I Don't Know What To Do*. Illus. Jane E. Nelson. Elgin, Ill.: Cook, 1984. 24p. God's Word in My Heart Series.

A black boy is uncomfortable as a stranger in a new school. He is very good in mathematics and faces a problem when some boys want to copy his homework answers. He asks God's help. Instead of gaining their friendship by helping them cheat, he does it by tutoring them. Attractive pictures alternatively in color and black and white. Preschool to third grade.

598. Murphy, Elspeth Campbell. *God Cares When I Don't Like Myself*. Illus. Jane E. Nelson. Elgin, Ill.: Cook, 1983. 24p. God's Word in My Heart Series.

A boy feels discouraged because he stepped on a neighbor's flowers, missed catching a baseball, was scolded by the school monitor. He thinks that if he disguised himself by turning purple, he could do everything right. But he realizes that his parents and God delight in him just as he is. Reassuring, conversational text. Neat illustrations done alternatively in black and white and color. Preschool to third grade.

599. Murphy, Elspeth Campbell. *God Cares When I'm All Tired Out*. Illus. Jane E. Nelson. Elgin, Ill.: Cook, 1983. 24p. God's Word in My Heart Series.

A little black girl shopping in a mall with her mother and grandmother gets bored and tired looking at grownup things. As she sits by a fountain to wait, she imagines Jesus letting her wade and then taking her on his lap and comforting her. Instructions to parents and teachers about helping children learn Bible passages. Gentle illustrations alternate color pages with those in black and white. Preschool to second grade.

600. Murphy, Elspeth Campbell. *God Cares When I'm Disappointed*. Illus. Jane E. Nelson. Elgin, Ill.: Cook, 1983. 24p. God's Word in My Heart Series.

A little girl longs to be the princess who rides on the swan float in the parade, but all she can do is watch the marchers go by. She consoles herself by talking to God, as she always can whenever she is sad and disappointed. Well-designed pictures in black and white and color. Kindergarten to third grade.

601. Murphy, Elspeth Campbell. *God Cares When I'm Sorry*. Illus. Jane E. Nelson. Elgin, Ill.: Cook, 1983. 24p. God's Word in My Heart Series.

A girl takes a brownie meant for her sister and blames the theft on the dog. Feeling guilty and sad, she confesses the truth and apologizes. She is grateful for God's ready forgiveness and unchanging love. Simple illustrations in color and black and white. Preschool to third grade.

602. Murphy, Elspeth Campbell. *God Cares When I'm Wondering*. Illus. Jane E. Nelson. Elgin, Ill.: Cook, 1984. 24p. God's Word in My Heart Series.

An Asian girl imagines what it would be like to be a bird and learns about them at the zoo and in the library. But she realizes that only God can know everything about birds and the rest of the world, as well. She is grateful that she was created curious and anxious to learn. Appealing artwork alternates black-and-white pages with those in color. Preschool to third grade.

603. Murphy, Elspeth Campbell. *God Cares When I'm Worried*. Illus. Jane E. Nelson. Elgin, Ill.: Cook, 1983. 24p. God's Word in My Heart Series.

A boy is upset and confused by the changes in his life when his family moves: a strange house, new children. He comforts his kittens and thinks of how God comforts him and gives him a peaceful feeling. Soothing pictures in color and black and white. Kindergarten to third grade.

604. Murphy, Elspeth Campbell. *God Cares When I Need to Talk to Somebody*. Illus. Jane E. Nelson. Elgin, Ill.: Cook, 1984. 24p. God's Word in My Heart Series.

When he is left out of show-and-tell at school, no one hears him ask for the ketchup at dinner, and he is tongue-tied when a famous football player greets him, a boy feels very discouraged. He is glad God always has time to listen to him and never makes him feel embarrassed. Competent illustrations done alternatively in black and white and color. Kindergarten to third grade.

605. Nystrom, Carolyn. *Growing Jesus' Way*. Illus. Wayne A. Hanna. Chicago: Moody, 1982. unp.

A little boy who has recently become a Christian emulates Jesus by helping a blind girl, sharing his lunch, protecting another child, resisting temptation, praying, etc. The artwork is basic in color and style. Preschool to first grade.

606. Nystrom, Carolyn. *What Is a Christian?* Illus. Wayne A. Hanna. Chicago: Moody, 1981. unp.

Scattered thoughts about how to follow Jesus: caring for other people, appreciating God's creation, listening carefully to Bible stories, obeying parents. Three basic steps to Christianity involving repentance, confession, and belief in Jesus' redeeming sacrifice are interpreted for young children. Simple pictures in primary colors of a little boy in daily life. Preschool to second grade.

607. Stafford, Tim. *The Trouble with Parents*. Grand Rapids, Mich.: Zondervan, 1978. 159p.

Focuses on anecdotes and incidents demonstrating problems of divorce, nagging, lack of trust, hostility, poor communication, etc., in various types of families, with suggestions on how to cope. Indicates that parents are imperfect and need tolerance and patience from their children. Christian faith will help. Understanding tone. Sixth grade and up.

608. Ward, Elaine. *Roots and Wings*. Illus. Ruth Lull. New York: Friendship, 1983. 14p.

Obviously didactic, very short stories center around common childhood problems such as adoption, divorce, moving, hospitalization. Contains discussion-starters. "Talk and think" questions to help children with similar problems express fear and anger and to help other children empathize with them. Positive suggestions for understanding and handling each difficulty. Realistic black-and-white drawings. Fourth to sixth grades.

609. Ziegler, Sandra. *Friends: A Handbook about Getting Along Together*. Illus. Seymour Fleishman. Elgin, Ill.: Child's World, 1980. 111p.

All kinds of friendships, with parents and pets as well as peers, are praised. Qualities of courtesy, generosity, consideration, etc., which make good friendships, are described. Suggestions for Bible readings. Lively cartoons in color and black and white. Kindergarten to fourth grade.

Fiction

610. Allred, Mary. *The Move to a New House*. Illus. Paul R. Behrens. Nashville: Broadman, 1978. 32p.

When Todd moves away from a house by the creek, and bulldozers begin draining off the water, he asks God to help him save his pet frog and to help him feel at ease in his new home. Reassuring tone. Unexceptional two-color pictures. Kindergarten to third grade.

611. Ashley, Meg. *The Deserted Rooms*. Ventura, Calif.: Regal, 1984. 139p. Boarding House Adventure Series.

In a wildly improbable plot thirteen-year-old Beth and her friend Joey, fifteen, follow cryptic, Scriptural clues which lead to an unusual treasure and foil evil crooks who plan to build a gambling casino near their northern Idaho home. Undisciplined writing style but fast paced. Fourth to sixth grades.

612. Ashworth, Mae Hurley. *Six Times True*. Illus. Allan Eitzen. New York: Friendship, 1973.

Collection of short stories about people serving God in various times and places. Includes Moses in his basket, David fleeing a vengeful Saul, persecuted Christian missionaries in Burma, Mennonites escaping from Russia, Zambian farm family aided by Canadian churches, Protestant and Catholic teenagers banding together for community service. Lively writing. Sixth grade and up.

613. Aven, Del. *Anna's Tree Swing*. Illus. Debra Aven. Nashville: Broadman, 1981. 32p.

Anna is upset when the big oak tree from which her swing hangs is seriously damaged by carpenter ants and must be cut down. She wonders why God didn't protect it. Her parents explain that human beings can't know God's plan for the world, must trust in his love, and can plant acorns. Two-color drawings. An easy reader. Kindergarten to third grade.

614. Bacigalupa, Drew. *The Song of Guadalupana*. Illus. Jeannie Pear. Huntington, Ind.: Our Sunday Visitor, 1979. 48p.

When Juan claims he hears the Virgin of Guadalupe singing in the valley where he herds goats, Manuelita, a poor child whose mother desperately needs work, asks him to pray for her to the Virgin. Later Manuelita discovers that an opera singer has rented a home and needs someone to keep house for her. A gentle miracle has occurred. Expressive, realistic full-page color illustrations of Mexican people and their village. Glossary of Spanish words. Kindergarten to fourth grade.

615. Baehr, Patricia. *Faithfully, Tru*. New York: Macmillan, 1984. 203p.

A fifteen-year-old sensitive but self-centered Catholic girl has a faith crisis when her life is disrupted by the appearance of a cynical father she thought dead, as well as the intrusion of an ill, elderly aunt and an unwed mother into her home. She emerges from her crisis with a truer, stronger belief. Faith healing sympathetically treated. Spare, effective style. Sixth grade and up.

616. Barrett, William E. *The Lilies of the Field*. Illus. Burt Silverman. Garden City, N.Y.: Doubleday, 1962. 92p.

Perfectly integrated novelette filled with humor, warmth,

decency, faith, and joy. Young black man, a devout Baptist, is touring the West in an old station wagon when he spies four nuns working on a farm. He stops to help them build a fence and ends up building them a Catholic chapel. Fine characterization. Sixth grade and up.

617. Bartholomew, Ralph. *The Gopher Hole Treasure Hunt*. Illus. Richard Mlodock. Wheaton, Ill.: Victor, 1977. 120p.

Jeff, twelve-year-old orphaned son of missionaries, has exciting, unlikely adventures in southern California searching for lost black opals and gold and catching bank robbers. He prays often for guidance, forgiveness, and help and converts a bad boy to Christianity. Action-filled narrative. Large type, short sentences. Fifth grade and up.

618. Boorman, Linda. *The Giant Trunk Mystery*. Illus. Marilee Harrald. Wheaton, Ill.: Victor, 1981. Horseshoe Bend Mystery Series.

During an 1898 Oregon influenza epidemic Susie Conroy, twelve-year-old redhaired preacher's daughter, finds the answer to why the widow's trunk is so heavy. The improbable plot is done in a lively, humorous style. Describes a first romance. Some discussion about Jesus' love. Fourth to sixth grades.

619. Boorman, Linda. *The Mystery Man of Horseshoe Bend*. Wheaton, Ill.: Victor, 1980. 100p. Horseshoe Bend Mystery Series.

Curious, mischievous Susie, part of preacher's large family in small Oregon town in 1897, longs for a bicycle. She watches a recently arrived bicycle salesman very closely and finds he is trying to steal her aunt's savings. Her family undertakes to reform him. Slight, easy reading. Fourth to sixth grades.

620. Buckingham, Jamie. *Jesus World*. Lincoln, Va.: Chosen, 1981. 132p.

Immensely wealthy Simon Pedersen is caught up in the dream of a television evangelist who wants to build a huge Biblical theme amusement park. Its purpose is supposedly to win souls to Christ, but big business concerns dominate it with frightening results. Simon withdraws and starts a modest ministry of his own, beginning with twelve men. A fast-paced and vivid story depicting conservative theology. Sixth grade and up.

621. Clifford, Laurie B. *The Peppermint Gang and Frog Heaven.* Wheaton, Ill.: Tyndale, 1984. 168p.

Jennifer Pepper, wily and full of get-rich-quick schemes, is a missionary pilot's daughter living in Central America. At Christmas she and her pals plan a gala celebration and gifts for poor families in the barrio, hoping to finance it by selling frogs they capture. God helps her help others. Humorous style of writing. Fourth to sixth grades.

622. Cooney, Ellen. *Small-town Girl.* New York: Dell, 1983. 184p.

Although somewhat restrained by her devout Catholic conscience, fiery Collie is shown charging through life as she attends parochial schools in the 1960s. She fights with anyone who opposes her, writes plays and poems, falls in love, and takes vengeance on her enemies. A vividly realized character. Absorbing and fast-paced story. Sixth grade and up.

623. Courtney, Dayle. *The Ivy Plot.* Illus. John Ham. Cincinnati: Standard, 1981. 192p. Thorne Twins Adventure Book Series.

Sixteen-year-old Christian twins thwart neo-Nazi organization with the help of a Jewish Nazi hunter and rescue a college dean's daughter, who was kidnapped to be exchanged for Nazi war criminal. Stiffly written yet easy to read. Full of action. Sixth grade and up.

624. Courtney, Dayle. *The Sinister Circle.* Illus John Ham. Cincinnati: Standard, 1983. 191p. Thorne Twins Adventure Book Series.

Lurid story of master criminal manipulating ring of teenage thieves through mind-altering drugs. Sixteen-year-old Thorne twins, firm Christians, involve themselves, rescue young runaway girl, and expose the ringleader. Although written in a brisk style, the plot is unconvincing. Sixth grade and up.

625. Croman, Dorothy Young. *Danger in Sagebrush Country: An Outlands Adventure.* Wheaton, Ill.: Tyndale, 1980. 131p.

Neatly written, obvious lesson in brotherly love. God-fearing Lutheran family rescues staunch black Baptists from rough treatment in 1884 Spokane, Washington. Adventures ensue and include the finding of stolen loot from bank robberies. In a pat ending the reward money enables the black family to buy a farm and seek a decent life away from prejudice. Fourth to sixth grades.

626. Dengler, Sandy. *3-in-1 Pioneer Family Adventures*. Chicago: Moody, 1979. unp.

Three separate books combined into one volume about the Tremain family, who emigrated from Illinois to West Texas in 1881. *Summer of the Wild Pig* tells about twelve-year-old Dan, who adopts a javelina (the wild pig of the title), helps train a race horse, and explores the meaning of faith in God with his friend Matthew Carson. *The Melon Hound* involves Dan in a mystery of stolen jewels. The born again Carson family wins Dan's parents to Christ. In *The Horse Who Loved Picnics* the Carsons move to Arizona and the Tremains wonder if they should follow. Convincing details of hardscrabble farming in dry, dusty terrain. Easy to read. Fourth to sixth grades.

627. Donahue, Marilyn Cram. *To Catch a Golden Ring*. Elgin, Ill.: Cook, 1980. 223p.

Thirteen-year-old Angie and her friend Con live in a Los Angeles slum. While running away from an abusive stepfather, Con falls under a train and loses his legs. Angie is intensely loyal and inspires him to put his life back together. During the crisis Angie asks God's help and is given strength to mature and change. Gritty, realistic details. Well written and absorbing. Fifth grade and up.

628. Durrett, Deanne. *My New Sister, the Bully*. Nashville: Abingdon, 1985. 128p.

When eleven-year-old Tom's mother remarries, he feels very much an outsider in the new family. Stepsister Lydia picks on him constantly. Although he is a committed Christian, Tom begins to hate her. A kindly old man counsels him and explains that Lydia has the same fear of rejection that he has, which is why she misbehaves. Lydia is the best realized character. The others are merely symbols presenting the problem and its Christian solution. Crisp style. Fourth to sixth grades.

629. Ellis, Joyce K. *Snowmobile Trap*. Nashville: Nelson, 1981. 166p.

Stacy, thirteen, is self-centered and careless. With her usual disregard of the consequences of an act, she dares her friend Ryan to speed in a snowmobile. It wrecks and he is paralyzed. Stacy feels so guilty that she can not enjoy her new horse until she is forgiven by God, Ryan, and herself. Fifth grade and up.

630. Epp, Margaret. *Sarah and the Darnley Boys*. Illus. Joe Van Severen. Wheaton, Ill.: Victor, 1981. 120p. Prairie Adventure Series.

Conservative, loving Scottish Christian family works together on a Canadian farm in 1920s. Vivid evocation of rural life. Plot centers around eleven-year-old Sarah's experiences with a strict teacher and some rowdy boys in a one-room schoolhouse. Believable, appealing characters. Black-and-white illustrations. Fourth to sixth grades.

631. Epp, Margaret. *Sarah and the Lost Friendship*. Wheaton, Ill.: Victor, 1979. 131p. Prairie Adventure Series.

Although they are supposed to be good Christians, fiery ten-year-old Sarah and her former best friend, Susan, are jealous and hateful toward one another until gentle pressure from family and friends reconciles them. Rural western Canada in 1926 is pictured with charm. Shows the beauty of changing seasons and rigors and rewards of farm life. Conservative religious tone. Fourth to sixth grades.

632. Evans, Shirlee. *Tree Tall and the Whiteskins*. Illus. James Ponter. Scottdale, Pa.: Herald, 1985. 104p.

Twelve-year-old Tree Tall becomes friends with kindly Christian family settling in Oregon. Curious, he asks about their strange praying, and they tell him about Jesus' love for all people. Later, when his tribe is forcibly relocated to a reservation, his new friends help them. Convincing treatment of Native Americans and their painful situation at this time. Realistic, humorous characterizations of young boys. Black-and-white drawings. Fourth grade and up.

633. Forti, Kathleen J. *The Door to the Secret City*. Illus. James F. Brisson. Walpole, N.H.: Stillpoint, 1984. 135p.

Three stories about Freddie, an exuberant, boastful, self-centered boy, and his guardian angel, Daniel. Freddie learns to share when he is hurt falling from a tree and has an out-of-body experience in a heaven-like City of Crystal. When he has a terrible nightmare, Freddie learns caring sympathy for others. Freddie also learns to practice faith healing on his broken hand. Didactic messages are well integrated. Lively, informal style. Fourth to sixth grades.

634. Gaeddert, LouAnn. *Daffodils in the Snow*. New York: Dutton, 1984. 114p.

In a small Kansas town in the 1950s Marianne, a sheltered and spiritual seventeen-year-old, announces that God is the father of her unborn child. Disowned by her rigidly pious father, she marries an unusually caring person. When the baby, Christopher, arrives, miraculous happenings associated with him begin to occur. Thoughtful, well-written speculation on what might happen with a Second Coming, from mobs demanding to be healed to the disbelief of the high-ranking clergy. Mature readers, sixth grade and up.

635. Graeber, Charlotte. *The Best Bike Ever. The Hand-Me Down Cap. The Hard Luck Mutt. I'm So-So, So What? The Muscle Tussle. My Mr. T. Doll*. Illus. Joe Boddy. Nashville: Nelson, 1985. unp.

Appealing, burly, and bejeweled Mr. T. of television fame gives sound Christian advice to young children. Lessons include sharing; not worshipping material things; wearing hand-me-down clothes cheerfully while appreciating family love; being kind to animals because "God don't make trash"; asking God for courage to perform in a gymnastics show; using your mind instead of your fists; and remembering there is a "big Dad" in heaven who cares about fatherless girls. Easy to read. Lively, colorful pictures. Kindergarten to fourth grade.

636. Grant, Myrna. *Ivan and the Daring Escape* (1976, 167p.). *Ivan and the Moscow Circus* (1980, 160p.). *Ivan and the Star of David* (1977, 142p.). Illus. Joe De Velasco. Wheaton, Ill.: Tyndale. Ivan Series.

Ivan and his family are part of a Russian Protestant community in Moscow. They love their country but not its repressive government. Ivan is involved in courageous rescues of persecuted young people--a Jewish girl wishing to escape to Israel, the son of a political prisoner confined in a reformatory-type school, an acrobat and his uncle wanting to flee to Canada. Authentic backgrounds. Briskly written, interesting, and easy to read. Prayer and conversion figure prominently. There are additional titles in this series. Black-and-white drawings. Fourth grade and up.

637. Gray, Margaret. *The Donkey's Tale*. Ventura, Calif.: Regal, 1984. unp.

Ordinary girl appears to be painting a mural indoors when a door in the wall opens on the world, and she is asked to help others. She is too tongue-tied to speak and too weak to act until a donkey appears and encourages her by painting with its tail scenes from Palm Sunday, when it was given special strength to carry Jesus into Jerusalem. Clear-cut illustrations in muted colors. Kindergarten to third grade.

638. Greene, Jacqueline Dembar. *The Leveller*. New York: Walker, 1984. 117p.

Sprightly tale of Tom Cook, young man in 1779 Massachusetts who "levels" society by transferring certain rich families' possessions to needy people in tricky, amusing ways. Although his mother had promised him to the Devil in exchange for his recovery from severe illness, he confounds Beelzebub with his good deeds, constant Bible reading, and quick wits. Based on local legend. Well written. Fifth grade and up.

639. Hein, Lucille E. *A Tree I Can Call My Own*. Illus. Joan Orfe. Valley Forge, Pa.: Judson, 1974. unp.

Small boy loves a special apple tree which gives him fruit and also an exciting place to play all year. He observes its seasonal changes and appreciates it as a gift of God. Interesting details but message is obscured by too much text, cluttered format. Undistinguished pictures. Kindergarten to third grade.

640. Henderson, Lois T. *The Blessing Deer*. Elgin, Ill.: Cook, 1980. 207p.

Deeply disturbed by racial prejudice in the United States, motherless Ellen leaves her father in Washington and seeks peace and love with her aunt's family in Canada. But she finds white-Indian conflict there. Motivated by Christian love, Ellen learns to face the problem positively. Good readers fifth grade and up.

641. Henderson, Lois T. *A Candle in the Dark*. Elgin, Ill.: Cook, 1982. 159p.

Christy, a courageous eighth-grader, has always attended special schools for the blind. When her mother remarries, she agrees to tackle public junior high. Her strong Christian faith, bright mind, and determination help her overcome obstacles until she adjusts to new life and friends. Perceptive portrayal of blind student's challenges. Contains humor. Informal style. Realistic but positive attitude. Fifth grade and up.

642. Holland, Isabelle. *God, Mrs. Muskrat, and Aunt Dot*. Illus. Beth Krush and Joe Krush. Philadelphia: Westminster, 1983. 78p.

Narrative in the form of a long letter from eleven-year-old Rebecca to God. Orphaned, she has been taken in by aunt and uncle. She is so hostile that she has no friends. She has two Gods: one, the loving God who rules all nature; the other, the cold, rigid God of the church, who has many rules. An imaginary anthropomorphic muskrat lady, who is warm and understanding, is Rebecca's solace. Eventually Rebecca accepts reality and her relatives' love. Empathetic, pictorial, flowing style. Lively black-and-white drawings well keyed to text. Fourth to sixth grades.

643. Holland, Isabelle. *Green Andrew Green*. Illus. Pat Steiner. Philadelphia: Westminster, 1984. 80p.

Andrew has turned green, resents his condition, blames God for not helping him. He has adventures inside magic television sets, wishes for power, and begins to hate everyone. When he meets a scrawny cat he likes, his aunt won't let him keep it. People say they love him and that God loves him, but this love seems to be equated with punishment. He is offered the power he craves, but he must sacrifice the cat's life to obtain it. Real love triumphs. Many lively black-and-white drawings. Fourth to sixth grades.

644. Horvat, Dilwyn. *Operation Titan*. Westchester, Ill.: Crossway, 1984. 125p.

When the repressive Empire assumed control of the galaxy, a group of Christians hid themselves away on a secret planet called Ekklesia. A traitor schemes to expose them, and Paul Trentam and his fourteen-year-old son must penetrate the Empire stronghold, rescue refugees, and fly them to Ekklesia. The convoluted, improbable plot is not unusual for science fiction and it has convincing technical details. The book also features prayer and persecution. It is high in interest, but low in readability. Sixth grade and up.

645. Howe, Fanny. *Taking Care*. New York: Avon, 1985. 160p.

Self-centered, ill-tempered Pamela, sixteen, is the daughter of alcoholic parents. Her life is empty and useless until she feels a need for God. While preparing for confirmation in the Roman Catholic church, she is required to do hospital work, learns compassion, and finds love. Slight, unconvincing romance for older girls, sixth grade and up.

646. Howe, Norma. *God, the Universe, and Hot Fudge Sundaes.* Boston: Houghton Mifflin, 1984. 182p.

Alfie, sixteen, undergoes a spiritual crisis when her little sister dies and she attends a Creation versus Evolution trial where she encounters a handsome graduate student with scientific arguments. There is conflict with her mother, who is dominated by a Conservative Christian group. Diffuse plot is weighted by author's message. Easy, informal style. Sixth grade and up.

647. Jenkins, Jerry B. *Allyson* (1981, 185p.). *Erin* (1982, 167p.). *Hilary* (1980, 159p.). *Karlyn* (1980, 159p.). *Margo* (1979, 191p.). *Paige* (1981, 158p.). *Shannon* (1982, 157p.). Chicago: Moody. Margo Mystery Series.

Margo and Philip, young detectives at the Haymeyer agency in Chicago, are Fundamentalist Christians who investigate a series of crimes in this series: Margo's mother murders her lover; Margo is defrauded of an inheritance; Karlyn is harassed by a mysterious prowler; Allyson's father may be a former Nazi; deranged Paige assumes the identity of a dead woman; Shannon is pursued by a clever maniac; teenage gymnast Erin is accused of killing a gangster. Bizarre, unconvincing premises. Wordy and often slow-moving. Sixth grade and up.

648. Jenkins, Jerry B. *Daniel's Big Surprise.* Illus. Richard Wahl. Cincinnati: Standard, 1984. Bradford Family Adventure Series.

Unlikely plot. Eleven-year-old Daniel is lonely in his new house in the country and decides to visit a state orphanage every day. He becomes strongly attached to a lively little Latino girl and is delighted when his family adopts her. Strong emphasis on Christian prayer, forgiveness, and service. Black-and-white drawings. Fourth to sixth grades.

649. Johnson, Lissa Halls. *Runaway Dreams.* Ventura, Calif.: Regal. 154p.

Although Pam, sixteen, comes from a so-called Christian

home, there is no demonstration of Christian living or loving there. At church camp she meets Carly, another unhappy rebel, and eventually runs away from home to live with Carly in a California beach resort on a bare sustenance level. Pam alternately despairs because God doesn't make her life easy (but takes no positive steps on her own) and exults in the beauty of his creation. Undisciplined writing. Unconvincing plot. Sixth grade and up.

650. Jorgensen, Dan. *Sky Hook*. Elgin, Ill.: Cook, 1985. 128p.

Eighth-grade girls' basketball team members at first are hostile toward one another, but by the end of a winning season all have become loyal friends. Andrea prays for and cares about her teammates, and her influence is effective. There is knowledgeable basketball description and a lively, matter-of-fact style. The Christian values are well integrated into story. Fifth grade and up.

651. Kauffman, Joel. *Wolfhunter*. Nashville: Abingdon, 1986. 110p.

Twelve-year-old Josh, dared by his friends to shoot a wild dog, is inspired by prayer to conquer her with love instead. Once Wolf is tamed, however, Josh won't accept responsibility for her. When his friends hunt her down, he realizes that love requires constant caring. He knows he has been forgiven by a loving Wolf and must forgive his friends before he can feel peace of mind. An introspective work, with a realistic setting of woods and wildlife. Fourth to sixth grades.

652. Kehle, Roberta Lunsford. *The Blooming of the Flame Tree*. Westchester, Ill.: Crossway, 1983. 140p.

Tron and his family, educated Christians, flee the Communist invasion of Laos. After a harrowing sea voyage and internment in Malaysia, they are accepted as immigrants to the United States. The story is tight, gripping, and authentic to this point. Becomes contrived after their arrival in Seattle. Children are ostracized at school until they earn classmates' respect through their kite-flying and shadow-puppet skills. Fifth and sixth grades.

653. Kerr, M.E. *Is That You, Miss Blue?* New York: Harper & Row, 1976. 176p.

Intensely religious, lonely science teacher at fashionable

girls' prep school is fired because she sees and talks to Jesus. Two maverick students--a preacher's daughter who denies God because of the hypocrisy she sees in the Episcopal church and a girl who believes in God although she comes from an atheist family--admire Miss Blue's gentle Christian eccentricity and fine teaching ability and take appropriate vengeance on the school by obtaining a special parting gift for her. Masterfully written. Sixth grade and up.

654. Lambert, Regina. *Valerie's Adventure at Crystal Lake*. Chicago: Moody, 1980. 126p. Valerie Series.

While searching for her little brother, lost in the wilderness, Christy and her friends ride into danger in the north woods. Little Nathan is being held by drug smugglers busy recovering cocaine and hashish from a crashed plane. With daring ingenuity the girls effect his rescue and capture the gang. Narrow Christian outlook. Stresses conversion. Easy to read and fast moving. Fourth grade and up.

655. Lambert, Regina. *Valerie's Adventures at Last Chance Mine*. Chicago: Moody, 1982. 126p. Valerie Series.

Valerie and Brad, high school seniors, are helping with a children's picnic when five boys become trapped in an old mine they were exploring. Cave-ins and rising water are endangering their lives, and Val must climb up an airshaft to rescue them. One of the boys facing death accepts Jesus. Conservative Christian tone. Fourth grade and up.

656. Lawhead, Stephen R. *In the Hall of the Dragon King* (1982, 351p.). *The Sword and the Flame* (1984, 313p.). *The Warlords of Nin* (1983, 367p.). Westchester, Ill.: Crossway. Dragon King Trilogy Series.

Fantasy series begins when fifteen-year-old Quentin, an acolyte of the god Ariel, is suddenly propelled into a new life of excitement and danger serving the royal family of legendary Mensandor. He is adopted as a prince, has adventures as a bold young knight, and eventually assumes the throne. Important sub-theme is Quentin's introduction to the One True God by a holy hermit and his assumption of a prophetic savior role toward his people. Medieval style setting. Vivid, detailed writing. Sixth grade and up.

657. Leppard, Lois Gladys. *Mandie and the Cherokee Legend* (1983, 138p.). *Mandie and the Ghost Bandits* (1984, 126p.). *Mandie and the Secret Tunnel* (1983, 141p.). Minneapolis: Bethany House. Mandie Series.

In early twentieth-century North Carolina eleven-year-old Mandie is supposedly orphaned at the death of her father. But when she seeks shelter with her Uncle John, she finds a beautiful mother as well. Other adventures include the exciting discovery of a gold nugget treasure, robbery and kidnapping, visits with the Cherokees. There is a good deal of stereotyping in this slight but pleasant series. The unbelievable plots rely heavily upon coincidence. Christian principles always underlie Mandie's behavior. Prayer and trust in God are stressed. Fourth to sixth grades.

658. Lutrell, Wanda. *The Legacy of Drennan's Crossing.* Wheaton, Ill.: Tyndale, 1985. 448p.

Phillip Moore, fourteen, is growing up on a Kentucky farm during World War I and is strongly influenced by an old man with a deep love of nature and God. When the old man is murdered, Phillip cannot understand how God could allow such goodness to be destroyed, especially after the killer is acquitted because of perjured testimony. Another test of Phillip's faith is the loss of many friends killed in battle. An excellent picture of a mischievous, imaginative adolescent in an authentic setting. Sixth grade and up.

659. McKissack, Patricia. *It's the Truth, Christopher.* Illus. Bartholomew. Minneapolis: Augsburg, 1984. 32p.

Determined to tell people the truth no matter how much it hurts (them), Christopher insults and embarrasses his friends with true but unkind comments. His mother tells him he must have a loving heart along with an honest mind. He apologizes to all and thanks God. Cartoon illustrations in color and black and white. Kindergarten to third grade.

660. McKissack, Patricia. *Lights Out, Christopher.* Illus. Bartholomew. Minneapolis: Augsburg, 1984. 32p.

A mean little redhaired boy preys on the fears of his friends during an overnight camping trip and feels superior until the fog rolls in at bedtime and frightens him. His friends help him by turning on all their flashlights, and he thanks God for them. An unconvincing story. Has large sketchy drawings done alternatively in black and white and color. Kindergarten to third grade.

661. Magorian, Michelle. *Good Night, Mr. Tom.* New York: Harper & Row, 1981. 318p.

Nine-year-old Willie Beech is victim of a mother so obsessed with sin and evil that she beats him cruelly for imagined transgressions. Evacuated from London during the World War II blitz, he is placed with a lonely old man, and both are transformed by a growing love for one another. The example of deranged religious fanaticism is chillingly portrayed. The book is beautifully written, moving, and satisfying. Fourth to sixth grades.

662. Marshall, Catherine. *Christy.* New York: Avon, 1978. 501p.

Idealistic young woman becomes the teacher and friend of proud, primitive mountain people in a remote area of Tennessee, where she finds great spiritual rewards and romance, along with pain and danger. Sensitive, authentic, filled with the beauty of the Great Smokies and the tragedy of poor and ignorant people. Good readers sixth grade and up.

663. Marshall, Catherine. *Julie.* New York: McGraw, 1984. 364p.

A gripping, romantic, and wholesome story. Seventeen-year-old Julie Wallace helps her father, a former clergyman, run the newspaper in a small Pennsylvania town. Their articles criticizing the local steel industry for anti-union activities and for allowing a potentially dangerous earth dam to hold back the waters of their exclusive club's lake bring violent retribution by hired thugs. Eventually a huge flood results in many deaths. One of the love interests is the crusading young pastor of Julie's church. Good characterization, setting, and pace. Sixth grade good readers and up.

664. Martin, Dorothy. *Mystery of the Missing Bracelets.* Chicago: Moody, 1980. 123p. Vickie Series.

When several articles of valuable jewelry are missing, Vickie wonders if her houseguest, Betty Lou, is responsible. Actually Vickie's friend Diane has been hiding the things under her mattress because she is jealous of Betty Lou. Vickie and her warm, loving Christian family support Diane after she finally confesses and repents. Slight but adequate story. Fourth to sixth grades.

665. Martin, Guenn. *Remember the Eagle Day*. Scottdale, Pa.: Herald, 1984. 125p.

Seventh-grader Melanie cultivates the friendship of a reclusive old man during the summer she and her family live on an island off the coast of Alaska. He has been embittered by the deaths of his wife and child, and Melanie has been sent by God to reconcile him. She succeeds. Shows Christian caring and prayer. Lively style, absorbing and authentic details of Alaska countryside and culture. Up-to-date details of conservative young teenager's interests. Fifth grade and up.

666. Matranga, Frances Corfi. *The Mysterious Prowler*. Illus. Joe Van Severen. Wheaton, Ill.: Victor, 1984. 120p.

While the Cristinas are staying at the home of friends in the Catskill mountains, twelve-year-old Nina, an amateur detective, becomes involved in the mystery of who is stealing food and small items from the house. With God's help she finds the answer and a new family for an abused orphan child. Mild, improbable, but readable. Fourth to sixth grades.

667. Matranga, Frances Corfi. *The Secret Behind the Blue Door*. Grand Rapids, Mich.: Baker, 1981. 148p.

Twelve-year-old Nina, a born again Christian, investigates the mystery of an orphan boy imprisoned in a nearby mansion. Nina's courage and forgiving behavior impress others so much that they wish to convert to Christianity. Unlikely plot, but fast-moving and easy to read. Fourth to sixth grades.

668. Moncure, Jane Belk. *My Baby Brother Needs Me*. Illus. Frances Hook. Elgin, Ill.: Child's World, 1979. 30p.

In attractive pictures of an idealized family a little girl loves and cares for her little brother and knows that God does the same. She looks forward to the time when the baby will be old enough to do exciting things with her. Simple text. Preschool to kindergarten.

669. Moncure, Jane Belk. *When I'm Afraid*. Illus. Frances Hook. Elgin, Ill.: Child's World, 1979. 30p.

Frightened by experiences such as being alone in the house, fearing the dark, feeling threatened by a big dog, climbing a high slide, a little girl is comforted by her parents. They talk about her fears and ask God to help her overcome them. Pretty, expressive pictures in soft colors. Preschool and kindergarten.

670. Moore, Ruth Nulton. *Danger in the Pines*. Scottdale, Pa.: Herald, 1983. 166p.

Jeff, age fourteen, has lost faith in God because his beloved father died. When his mother falls in love with a caring man, resentful Jeff runs away and gets lost in the New Jersey Pine Barrens wilderness area. He has many adventures including the rescue of a retarded child, as he escapes from a forest fire and a pack of feral dogs. He prays to God for help and finally accepts his mother's new love interest as good person and role model. Exciting and fast moving but the characters are flat. Has an excellent sense of setting. Fifth grade and up.

671. Moore, Ruth Nulton. *Mystery of the Missing Stallions*. Illus. James Converse. Scottdale, Pa.: Herald, 1984. 136p. Sara and Sam Series.

While helping reunite Huy, a young Vietnamese refugee, with his little brother, who has been taken in as a foster child and become a Christian, teenage twins, with prayer and determination, solve the mysterious disappearance of valuable saddlehorses from the farm where Huy works. A slight plot, in readable style, has a happy ending all around. Fifth grade and up.

672. Murphy, Elspeth Campbell. *Mary Jo Bennett*. Illus. Tony Kenyon. Elgin, Ill.: Cook, 1985. 108p. Kids from Apple Street Church Series.

Prayer journal letters to God from Mary Jo, a minister's boisterous and impulsive daughter, tell how she tries to moderate her behavior in school to earn a trip to her grandparents' house and a ride on a horse. Prissy tattletale Vanessa is one of Mary Jo's main stumbling blocks, but in the end they begin to appreciate one another. Lively, funny, easy to read, with black-and-white drawings. Third to fifth grades.

673. Myra, Harold. *Today Is Your Super-Terrific Birthday*. Illus. Dwight Walles. Nashville: Nelson, 1985. 32p.

Greg has a birthday party with an international theme. Everyone is having fun but Katy, whose parents have just divorced. Greg's father cheers her by talking with the children about how the birth of every person is an awesome event because he or she is special to God and can live forever in heaven, if a Christian. This obviously didactic work has adequate color illustrations. Kindergarten to third grade.

674. Naylor, Phyllis Reynolds. *Change in the Wind: True-to-Life Stories of How Teenagers Deal with Feelings, Problems, Questions*. Minneapolis: Augsburg, 1980. 127p.

A collection of very short story-lessons in which young people show consideration for others, overcome prejudice, learn to understand their parents. Some examples are: a girl gives up a Thanksgiving trip to care for a blind friend; a boy devotes his summer to his paralyzed father; a boy visits a lonely old grandmother. Moral tone. Fifth grade and up.

675. Nelson, Carol. *Dear Angie, Your Family's Getting a Divorce*. Elgin, Ill.: Cook, 1980. 119p.

Seventh-grader Angie is crushed by her parents' separation. Then when she feels partly responsible for the death of a little boy, Angie is close to a breakdown. But her strong faith reawakens, and she works hard to reunite her parents. Well-realized main character, realistic dialogue, wry humor, but rather lurid plot. Fifth grade and up.

676. Oke, Janette. *Love Comes Softly* (1979, 188p.). *Love's Enduring Promise* (1980, 206p.). *Love's Long Journey* (1982, 207p.). *Love's Unending Legacy* (1984, 224p.). Minneapolis: Bethany House. Love Comes Softly Series.

A young, pregnant widow is stranded on the prairie and in desperation accepts the proposal of strong, gentle Christian widower looking for someone to mother his little girl. They fall deeply in love, raise a fine family, and the series progresses to succeeding generations. Illustrates high ideals and old-fashioned values. Nineteenth-century pioneer settings. Homely details of honest toil and joys of parenthood. Warm, enthusiastic, sentimental tone. There are more books in the series. Sixth grade and up.

677. Oxley, Dorothy. *Winter Song*. Westchester, Ill.: Crossway, 1984. 137p.

After moving from Cornwall to Buckinghamshire in England, energetic new Christian Fran Tremayne, who is thirteen years old, counts on God to help her arrange for the performance of a beautifully written rock opera celebrating peace and to reunite its radical composer with his estranged parents. Vivid setting of English country life. Skillful writing helps overcome the deficit of the unlikely plot. Uses British vocabulary. Fifth grade and up.

678. Oxley, Dorothy. *Summer Dreams*. Westchester, Ill.: Crossway, 1984. 128p.

In a Cornwall, England, village a spunky and hot-tempered tomboy becomes involved with entertaining a group of wheelchair-bound, severely handicapped children. After saving the life of a drowning boy, Daffy finds herself drawn more and more strongly toward committing her life to Jesus. Brisk pace, witty and sharp outlook, very British. First published as *Wheelchair Summer*. Fifth grade and up.

679. Peretti, Frank E. *The Door in the Dragon's Throat*. Westchester, Ill.: Crossway, 1985. 125p. Cooper Family Adventure Series.

Based upon Revelation 9, in which a star fallen from heaven is given the key of the shaft of an abyss filled with fierce creatures waiting to be loosed upon mankind. The plot concerns a Christian archaeologist and his teenage children, who are summoned to a poor Arab country to investigate a mysterious, huge shaft with a large door at the bottom. Behind it reputedly lies Nimrod's treasure. With Jesus' help, they successfully combat the forces of evil. It is an overwritten and unconvincing book with one-dimensional characters. Fourth grade and up.

680. Peretti, Frank E. *Escape from the Pit of Aquarius*. Westchester, Ill.: Crossway, 1986, 160p. Cooper Family Adventure Series.

Dr. Jake Cooper, an archaeologist, and his teenaged children, all born again Christians, investigate the disappearance of a missionary on the South Pacific island of Aquarius where they find an Anti-Christ figure leading a cult group of white middle-class people in firewalking, human sacrifice, and other bizarre activities. Implausible, lurid, but fast paced. Fourth grade and up.

681. Phillips, Carolyn E. *Our Family Got a Divorce*. Illus. Roger Bradfield. Glendale, Calif.: Regal, 1979. 110p.

When Chip's parents divorce, his mother and grandmother

gently encourage him to express his normal feelings of anger, grief, and fear. They also assure him that Jesus will always be an unchanging, loving presence in his life and that God's plan for us is sometimes hard to accept. Sketchy black-and-white pictures. Kindergarten to fourth grade.

682. Pollock, Penny. *Emily's Tiger*. Illus. Judy Morgan. New York: Paulist, 1985. unp.

Ancient ecumenical rite of Blessing of the Animals inspires Emily to smuggle her favorite toy tiger, which has been chewed up by a bulldog, into church. When told by the priest that the blessing is only for real animals, she explains that Tiger is real because he shares so much of her life. He is blessed and later repaired. This is a tender, funny, true-to-life rendition of a child's innocent love and faith. Flat but lively black-and-white pictures. Preschool to third grade.

683. Rhiner, Gladys. *Jimmy Goes to the Country*. Illus. Ronald R. Hester. Nashville: Broadman, 1981. 32p.

Little Jimmy visits his grandparents' farm, is rescued from attack by a sow, attends an old-fashioned country church, and finally thanks God for all the pleasures of the trip. A mild little book that has simple three-color drawings. Preschool to first grade.

684. Roddy, Lee. *The City Bear's Adventures* (132p.). *Dooger, The Grasshopper Hound* (132p.). *The Ghost Dog of Stoney Ridge* (132p.). *The Hair-pulling Bear Dog* (144p.). Wheaton, Ill.: Victor, 1985. D.J. Dillon Adventure Series.

Continuous saga of committed Christian D.J. Dillon, thirteen, and his twelve-year-old pals Alfred and Kathy as they enjoy mystery and adventure in California's Sierra Nevada mountains. With the help of brave dogs they confront a fearsome forest fire, a nefarious scheme to seize control of a lumber mill by polluting a lake, and attacks of fierce bears. The books contain interesting details of hunting with hounds, and have contrived but quick-moving plots. There is a glossary of mountain area terms. Fourth grade and up.

685. Schell, Mildred. *The Shoemaker's Dream*. Illus. Masahiro Kasuya. Valley Forge, Pa.: Judson, 1982. unp.

After reading his Bible, Martin dreams that Jesus will

visit him the next day. While watching for him, Martin cares for an old man, a soldier's wife and baby, and a boy who tries to steal an apple from an old woman. Disappointed that Jesus never comes, Martin dreams again and discovers that he has served the Lord by helping others. Simply and tenderly told. Based on a Tolstoy story. Misty, softly colored pictures in primitive style. Kindergarten to third grade.

686. Schloneger, Florence. *Sara's Trek*. Illus. Sidney Quinn. Newton, Kans.: Faith and Life, 1981. 105p.

Eleven-year-old Sara is the daughter of Mennonites who have fled Russia during World War II and settled in Poland. Fleeing again to avoid repatriation at the war's end, Sara becomes separated from her parents, survives because of the kindness of many strangers, and eventually reaches Canada. Well-written, absorbing, pro-German. Sixth grade and up.

687. Schraff, Anne E. *Caught in the Middle*. Grand Rapids, Mich.: Baker, 1981. 98p.

High school track star and sincere Christian Daniel rescues Cheryl, a poor and unpopular girl, from a beating by Ed, a vicious boy from a wealthy family. Pressure from Ed's influential parents forces Daniel and Cheryl to drop charges against him. Then a tragic accident changes all their lives. Too contrived at the end, but fast moving and easy to read. Fifth grade and up.

688. Shelby, Kermit. *Big Shake and the Night of Terror*. Illus. Robert G. Doares. Grand Rapids, Mich.: Baker, 1972. 128p.

During a series of severe earthquakes in Missouri in 1811 twelve-year-old Mack and his Seminole pal, New Leaf, rescue injured people, two horses, and a puppy; help rebuild the devastated community; and are kidnapped by the Choctaws. Amid the excitement New Leaf is converted to Christianity. A true incident provides the unusual background for boys' adventures. Rapid pace. Black-and-white drawings. Fourth to sixth grades.

689. Shelby, Kermit. *Snowfire*. Grand Rapids, Mich.: Baker, 1973. 160p.

Enthusiastically overwritten account of beautiful white mustang and all the people who covet him and suffer as a consequence. Several--a proud Native American chief, a kindly Italian father, and an evil rodeo rider--are converted through contact with the horse and the good Christian people who love him. Didactic plot but appealing to horse lovers. Fourth to sixth grades.

690. Sommer, Susan. *And I'm Stuck with Joseph*. Illus. Ivan Moon. Scottdale, Pa.: Herald, 1984. 126p.

Instead of a longed-for baby sister, eleven-year-old Sheila has to cope with an uncontrollably naughty three-year-old boy her parents decide to adopt. She also has unpleasant problems at school and can not understand why God has made her life so uncomfortable. Insightful characterizations of all the children, especially the anxious, hyperactive, destructive Joseph. Realistic, interesting farm setting. Fourth to sixth grades.

691. Spencer, Chris. *Starforce Red Alert*. Westchester, Ill.: Crossway, 1983. 144p.

Christian science fiction. Sixteen-year-old space pilot Zak and friends search for Zak's missionary astronaut father, whom they find on a beautiful planet where the inhabitants have reached the same crisis about the knowledge of good and evil as Adam and Eve. The earth people have been sent by God with tapes of the Bible to rescue them from Satan. Good technical details, pace, and suspense. Obvious message. Fifth grade and up.

692. Spyri, Johanna. *Heidi*. New York.: Grosset, 1925. 305p.

Strong faith in God pervades this story of a little Swiss girl sent to live with her misanthropic grandfather on an Alpine peak and then torn from her happy life there to be the companion of an invalid in Frankfort. Heidi's prayers, patience, and trust produce joyful results for all. Old-fashioned charm in plot and style. Fourth grade and up.

693. Stahl, Hilda. *Elizabeth Gail and the Frightened Runaways* (1981, 127p.). *Elizabeth Gail and the Secret Love* (1983, 121p.). *Elizabeth Gail and the Silent Piano* (1981, 127p.). *Elizabeth Gail and the Summer for Weddings* (1983, 126p.). *Elizabeth Gail and the Time for Love* (1983, 119p.). *Elizabeth Gail and Trouble from the Past* (1981, 125p.). Wheaton, Ill.: Tyndale. Elizabeth Gail Series.

Libby, a foster child adopted by a caring Christian family, has problems learning to trust and love others and control her temper. Once she is converted to Christianity, she is able to face life's setbacks and help others. During the extended series she grows up and marries. A troubled person is usually converted in each book. The books depict a comfortable farm setting, contain wholesome values, have farfetched plots, and are fast paced. High interest, low readability. Fourth grade and up.

694. Stahl, Hilda. *Teddy Jo and the Ragged Beggars* (1984, 121p.). *Teddy Jo and the Stolen Ring* (1982, 121p.). *Teddy Jo and the Strange Medallion* (1983, 127p.). Wheaton, Ill.: Tyndale. Teddy Jo Series.

The heroine is a middle elementary student when she becomes a Christian under the influence of her grandfather. Eventually she is able to convert her entire family. She befriends elderly ladies, becomes reconciled with her arch-enemy, helps a friend overcome the stress of discovering she is adopted, etc. Understands a young girl's feelings and reactions, but other characters are cardboard. Emphatic style. Easy reading. Fourth to sixth grades.

695. Stewart, Allan. *Rick Shannon and the Case of the Missing Pilot*. Wheaton, Ill.: Tyndale, 1985. 127p.

While on a photography assignment for a newsmagazine, Rick, eighteen, becomes involved in the affair of an empty plane that has crashed into a mountain wilderness area. As he and his friend Marc, a helicopter pilot, are solving the mystery, Rick has a chance to show Marc true Christian faith. Mild, easy-to-read adventure. Fifth grade and up.

696. Stoddard, Sandol. *God's Little House*. Illus. Jane Winthers Newman. Mahwah, N.J.: Paulist, 1985. unp.

A lost child comes upon an old woman in a tiny cottage and decides to stay with her. There she learns to heal and pray and praise God. She finds God in her daily life of baking, spinning, and singing. Handsome, old-fashioned black-and-white drawings and elegant typeface help express the simple, gentle verse message. First to third grades.

697. Thomas, Joan Gale. *If Jesus Came to My House*. New York: Lothrop, 1951. unp.

Imagining that if he had the child Jesus for a playmate, he would give him the best toys and the comfy rocker for a seat, a little boy decides that he should treat all his friends with kindness and generosity, just the way he would have received Jesus. Verse form. Winsome three-color drawings. Preschool and kindergarten.

698. Tolstoy, Leo. *Martin the Cobbler*. Illus. Billy Budd Films, Inc. Minneapolis: Winston, 1982. 30p.

Adapted from the story of the sad old cobbler who has lost all his family and longs for death. One night in a dream he hears Jesus say he will visit him the next day. But Martin sees only an old man, a woman with a baby, and a young thief, all of whom he helps. Then he realizes that Jesus has been present in each one. Well expressed and touching. Illustrated in color with stills from an animated film using clay figures for the characters. Fourth to sixth grades.

699. Vogt, Esther Loewen. *Mystery at Red Rock Canyon*. Grand Rapids, Mich.: Baker, 1979. 99p.

Eleven-year-old boys at church camp slip off to explore a cave and are captured by teenage drug dealers who have stored marijuana and heroin there. After being rescued, one boy decides to accept Jesus, and the other, already a Christian, to be more obedient. Improbable, diffuse story. Fourth to sixth grades.

700. Ward, Jeannette W. *I Have a Question, God: A Story for Boys and Girls Who Are Adopted*. Illus. Bill Myers. Nashville: Broadman, 1981. 32p.

A girl, aged eleven, talks to God about her various feelings about being adopted. She is concerned about her birth parents, her problems with friends, and her resentment at the adoption of a little brother into her family. Fragmented, confusing flashback style mars author's genuine understanding of an adoptee's fears. Suitable two-color illustrations. Fourth to sixth grades.

701. Wirt, Sherwood Eliot. *The Doomsday Connection*. Westchester, Ill.: Crossway, 1986. 259p.

Warned that the world is about to end, a large cast of characters reacts in various ways. Included are a black minister, a Salvation Army commissioner, Bible college gospel singers, a prostitute, a preppie, a Soviet agent, and a Jewish lawyer. The main character is a bitter, self-centered fifteen-year-old boy. At the end they confront a taco-munching St. Columba and redemption. Crisp, descriptive style. Characters are contrived to suit the message. Sixth grade and up.

702. Wojciechowska, Maia. *How God Got Christian into Trouble*. Illus. Les Gray. Philadelphia: Westminster, 1984. 80p.

To help an eleven-year-old Christian communicate with him God assumes the form of José, a small Puerto Rican boy, for several days. When José accompanies Christian to his home, church, and school, some people believe José is God. A group of schoolchildren, for example, vow to protect abused children. Others are untouched. Discussions of evil, free will, life after death, etc., are logically included in the sprightly narrative. Action-filled black-and-white drawings. Fifth and sixth grades.

703. Zoller, Bob. *My Sister Is an Only Child*. Ventura, Calif.: Regal, 1983. 152p.

Unaware that his sister is ill with a brain tumor, Steve resents the attention given her, feels thoroughly unappreciated, runs away to his secret clubhouse, and is caught in a flood. A gentle, devout couple from the neighborhood helps the whole family become reconciled after the crises are resolved. Has an obvious plot but is skillfully written and suspenseful. Fourth to sixth grades.

John Bunyan

704. Finley, Tom. *Wilbur, Master of the Rats*. Illus. author. Ventura, Calif.: Regal, 1983. unp.

Inspired by Bunyan's *The Holy War*. Black-and-white illustrations in comic strip format. In the city of Mansoul the populace is protected from enslavement by Diabolus because King Shaddai has sent them his son Emmanuel and another helper, Lady Solace (Father, Son, and Holy Spirit). Young Wilbur prevents Diabolus from reentering the city by means of his henchman, Unbelief. Mad Magazine type humor, grotesque villains, much text, unmistakable message. Fifth grade and up.

705. Fuller, Ronald. *Pilgrim*. Illus. Pat Marriott. Ownings Mills, Md.: Stemmer House, 1980. 48p.

Based on *Pilgrim's Progress*. Christian, formerly known as Graceless, repents and leaves the city of Destruction, aided by Evangelist, to seek eternal life in the Celestial City. He encounters geographical hazards, giants and demons, and cruel people who try to turn him from his path. Satirizes hypocrisy, formalism, envy, sloth, and other religious and personality faults. Flowing, well-written prose. Large, very colorful matte finish watercolors are undistinguished. Pilgrims wear Biblical dress, but other characters are in Elizabethan clothing. Picture book format but the text is for fifth grade and up.

706. Hunkin, Oliver. *Dangerous Journey*. Illus. Alan Parry. Grand Rapids, Mich.: Eerdman, 1985. 126p.

Shortened version of *Pilgrim's Progress*. Christian, young husband and father, seeks salvation and sets out on a long, dreadful journey to find the Celestial City. Stalwart figures such as Evangelist are his guides. Scurvy villains and slavering monsters plague his route. Combines religious allegory, adventure story, historical commentary, and satire. Effective illustrations sweep across the pages with fluid energy and fascinating detail. Villains are wittily evil, vitally vulgar. Gloomy backgrounds sustain mood. Stately prose and impressive format. Fifth grade and up.

Clergy

707. Bach, Alice. *He Will Not Walk with Me*. New York: Delacorte, 1985. 182p.

Drawn into volunteer work at Communion House, a downtown Manhattan soup kitchen and shelter for street people, by her intense admiration for the loquacious and charismatic minister of her church, sixteen-year-old Hallie is bitterly disappointed by his subsequent lack of interest in her job there. The truly caring nuns, priest, and seminarian staffing the mission are the ones who really earn her admiration. Convincing setting and presentation of homeless eccentrics. Other characters serve as vehicles for the heavy message. Sixth grade and up.

708. Branscum, Robbie. *The Saving of P.S*. Illus. Glen Rounds. New York: Dell, 1977. 127p.

Twelve-year-old, motherless Priscilla Sue, fiercely jealous when her preacher father courts and marries a widow with two daughters, runs away from their Arkansas farm. The hardship and loneliness she experiences and the joy of all her family when she is finally found help her realize that she is worthy of God's love and theirs. Well-realized characters and setting. Moving and humorous. Scratchy but eloquent black-and-white sketches. Fourth to sixth grades.

709. Fox, Paula. *One-Eyed Cat.* Scarsdale, N.Y.: Bradbury, 1984. 216p.

Congregationalist minister's son is inexorably tempted by an air rifle, a gift on his eleventh birthday. Its use has been forbidden until he is fourteen, but he sneaks out with it one night and shoots at something moving in the dark. When he finds out he has half-blinded a cat, his whole life is devastated by guilt. His patient, self-sacrificing, exasperatingly reasonable father has set extremely high standards of reverence for life, honesty, and tolerance which the boy believes he has desecrated. Universal details of small-town church life. In-depth characterization. Introspective mood. Fifth grade and up.

710. Huntington, Lee Pennock. *Maybe a Miracle.* Illus. Neil Waldman. New York: Coward, 1984. 95p.

Dorcas, a ten-year-old minister's daughter, fervently prays that her grownup friends, Dr. and Mrs. Abbot, will have a much-desired baby. A foundling infant is left on the doctor's doorstep and becomes their adopted daughter. Set in a rural town during the Depression. Depicts a cozy family life with firm but caring parents. Gentle faith, positive tone. Fourth to sixth grades.

711. Kerr, M.E. *What I Really Think of You.* New York: Harper & Row, 1982. 208p.

The daughter of the leader of an emotional, charismatic sect and the son of a wealthy, prominent television evangelist meet one summer, and profound changes take place in both families as a result. Understanding portraits of the people involved in both types of ministries. Masterfully written. Sixth grade and up.

712. Lorimer, L.T. *Secrets.* New York: Holt, 1981. 192p.

Sixteen-year-old Maggie's father is a popular, charming minister but disturbs her with his flashes of irresponsibility and easy lies. Her mother is bitter and strict. Maggie rebels by dating a motorcycle bum, but eventually must confront her family's tragic secrets. Spare, effective style creates a somber mood. Sixth grade and up.

713. Naylor, Phyllis Reynolds. *A String of Chances.* New York: Atheneum, 1982. 244p.

Evie, sixteen and the daughter of a conservative minister, leaves her home in a small Maryland community for the first time to spend the summer helping her pregnant cousin. The joyful birth and then the tragic death of little Josh imperil her faith in God. She also experiences a new freedom from her loving but demanding family and a first love. These events jolt her forward into new maturity. Competently written, affecting, readable. Sixth grade and up.

714. Neufeld, John. *Edgar Allen*. New York: Phillips, 1968. 95p.

A minister and his family adopt a tiny black boy, whom all but the older daughter learn to love at once. But opposition from prejudiced parishioners and townspeople persuades him to return the child to the adoption agency. His younger children are greatly dismayed, and the town then turns against him for not upholding Christian principles. Low-key, nonjudgmental, but penetrating. Fifth grade and up.

715. Newton, Suzanne. *I Will Call It Georgie's Blues*. New York: Viking, 1983. 197p.

An aging, fearful Baptist minister demands perfection from his family in order to impress the congregation and the community with his competence. All the children are drastically affected, especially seven-year-old Georgie, who feels so unloved he begins to lose his sanity. This tragedy eventually begins to draw the Sloans together. Pressures on a minister's family realistically presented. Absorbing and touching. Fifth grade and up.

716. Van Leeuwen, Jean. *Seems Like This Road Goes on Forever*. New York: Dial, 1979. 214p.

Mary Alice, seventeen, is hospitalized after an automobile accident and refuses to respond to anyone but a psychologist who finally wins her trust. Her minister father is withdrawn, fanatic, demanding perfection. Her mother is absorbed in church activities, undemonstrative, concerned mainly with appearances. They wish to force her into a rigid religious mold but are otherwise indifferent to her needs. Disturbing picture of the effect of self-absorbed, outwardly model Christian parents on their children. Sixth grade and up.

717. Wallace-Brodeur, Ruth. *Callie's Way*. New York: Atheneum, 1984. 119p.

Twelve-year-old Callie would like to hide the fact she

is a minister's daughter and be a real preteen who notices boys, likes rock music, and seeks refuge in the easygoing atmosphere of her best friend's home. Her father is mild and colorless, her mother an otherworldly music teacher, and her sister a fiercely dedicated violinist. By the end of the book, Callie has begun to take charge of her own life and earn the respect of her family. Good portrayal of congregational busybodies, smarmy Sunday School chairman, and other challenges of church-related living. Fourth grade and up.

VI
CHRISTIAN CHURCH

718. Henderson, Felicity. *Learning about the Church*. Illus. Michael Grimsdale. Belleville, Mich.: Lion, 1984. 30p.

Stresses the universality of Christianity by showing various types of churches; all ages, colors, and sizes of people; varied ways of praying, witnessing, receiving communion, being baptized and confirmed. Vividly colored pictures of New Testament scenes and modern people worshiping and having fellowship. Glossary. Scriptural references. Kindergarten to fourth grade.

719. Hickman, Martha Whitmore. *When Our Church Building Burned Down*. Illus. Sandra Speidel. Nashville: Abingdon, 1986. unp.

Sammy and his family hear sirens close by and rush out to find their church on fire. Only a few things are saved. Even though the building is gone, the church continues to meet in a local restaurant. Thus Sammy is reassured that its real body is the congregation. Has a matter-of-fact tone and believable premise. It is clearly written and has sketchy, action-filled two-color drawings. Kindergarten to fourth grade.

720. Hogan, Bernice. *The Church Is a Who*. Illus. John Steiger. St. Louis: Bethany Press, 1979. 31p.

Churches have various "whats" such as crosses, pews, and hymnbooks and "wheres" in cities and countrysides from Africa to Arizona, but their "whos" are their most important parts. "Whos" include not only teachers and pastors but all the members wherever they are and whatever they do. A useful but wordy book containing plain, coloring book style illustrations in three colors showing cartoon type figures of various races. Kindergarten to third grade.

721. Nystrom, Carolyn. *What Is a Church?* Illus. Wayne A. Hanna. Chicago: Moody, 1981. unp.

Churches come in various sizes, from cathedrals to store fronts, but basically are made up of people who follow Jesus and help others in all kinds of ways. A little boy reviews the various activities in his own church and reminds us that all believers will live together in heaven. Bible verses cited. Simple language. Bright cartoon-style pictures. Preschool to first grade.

MISSIONS

722. Burkholder, Ruth Cook. *Mi Jun's Difficult Decision.* Illus. Chung Soon O'Dwyer. New York: Friendship, 1983. 14p.

A Korean-American girl in the sixth grade learns about Korean customs, religions, and history from her cousin's letters. Both are Protestant Christians. The letters persuade her she will enjoy living with her cousin for six months and finding out more about her ancestral land. Mildly interesting. Black-and-white drawings with Oriental flavor. Contains suggested activities. Fourth to sixth grades.

723. Burkholder, Ruth Cook. *Won Gil's Secret Diary.* Illus. Chung Soon O'Dwyer. New York: Friendship, 1983. 14p.

Eight-year-old Korean Protestant boy decides to write about a year of national holidays: New Year's, Easter, the Tano spring festival, a child's first birthday, and Chusok, the fall Thanksgiving festival. Several have Christian emphasis interwoven with Korean tradition. Discussion questions and activities for each. Full-page black-and-white drawings in Oriental style. First to fourth grades.

724. Nystrom, Carolyn. *Jesus Is No Secret.* Illus. Wayne A. Hanna. Chicago: Moody, 1983. unp.

Evangelism is discussed. Includes early days of the Apostles, Pentecost, and Paul; activities of today's missionaries and how the church supports them; problems Christians have trying to share their faith without being offensive. Simply told from a little boy's viewpoint. Basic, color-splashed illustrations. Kindergarten to second grade.

725. Ross, Uta v.O. *The Boy Who Wanted to Be a Missionary*. Illus. Debbie Dieneman. Nashville: Abingdon, 1984. unp.

Basic evangelism explained. Eight-year-old Jimmy is powerfully attracted by the life of a missionary in Africa. He dreams of preaching, fighting lions, impressing everyone. When a new boy with a broken leg moves into the neighborhood, however, Jimmy learns that mission work begins by befriending others close to home. Short, easy-to-read sentences. Faint but agreeable black-and-white drawings in semi-cartoon style. Kindergarten to third grade.

VII
CHRISTIAN BIOGRAPHY

Collective

726. Flynt, Faye De Beck. *They Dared to Cross Frontiers*. Illus. Anne Gayler. New York: Friendship, 1975. 56p.

Short, well-written accounts of the brave exploits of American Christians. Includes John Woolman, Quaker called to witness to the Indians; Frederick Douglass, escaped slave who became a fiery Abolitionist speaker; John Eliot, evangelist to the Algonquins; Cherokee Bible translator Sequoyah; Martha Berry and her boarding school for poor mountain children; Mary McLeod Bethune's work in black education; Martin Luther King and anti-segregation. Fifth grade and up.

727. Hanley, Boniface. *No Strangers to Violence, No Strangers to Love*. Notre Dame, Ind.: Ave Maria, 1983. 224p.

Interestingly written brief biographies of six Roman Catholic men and women who led lives of piety, sacrifice, and courage in the twentieth century. Most are priests, some martyrs. Includes missionary doctor Thomas Dooley, Jewish convert and nun Edith Stein, missionary to North Africa Charles de Foucauld, missionary to China Vincent Lebbe, Austrian opponent of Nazism Franz Jaegerstaetter, French comedienne Eve Lavalliere, Dutch priest Titus Brandsma in Dachau, and Father Miguel Pro, executed during the anticlerical period in Mexico. Black-and-white photographs. Fifth grade and up.

728. Lehn, Cornelia. *Peace Be with You*. Illus. Keith R. Neely. Newton, Kans: Faith and Life, 1980. 126p.

The strong conviction that hatred and violence are evil is shared by the peacelovers over the centuries included in this survey. Biographical incidents begin with Pontius Pilate being pressed by the Jews to remove the statue of the Roman emperor from Jerusalem and go on to well-known persons such as Servitor, St. Patrick, Telemachus, Menno Simons, and Jane Addams; lesser-known persons such as

Baiko San, a Buddhist lady, and Cheyenne maiden Sweet Medicine; and end with Mother Teresa. Many are Mennonites. Fifth grade and up.

Individual

729. Andrew, Brother. *God's Smuggler*. Carmel, N.Y.: Guideposts, 1967. 241p.

After an early life of reckless dissolution as a commando in the Dutch East Indies, Andrew is converted in a veterans' hospital and begins evangelizing factory workers in Holland. Later he becomes involved with Christians in Iron Curtain countries, preaching and distributing Bibles. He always feels both propelled and protected by God in this work. Lively, pictorial, forward-moving style. Sixth grade and up.

730. Barrett, Ethel. *Fanny Crosby*. Ventura, Calif.: Regal, 1984. 144p.

Relentlessly cheerful and uplifting fictionalized life of the blind poet and composer of thousands of songs and popular hymns. Fast-paced and animated first-person narrative from age five forward. Contains humor and romance. Includes words and music of sixteen of Crosby's best-known hymns. Fourth grade and up.

731. Barrett, Ethel. *Steve Paxon: Can't Lose for Winning*. Ventura, Calif.: Regal, 1985. 154p.

Handicapped by a crippled foot and a stammer, Paxon nevertheless learned to sing and play the fiddle and the hatting trade. After marriage he felt the call to teach boys in church, which led to his conversion and a vocation as a Sunday School missionary. Sunny, positive tone. Interesting and easy to read. Fifth grade and up.

732. Blackwood, Cheryl Prewitt, and Kathryn Slattery. *A Bright-Shining Place*. New York: Ballantine, 1981. 233p.

The story of the 1980 Miss America. The daughter of Mississippi country store keeper, she sings in a family gospel group and is injured badly in an auto accident. She receives the Holy Spirit and instantly one leg, which was shorter than the other, lengthens, and her limp is healed. She enters a series of beauty pageants, believing it is God's will that she become Miss America. Contains prayer, faith healing, speaking in tongues, strong faith, and high morals, written with enthusiasm. Black-and-white photographs. Sixth grade and up.

733. Corfe, Thomas Howell. *The Murder of Archbishop Thomas*. Minneapolis: Lerner, 1977. 50p. Cambridge Topic Book Series.

Short biography of Thomas à Becket, Archbishop of Canterbury. Interesting details of twelfth-century England and King Henry II's personality, possessions, and problems. Many black-and-white photographs, maps, and drawings. Index. Fifth grade and up.

734. Cottrell, Stan. *No Mountain Too High*. Old Tappan, N.J.: Revell, 1984. 221p.

The author, from poor but proud rural Kentucky background, has burning desire to get ahead in life. Begins running and winning long distance races early in life, gets a college scholarship, pursues business and athletic career, but can't find real success until he seeks God's guidance. Declarative, readable, self-centered style. Photographs. Sixth grade and up.

735. Cruz, Nicky, and Jamie Buckingham. *Run Baby Run*. Plainfield, N.J.: Logos, 1968. 240p.

A Puerto Rican street gang leader is converted by David Wilkerson and brings the power of Christian love to desperate, lonely, sorrowful, poor urban minority youths. The occasional graphic scenes of sex and violence are natural to the situation. The book is convincing. It stresses a Pentecostal type of religious experience. Sixth grade and up.

736. Cunningham, Glenn, and George X. Sand. *Never Quit*. Lincoln, Va.: Chosen, 1981. 143p.

Although terribly burned in a schoolhouse accident in childhood, Cunningham overcomes injuries, constant pain, and frequent illnesses to compete in the Olympics and other track events in the 1930s. Strongly depicts a life of discipline, frugality, persistence, and gradually increasing religious faith. He founds a youth ranch for problem and needy children. Some black-and-white photographs. Sixth grade and up.

737. Davids, Richard C. *The Man Who Moved a Mountain*. Philadelphia: Fortress, 1972. 253p.

Rousing, gripping life of quick-shooting, hard-drinking mountain lad, Bob Childress, from the Virginia Blue Ridge area, who is led to an amazing ministry as a founder of churches, schools, and Sunday schools. He is a fearless evangelist who stands up to rough mountain men and earns their respect and a civic leader who brings investments and gainful work into the poor community. Loved fiercely by his congregations. Vivid, pictorially beautiful style with exciting subject matter. Good readers sixth grade and up.

738. Di Franco, JoAnn, and Anthony Di Franco. *Mister Rogers: Good Neighbor to America's Children*. Minneapolis: Dillon, 1983. 56p. Taking Part Books Series.

Presbyterian minister whose mission is to serve children and families through mass media. Mild, low-key, earnest biography of Fred Rogers stresses care with which the "Mister Rogers' Neighborhood" television programs are prepared to teach, entertain, and reassure their audiences and Rogers' serious commitment to his work. Large black-and-white photographs. Third to fifth grades.

739. Eareckson, Joni, and Joe Musser. *Joni*. Grand Rapids: Zondervan, 1976. 190p.

Pretty, popular, athletic, affluent Joni at age seventeen becomes paraplegic from a diving accident. She suffers for months, and her prayers for healing are not answered. Always a Christian, she now uses her life as an artist, writer, speaker to show how faith can overcome a handicap. The photographs of a beautiful, lithe girl riding and tumbling before the paralysis become heartbreaking in the context. Sixth grade and up.

740. Evans, James S. *An Uncommon Gift*. Philadelphia: Westminster, 1983. 180p.

Son of a wealthy and supportive California family, attractive and determined James suffers both dyslexia and hyperkinesia and has struggled throughout his entire life to control them and achieve his goals. His strong personal faith in Jesus Christ has carried him through depressing times and given him the courage to keep trying. Forthright, absorbing autobiography. Sixth grade and up.

741. Flynn. *Mister God This Is Anna*. New York: Ballantine, 1976. 180p.

Short, wrenching, amazing life of a six-year-old waif abandoned in England, rescued by a young man, and warmly received by his family. Her astounding knowledge of God's love and fresh, touching, profound views of life as a gardener, mathematician, poet, and philosopher constantly enrich the lives of those around her. Tragically, her glory is quenched in a fatal accident. Fifth grade and up.

742. Graham, Robin Lee. *The Boy Who Sailed 'Round the World Alone*. Waco, Tex.: Word, 1985. 165p.

Youth edition. The exciting saga of a sixteen-year-old who spends five years sailing a sloop alone from California westward to Hawaii, Samoa, other South Pacific islands, Australia, South Africa, the Galapagos, and back to Long Beach. Once home again his life loses meaning. He is about to commit suicide when he asks God, who has protected him all along, to give him direction. Black-and-white photographs. Fifth grade and up.

743. Gray, Ronald. *Christopher Wren and St. Paul's Cathedral*. Minneapolis: Lerner, 1982. 51p. Cambridge Topic Book Series.

A biography of Wren is included in a general discussion of the history and construction of the cathedral and Wren's other churches, examination of Gothic and Renaissance buildings, and information on seventeenth-century London. Many black-and-white photographs and drawings. Contains a glossary and an Index. Fifth grade and up.

744. Holdren, Shirley, and Susan Holdren. *Why God Gave Me Pain*. Chicago: Loyola, 1984. 115p.

The last two years of Susan's life, as chronicled by her mother. Attacked by lymphoblastic leukemia at eighteen, Susan maintains a courageous, optimistic attitude throughout chemotherapy and other drug treatment, severe pain, and the distressing reappearance of cancer cells after brief remission periods. She experiences great spiritual growth and accepts death trustingly. Written in a simple, very moving style. Sixth grade and up.

745. Jenkins, Peter. *A Walk Across America*. New York: Fawcett, 1979. 320p.

Vivid first-person account. A confused and rootless young man sets out on foot to learn about the United States. At first disillusioned and cynical, his morale and patriotism soar after he has had all kinds of adventures from New York to New Orleans and made a variety of friends. His exhilarating and maturing experiences lead him to accept Christ. Sixth grade and up.

746. Miller, Barbara, and Charles Paul Conn. *Kathy*. Old Tappan, N.J.: Revell, 1980. 160p.

Calling herself God's representative, Kathy makes a miraculous recovery after being mangled by a car when she is thirteen. Former competitive swimmer and runner, she struggles through a long medical ordeal but eventually achieves mental, psychological, and physical rehabilitation and can run again. Black-and-white photographs. Fifth grade and up.

747. Milne, Darla. *Second Chance: The Israel Narvaez Story*. Wheaton, Ill.: Tyndale, 1979. 286p.

While president of the Mau Mau street gang, Narvaez receives Christ at an evangelistic meeting conducted by David Wilkerson. Soon after he backslides and is jailed at age sixteen. A tough survivor, he determines never to return to prison after his release, regains his faith, and eventually begins his own ministry in Washington. Includes prison details. Fast, easy reading. Sixth grade and up.

748. Noel, Gerard. *Cardinal Basil Hume*. Illus. Nicholas Day. North Pomfret, Vt.: David and Charles, 1984. 60p. Profiles Series.

Kindly, informal biography of British Roman Catholic demonstrates his early propensity toward the priesthood, his down-to-earth personality, his strong ecumenical leanings. Includes details of his seminary training and of his personal philosophy. Written in a simple, straightforward style. Photographically realistic black-and-white drawings. Fifth and sixth grades.

749. O'Neill, Cherry Boone. *Starving for Attention*. New York: Continuum, 1982. 187p.

Well-written, moving, effective treatise on anorexia nervosa by Pat Boone's oldest daughter. Brought up in the glow of success and comfort, Cherry is an overachiever whose impossible standards for herself lead to behavior that horrifies her husband and family. Their strong support and her own solid Christian faith eventually help her to achieve remission. Honest and graphic. Black-and-white photographs. Sixth grade and up.

750. O'Neill, Judith. *Martin Luther*. Minneapolis: Lerner, 1975. 51p. Cambridge Topic Book Series.

Evenhanded yet affective account of Luther's life and

the early Reformation. Good historical writing reinforced by numerous black-and-white paintings, drawings, engravings, maps, cartoons, photographs, and woodcuts of Luther, his contemporaries, and the setting in which he lived and worked. Index. Fifth grade and up.

751. Phillips, Carolyn E. *Michelle*. New York: New American Library, 1980. 148p.

An eight-year-old girl suffers leg amputation and painful chemotherapy as a result of bone cancer. Her personal relationship with Jesus provides comfort and strength. A realistic, outgoing, caring person, she has great energy and determination. She skis, rides, skates, and swims. Although overwritten and sentimental, Michelle's personality shines through to make the biography truly moving. Contains photographs. Fifth grade and up.

752. Ready, Dolores. *Traveler for God: A Story about John Neumann*. Illus. Constance Crawford. Minneapolis: Winston, 1977. unp.

Incomplete account of the Bohemian Roman Catholic priest who emigrated to America in 1836 to minister to German-speaking congregations who were often victims of prejudice in their communities. Text stresses his sea voyage and early pastorate in Williamsville, New York. A one-page biographical sketch at the end briefly details his entire life. Has flat, pebbly-textured illustrations in crayon colors and black and white. Kindergarten to third grade.

753. Rogers, Dale Evans. *Angel Unaware*. New York: Pyramid, 1963. 64p.

Robin Rogers, a Downs Syndrome child of Roy and Dale, talks about her short, two-year life as she remembers it in Heaven. Her complete innocence and need for unconditional love bring everyone whose lives she touches closer to God. Also emphasizes to parents the joys possible in the relationship with a retarded child. Fifth grade and up.

754. Sabin, Louis. *Narcissa Whitman: Brave Pioneer*. Illus. Allan Eitzen. Mahwah, N.J.: Troll, 1982. 48p.

Mainly deals with her childhood, the never ending chores of a farm family, her desire to be a teacher and work with Indians, and her education. Only brief mention of her emigration west over the Rocky Mountains and her mission to the pioneers and Indians. Pictorial details of early nineteenth-century farm life. Simple, large black-and-white drawings. Kindergarten to fourth grade.

755. Simonides, Carol. *I'll Never Walk Alone: The Inspiring Story of a Teenager's Struggle against Cancer*. New York: Continuum, 1983. 183p.

Thirteen when she loses a leg to the first of many cancers, Carol is sustained by an unquenchable spirit and strong faith. She becomes a cheerleader, graduates from high school, appears on television shows, marries, and generally crams much living into the five years remaining to her, in spite of prolonged chemotherapy and various operations. Uplifting. Photographs. Sixth grade and up.

756. Story, Bettie Wilson. *Gospel Trailblazer: The Exciting Story of Francis Asbury*. Illus. Charles Cox. Nashville: Abingdon, 1984. 125p.

Father of American Methodism. Born in England in 1745 into poor but pious family, meagerly educated, zealously religious, Asbury overcame obstacles of poor health, rugged terrain, and suspicious settlers to ride the circuit and save souls in Pennsylvania, Virginia, the Carolinas, Kentucky, and Tennessee. With steely determination and sacrificial example he survived power struggles to become the principal leader of the fledgling American Methodist church and prevailed in the ministry for fifty-four years. Written in a dry and factual style and contains appropriately somber black-and-white drawings. Fourth grade and up.

757. Vernon, Louise A. *The Beggars' Bible*. Illus. Jeanie McCoy. Scottdale, Pa.: Herald, 1971. 136p.

In fourteenth-century England a poor boy of thirteen who has a burning desire to study at Oxford is attracted to the scholar John Wycliffe, who is calling for church reform and has a dream of providing the common people with Bibles they can understand. Despite opposition from a corrupt and hostile established church hierarchy, Wycliffe completes his Scripture translation and distributes it. A fast-moving narrative with black-and-white drawings. Fourth to sixth grades.

758. Vernon, Louise A. *The Bible Smuggler*. Illus. Roger Hane. Scottdale, Pa.: Herald, 1967. 140p.

Ten-year-old Collin becomes assistant to William Tyndale

during the period when he is translating the Bible into English in spite of strong opposition from Cardinal Wolsey. When Tyndale must flee to Europe, Collin goes with him and helps smuggle the finished books into England. Has crisp black-and-white pictures. Fourth to sixth grades.

759. Vernon, Louise A. *Key to the Prison*. Illus. Allan Eitzen. Scottdale, Pa.: Herald, 1968. 139p.

A twelve-year-old parson's son and his family follow the career of George Fox and the beginnings of the Quaker movement in the seventeenth century. Fox's prophetic and healing powers, his dignity and courage in enduring persecution, and his strong, simple faith are stressed. Lively style. Undistinguished black-and-white art. Fourth to sixth grades.

760. Wilkerson, David, and John Sherrill and Elizabeth Sherrill. *The Cross and the Switchblade*. Old Tappan, N.J.: Revell, 1963. 174p.

Impelled and supported by the Holy Spirit, Pennsylvania country pastor David Wilkerson travels to New York to minister to street gangs and drug addicts. He preaches God's love and forgiveness. Many are saved and in turn witness to others. Direct and absorbing narrative. Sixth grade and up.

761. Wolcott, Leonard T., and Carolyn E. Wolcott. *Wilderness Rider*. Nashville: Abingdon, 1984. 144p.

The life of Methodist circuit rider Noah Fidler, who traveled Maryland, Virginia, and Pennsylvania in the early nineteenth century. Begins when he was ten and extends through his marriage and final retirement. A good reconstruction of the era and the dangers and rewards of serving people scattered in the wilderness; written in a lively, pictorial style. Fifth and sixth grades.

762. Woodson, Meg. *I'll Get to Heaven before You Do!* Nashville: Abingdon, 1985. 92p.

Thirteen-year-old Peggie, suffering from cystic fibrosis, begins facing a probable early death squarely, with both regret and a determination to make the most of what she has. Her strongly developing Christian faith helps her accept her condition. Gives poignant details of her daily problems at home and school, as tellingly written by her mother. Sixth grade and up.

JOHN PAUL II

763. Bonic, Thomas. *His Holiness Pope John Paul II*. Toronto: Grolier, 1984. 48p. Picture-Life Series.

A dramatic beginning describing the suspenseful election of the new Pope introduces a warm, vital biography emphasizing the Pope's concern for people and special fondness for youths and children. The assassination attempt and its aftermath are especially well handled. Admiring, enthusiastic tone. Good color photographs show the Pope reaching out to both individuals and crowds. Index. Third to fifth grades.

764. DiFranco, Anthony. *Pope John Paul II: Bringing Love to a Troubled World*. Minneapolis: Dillon, 1983. 72p. Taking Part Books Series.

A thorough and interesting coverage of the Pope's childhood, education, love of the theater and sports, experiences in World War II, rapid rise in the church hierarchy, election as Pontiff, outreach, conservative theology, attempted assassination, and daily routine. A fact-packed narrative that stresses the Pope's optimistic sense of goodness and hope. Contains color and black-and-white photographs. Fourth to sixth grades.

765. Douglas, Robert W. *John Paul II: The Pilgrim Pope*. Chicago: Children's Press, 1980. 32p.

The Pope's versatility, his love of people, and his desire to avoid a life of pomp and ceremony are stressed in a clear, well-presented, and admiring overview. Also emphasizes his travels, the ways he relates to his worldwide flock, and how he is received in various countries. No coverage of the assassination attempt. Large, attractive color photographs of papal activities, including closeups. Contains black-and-white photographs and drawings, as well. Second to fourth grades.

766. Grant, Steven. *The Life of Pope John Paul II*. Illus. John Tartaglione and Joe Sinnott. New York: Marvel, 1982. 64p.

In comic book format tells the story of a newspaper reporter attending the Pope's appearance at Yankee Stadium in 1979. He reviews the Pontiff's life from early childhood onward, stressing his intelligence, love of sports, dedication to the church, and modesty. Impressed by the Pope's magnetism and goodness, the reporter is horrified at the assassination attempt. A reverent, thorough, and admiring assessment. The artwork is done in a forceful style. Fourth to sixth grades.

767. Sullivan, George. *Pope John Paul II: The People's Pope*. New York: Walker, 1984. 137p.

A capably written, laudatory, and interesting life of Karol Wojtyla. Begins with the death of John Paul I and the election of the first non-Italian pope in centuries. Reviews his childhood and early career and discusses his emphasis on traditional Roman Catholic values. Black-and-white photographs. Fifth and sixth grades.

JOHN NEWTON

768. Dick, Lois Hoadley. *Devil on the Deck*. Old Tappan, N.J.: Revell, 1984. 190p.

A fictionalized, fast-paced account of the early years of the composer of "Amazing Grace" and other well-known hymns, whose life progresses through violent and dangerous adventures as a seaman and in the slave trade. Although he is aware of his sins and in love with a gentle English girl, he is not able to reform until his desperate prayer in a violent storm is answered. Then he experiences conversion. Fifth grade and up.

769. Strom, Kay Marshall. *John Newton: The Angry Sailor*. Chicago: Moody, 1984. 125p.

Impressed into the British navy at eleven, Newton is turned into a proud, defiant, reckless seaman by its cruelties. When his life is repeatedly and miraculously spared, he finally repents and accepts Christ. Eventually he becomes a distinguished hymn writer and minister of the eighteenth-century. Fast-moving, brief, and easy to read. Fifth to sixth grades.

CORRIE TEN BOOM

770. Ten Boom, Corrie, and John Sherrill and Elizabeth Sherrill. *The Hiding Place*. Washington Depot, Conn.: Chosen, 1971. 221p.

Loving and committed Christians, two middle-aged women and their elderly father hide Jews in their home during the Nazi occupation of Holland. Betrayed and imprisoned in concentration camps, the father soon dies, but the sisters spread the message of Jesus' love to the inmates of infamous Ravensbruck. Betsie also dies in prison, but Corrie continues the family mission to share their faith and forgive their enemies. This is a vivid, enthralling, and genuinely inspiring work written in a down-to-earth style. Fifth grade and up.

771. Watson, Jean. *Watchmaker's Daughter: The Life of Corrie Ten Boom for Young People*. Old Tappan, N.J.: Revell, 1982. 159p.

A fictionalized and abridged but generally faithful version of *The Hiding Place* (item 770). Courageous Dutch Christians in World War II secrete Jews in their home until a Nazi informer has them arrested. Although suffering and starving, Corrie and her sister never waver in the faith. They comfort and convert fellow inmates in the concentration camp where they are sent. This is a clearly written, moving, absorbing work. Black-and-white drawings. Fourth grade and up.

MOTHER TERESA

772. Gonzalez-Balado, Jose Luis. *Mother Teresa: Always the Poor*. Liguori, Mo.: Liguori, 1980. 112p.

A short and simply told biography of the Albanian nun and her Missionaries of Charity in India. There is also a description of the offshoot Missionary Brothers' work, the Contemplative Sisters, the lay Co-Workers, and others who provide prayer support and care for poor people throughout the world and contains the tenets of the Co-Workers and the sayings of Mother Teresa. Written in an admiring, spiritual tone. Fifth grade and up.

773. Greene, Carol. *Mother Teresa: Friend of the Friendless*. Chicago: Children's Press, 1983. 32p.

Brief but good overview of her life and work. Very easy to read and interesting and illustrated with black and white photographs of her activities and a few drawings of Mother Teresa in her early years. Includes a list of important dates. Kindergarten to fourth grade.

774. Lee, Betsy. *Mother Teresa: Caring for All God's Children*. Illus. Robert Kilbride. Minneapolis: Dillon, 1981. 48p. Taking Part Books Series.

Opens with the child, Agnes, celebrating Easter in Yugoslavia and follows her life after age eighteen as a Loreto nun and teacher in Darjeeling and Calcutta. A strong call to serve the poor impels her to leave the convent in 1948. Most of the book deals with her saintly missionary work in India and abroad. The book is well-organized and clear and written in a respectful tone. It has unusual, blocky, almost Cubist illustrations. Third to fifth grades.

775. Leigh, Vanora. *Mother Teresa*. Illus. Richard Hook. New York: Bookwright, 1986. 32p. Great Lives Series.

This absorbing, fast-paced presentation of principal events of Mother Teresa's life captures the essence of her work and personality. It is done sympathetically and appreciatively. Busy but interesting format with many strong, realistic color illustrations and black-and-white and color photographs. Contains a list of important dates, a glossary, a reading list and an index. Fourth to sixth grades.

776. Michelinie, David. *Mother Teresa of Calcutta*. Illus. John Tartaglione and Joe Sinnott. New York: Marvel, 1984. unp.

Uses a comic book format. A cable news correspondent and his photographer gather data on Mother Teresa's life as they visit Skopje, Loreto Abbey in Ireland, Calcutta, and Beirut. They tell her story as they travel about. The action-filled illustrations vary from closeups to panoramas. Fourth to sixth grades.

JOHN WESLEY

777. McNeer, May. *John Wesley*. Illus. Lynd Ward. Nashville: Abingdon, 1951. 95p.

Emphasizes John Wesley's life and calling but discusses the faith and determination of the entire Wesley family. Founder of the Methodist Societies, John endured prejudice and privation throughout most of his life as he traveled and preached the length and breadth of England. This sympathetic and vividly told narrative is illustrated with vigor and skill. Third grade and up.

778. Vernon, Louise A. *A Heart Strangely Warmed*. Illus. Allan Eitzen. Scottdale, Pa.: Herald, 1975. 125p.

Robert, young peddler boy, and his father are drawn to

the Methodist religion by John Wesley's straightforward preaching, charismatic personality, unswerving purpose, and bravery under persecution by the traditional, official Church of England. Through this relationship Robert finally realizes what God wants him to do with his life. Contains interesting historical detail and plain black-and-white drawings. Fourth to sixth grades.

SAINTS

Collective

779. Charlebois, Robert, and Mary Sue Holden and Marilyn Diggs Mange. *Saints for Kids by Kids*. Liguori, Mo.: Liguori, 1984. 80p.

Three hundred Catholic children chose the saints, helped write their stories, and composed prayers to each. The book contains short sketches of St. Patrick, St. Nicholas, St. Cecilia, St. Bernadette, St. Elizabeth of Hungary, St. Anthony of Padua, St. Joan of Arc, and St. Thomas Aquinas told in a child's language and concepts. Saints' childhoods are particularly noted in this fresh and appealing work. It is illustrated with children's drawings in black and white. Second to fifth grades.

780. Nastick, Sharon. *So You Think You've Got Problems: Twelve Stubborn Saints and Their Pushy Parents*. Illus. James E. McElrath. Huntington, Ind.: Our Sunday Visitor, 1982. 91p.

Maurice, the writer's guardian angel, tells her stories of saints whose parents opposed their aspirations to a religious vocation. The women are usually fighting arranged marriages and the men brilliant secular careers. Included are less familiar saints such as Frances of Rome, John Calybites, and Rose of Viterbo, and better-known persons such as Thomas Aquinas and Catherine of Siena. The book is written in an informal, slangy style and has cartoon-style black-and-white drawings. Fourth grade and up.

781. Synge, Ursula. *The Giant at the Ford: And Other Legends of the Saints*. Illus. Shirley Felts. New York: Atheneum, 1980. 183p.

In graceful, straightforward prose, depicts St. Christopher as a giant serving the Lord by carrying people across a river; St. George as a Roman soldier killing the dragon while stationed in Libya; St. Jerome training a lion; St. Moling attempting to reform a fox; St. Warburgh chastising an unruly flock of geese. Stresses the virtues of tenderness toward animals, patience, modesty, forgiveness. Has some black-and-white drawings. Fifth grade and up.

782. Twomey, Mark J. *A Parade of Saints*. Illus. Placid Stuckenschneider. Collegeville, Minn.: Liturgical, 1983. 176p.

Brief but fact-packed biographies of saints of the Americas (Lily of the Mohawks, Mother Seton, Martin de Porres, Mother Cabrini, John Newman); New Testament saints, apostles, and evangelists; martyrs; bishops; founders of religious orders; doctors of the church. Also has the meaning and versions of saints' names, feast days, dates and a glossary. It is written in a crisp style in a very handsome format with two-color wood-cut style pictures. Fourth grade and up.

Individual

783. Laird, Elizabeth, and Abba Aregawi Wolde Gabriel. *The Miracle Child: A Story from Ethiopia*. New York: Holt, 1985. 32p.

The legend of the thirteenth-century saint of the Ethiopian Orthodox Church, Tekla Haymanot. The saint's parents, childless for years, are saved from evil King Matalome by Archangel Michael and given a special son, beloved by God. From the age of one Tekla performs miracles and grows up to be a famous priest. Written in a stately, storytelling prose and illustrated with ingenuously stylized scenes from an eighteenth-century illuminated Ethiopian manuscript in glowing colors, emphasizing scarlet, gold, and blue. Fourth to sixth grades.

784. De Paola, Tomie. *The Lady of Guadalupe*. Illus. author. New York: Holiday, 1980. unp.

Poetically retold legend of a church built especially for the Indians of Mexico on the hill of Tepeyac and inspired by the miraculous appearances of the Virgin to devout native, Juan Diego, in 1531. Juan is able to persuade the bishop to believe in the holy visitations after

Mary gives him a bouquet of Castilian roses, and a beautiful painting of her suddenly appears on his cactus-fiber robe. Carefully researched illustrations in soft colors of stocky Indian figures. Creates a pensive, spiritual mood. Kindergarten to third grade.

785. Fritz, Jean. *The Man Who Loved Books*. Illus. Trina S. Hyman. New York: Putnam, 1981. unp.

Text and pictures are perfectly harmonized in this gem about St. Columba, missionary and booklover. A genial, burly giant with a hair shirt under his robe, Columba tramps about Ireland searching out new manuscripts and then emigrates to Scotland where he converts the king and lives a long life on Iona, making numerous copies of the New Testament. The fine, flavorful writing evokes a legendary tone. Beautifully designed and balanced illustrations in warm brown tones of craggy people, curly waves, armies bristling with spears that brim with life and humor. Kindergarten to fourth grade.

786. Hodges, Margaret. *Saint George and the Dragon*. Illus. Trina Schart Hyman. Boston: Little, 1984. 32p.

George, the Red Cross Knight, does mighty and bloody battle with the dragon which has been wasting the Lady Una's kingdom, slays it, and marries the princess. Adapted from a portion of Spenser's *Faerie Queen*. Elegantly conceived, with flower bordered pages, delicate fairy folk, an ethereal Una, a stalwart knight, and a dragon of fire and ferocity; written in a dignified storytelling prose. Kindergarten and up.

FRANCIS OF ASSISI

787. Bawden, Nina. *St. Francis of Assisi*. Illus. Pascale Allamand. New York: Lothrop, 1983. unp.

Many legends of the saint--miraculous changing of chicken to fish on Friday, preaching to the birds, taming Brother Wolf at Gubbio, receiving the stigmata, etc.--are included in this short, lively, simply written biography. It is in picture book format with very large type and has ingenuous, appealing, richly colorful pictures filled with appealing animals. First to fourth grades.

788. Bulla, Clyde Robert. *Song of St. Francis*. Illus. Valenti Angelo. New York: Crowell, 1952. 71p.

Interesting, pictorial, well-constructed narrative details

Francis's progress from reckless boyhood to the gradual realization that he has been called by God to rid himself of his possessions, found a band of mendicant Brothers, and lead a holy life. Strong themes of service to others, love of God. Simple line drawings. Second to fifth grades.

789. Darian, Mujana. *St. Francis and You*. Illus. author. Huntington, Ind.: Our Sunday Visitor, 1979. 48p.

Highlights of the saint's life told in short, declarative sentences interspersed with didactic spiritual questions addressed to the young child reader. Strangely illustrated with photographs of intense, foreshortened brown sculptures of Francis with birds and animals, the leper, St. Clare, receiving the stigmata, etc. Contains a vocabulary list. Kindergarten to second grade.

790. De Paola, Tomie. *Francis: The Poor Man of Assisi*. Illus. author. New York: Holiday, 1982. unp.

In a reverent and simple text the book gives selected incidents from the lives of St. Francis and St. Clare, both of whom give away their riches to lead lives of poverty and holiness and found religious orders. Stocky, strong-faced people and authentic thirteenth-century backgrounds and costumes in richly colored illustrations. Kindergarten to second grade.

791. Duffy, Mary Jo. *Francis: Brother of the Universe*. Illus. John Buscema and Marie Severin. New York: Marvel, 1980. 48p.

Well-drawn, interesting comic book format biography tells of Francis's profligate youth, call by God, life of poverty, founding of monastic order, trip to Damietta, stigmata. Includes the Canticle of the Sun. Miracles stressed throughout. Written in a reverent tone. Fourth to sixth grades.

792. Luckhardt, Mildred Corell. *Brother Francis and the Christmas Surprise*. Illus. Hannah DeVries. Ramsey, N.J.: Paulist, 1983. unp.

St. Francis and his Little Brothers of the Poor want to give the people of Greccio a surprise Christmas gift that will make them see God's love alive in Jesus and feel more loving and joyful themselves. The Brothers choose to celebrate the Nativity with the first living creche. This vividly written work reflects the saint's personality and life of gentle goodness. It has soft-lined drawings in muted brown tones. All ages.

793. Mayer-Skimanz, Lene. *The Story of Brother Francis*. Illus. Alicia Sancha. Notre Dame, Ind.: Ave Maria, 1983. unp.

Finely written, simplified but comprehensive, this lengthy text is arranged on a page in free verse style using poetic language, repetition, rhythm. It sparkles with imaginative detail and dialogue. Contains bold, impressionistic watercolors. Third to sixth grades.

794. O'Dell, Scott. *The Road to Damietta*. Boston: Houghton Mifflin, 1985. 230p.

A skillfully written version of St. Francis's life seen through eyes of a self-centered, love-struck girl of thirteen who witnesses his dramatic renunciation of worldly possessions and his deeds of kindness; follows him to Egypt during the Fifth Crusade, where he hopes to convert the Sultan and bring peace to Christians and Moslems; and finally is herself changed into a spiritual and caring person. Describes the founding of Poor Clares and has excellent details of the Crusade, the thirteenth-century setting, and the medieval church. Fifth grade and up.

795. Sack, John. *The Wolf in Winter: A Story of St. Francis of Assisi*. Illus. Gloria Ortiz. Mahwah, N.J.: Paulist, 1985. 120p.

This is a vivid account of the saint's life immediately after his renunciation of worldly matters. He is ridiculed in Assisi, shelters for a while in a brutally run monastery, finally reaches Gubbio where he serves the wretched inmates of a leprosarium, and tames the marauding wolf. At the end he is thrust back into the world to complete an as yet unknown mission. Written in a poetic, powerful style with realistic, authoritative details. It is moving and absorbing. Has small, simple drawings. Sixth grade and up.

JOAN OF ARC

796. Boutel de Monvel, Louis Maurice. *Joan of Arc*. New York: Viking, 1980. 56p.

Written with old-fashioned charm, this facsimile of the 1896 French edition is stately, saintly, comprehensive, but sometimes apocryphal. Its elegantly detailed, subtly colored illustrations swirl with warhorses, bristle with lances, show menacing black-robed judges and shine with splendid court finery. The Introduction discusses Joan's place in history and Boutel de Monvel's life and evaluates the text and artwork. Fifth grade and up.

797. Storr, Catherine. *Joan of Arc*. Illus. Robert Taylor. Milwaukee: Raintree, 1985. 32p.

Unsentimentally told, this brief biography in picture book form begins with Joan hearing saints' voices as a girl in Domrémy and stresses her determination to carry out their instructions to save France. Harsh, powerful color illustrations show Joan, with fanatic eyes, in court and in battle, being shot in the throat, and weeping at the stake as the executioner lifts his torch. Violent fare for first to fourth grades.

PATRICK

798. Barth, Edna. *Shamrocks, Harps, and Shillelaghs: The Story of St. Patrick's Day Symbols*. Illus. Ursula Arndt. New York: Clarion, 1977. 96p.

St. Patrick's life and legends, along with the ways in which the holiday is celebrated and the history and meaning of the various symbols. Also discusses Irish culture and the plight of Irish Catholics under Protestant English rule in an attractive, interesting presentation with three-color drawings. Has an index and bibliography. Third to sixth grades.

799. Corfe, Thomas Howell. *St. Patrick and Irish Christianity*. Minneapolis: Lerner, 1973. 51p. Cambridge Topic Book Series.

Black-and-white maps, photographs, and drawings provide the vivid setting for the life and legends of Patrick. Also includes material on other Irish saints (Bridget, Columba, and Columban), monks, missionaries, architecture, culture, and history. Index. Fifth grade and up.

800. Kessel, Joyce K. *St. Patrick's Day*. Illus. Cathy Gilchrist. Minneapolis: Carolrhoda, 1982. 56p.

Ireland's patron saint is born in England of Roman parents, stolen as a slave by King Niall of Ireland in 400, escapes, is called by God to be a missionary, studies in

France, becomes a bishop, and successfully proselytizes initially hostile Irish. He fills the land with churches, unites people, performs miracles. The sturdy, spare black-and-white drawings are touched with green. First to fourth grades.

801. Roquitte, Ruth. *Saint Patrick: The Irish Saint*. Illus. Robert Kilbride. Minneapolis: Dillon, 1981. 48p.

All the known details of the saint's life and missionary work are well filled out with background material and presented in a simple, interesting way. Includes the snake legend. Has large, brilliant illustrations with blocky, primitive figures placed on one-dimensional backgrounds. First to fourth grades.

VIII
CHRISTIAN CHURCH HISTORY

802. Boyd, Anne. *Life in a Fifteenth Century Monastery*. Minneapolis: Lerner, 1978. 51p. Cambridge Topic Book Series.

Details of the buildings, inhabitants, daily life, financing, leadership, and history of the Benedictine Durham Priory in England are absorbing. Done in a crowded double column format, it has black-and-white maps, photographs, drawings, and an index. Fifth grade and up.

803. Cairns, Trevor. *Barbarians, Christians, and Muslims*. Minneapolis: Lerner, 1975. 100p. Cambridge Introduction to History Series.

In this once-over-lightly coverage of 392-814 C.E. with heavy British emphasis, barbarians of the forest and plain rampage through Europe and are gradually Christianized and the Christian faith spreads to the British Isles. The Byzantium empire rises. Islam is founded, and Arabic culture flowers. The Vikings are subdued. It has many paintings, maps, photographs, drawings, charts, diagrams in color and black and white and an index. Fifth grade and up.

804. Drury, John. *The Church and the Modern Nations*. Illus. Franco Vignazia. Minneapolis: Winston, 1982. unp. Illustrated History of the Church Series.

Rapid technological change challenges traditional faith from 1850 to 1920. With a definite Roman Catholic emphasis, this work discusses Bernadette of Lourdes, Pius IX and X, John Bosco, Leo XIII, Charles Lavigerie, Mother Cabrini, etc., and the Catholic church in the United States, South America, Ireland, England, Europe, as well as missions in Africa and Asia. Kierkegaard and other Protestant theologians mentioned, along with Marx and Engels, Schweitzer, Ghandi. Contains large, bright, simply designed illustrations. It has a chapter outline. Fourth grade and up.

805. Drury, John. *The Church Established: From 181 to 381*. Illus. Antonio Molino. Minneapolis: Winston, 1981. unp. Illustrated History of the Church Series.

The growth of Christianity in the Roman Empire: early Christian art; Constantine's conversion and influence; Arianism; the Council of Nicaea; the beginning of Monasticism. Contains a panoply of important persons such as Perpetua, Origen, Cyprian, Eusebius, and Martin of Tours in addition to other topics that are all discussed in an interesting way. Huge, brilliantly colored pictures in caricature style are interspersed throughout the text, making for easier reading. There is a chapter outline. Fourth grade and up.

806. Drury, John. *The Church in Revolutionary Times: From 1700 to 1850*. Illus. Franco Vignazia. Minneapolis: Winston, 1981. unp. Illustrated History of the Church Series.

Roman Catholic events and personalities, mainly in Europe, predominate. Discusses the effects of the Enlightenment and the Romantic Movement, Jansenism, Masonry, the French Revolution, and Liberalism. Touches upon the Industrial Revolution, the Oxford Movement, Methodism, missions in the Far East. Very large, amusing illustrations are not always tied to the text but give flavor and interest to each subject. Has a chapter outline instead of an index. Fourth to sixth grades.

807. Drury, John. *The Church in the Age of Humanism*. Illus. Sandro Corsi. Minneapolis: Winston, 1981. unp. Illustrated History of the Church Series.

More secular history than church history in the period 1300-1500. Includes the Black Death, rise of merchants and guilds, the Avignon papacy, the Great Schism, the growth of cities, the fall of Byzantine Empire, and much more. Personalities mentioned: Catherine of Siena, Meister Eckhardt, John Wycliffe, Jan Hus, Jeanne d'Arc, Savonarola, the Medicis, etc. Text concentrates on Italy but moves to Poland, Russia, Spain, the Congo, as well. Detailed color pictures are realistic yet exaggerated to witty caricature. There is a chapter outline. Fourth to sixth grades.

808. Drury, John. *The Church Today: From 1920 to 1981*. Minneapolis: Winston, 1982. unp. Illustrated History of the Church Series.

With the Roman Catholic church in forefront, the book includes the Liturgical Movement, Vatican II, modern popes, Dorothy Day and the Catholic Worker Movement, Teilhard de Chardin, American parochial schools, Mother Teresa, etc. It also contains capsules of recent events in Iran, Mexico, Africa, Russia, India. It deals also with events during World War II, focusing on the roles of various churches and clerics, and goes on to discuss Existentialism, Bultmann, Tillich. It is overloaded with facts, but is objective and absorbing. Eyecatching, clever color illustrations by various artists. Has a chapter outline. Fourth to sixth grades.

809. Drury, John. *The End of the Ancient World*. Illus. Franco Vignazia. Minneapolis: Winston, 1980. unp. Illustrated History of the Church Series.

Brief sketches of the lives, thoughts, and influence of John Chrysostom, Ambrose of Milan, Augustine, Jerome, Leo the Great, Clovis, etc. Discusses numerous schisms, including Pelagianism, Arianism, Nestorianism, Monophysitism, and the crystallization of doctrine. The period covered is 381-630 and includes the spread of Christianity to Britain, Gaul, and other Frankish territories; the end of Roman empire, the spread of barbarians, the growth of monasteries, the rise of Constantinople, Mohammed, and growth of Islam. The full, rich subject is successfully handled. Has huge, ebullient, blindingly colorful illustrations and sometimes confusing maps. There is a chapter outline. Fourth to sixth grades.

810. Drury, John. *The First Christians*. Illus. Antonio Molino. Minneapolis: Winston, 1979. unp. Illustrated History of the Church Series.

From the beginnings to 180 A.D. Much of the first half is a distillation of Gospels and Acts, with excerpts from Paul's letters and some of Revelation. Proceeds to destruction of the Temple in 70; persecutions of Christians under the crumbling Roman regime; has biographical sketches of Clement, Ignatius, Polycarp, Justin Martyr, etc.; describes the formation of the Christian canon; and indicates the spread of Christianity to central Europe, Spain, Middle East, Northern Africa. Contains large, simple pictures in bold colors. Somewhat choppy organization but straightforward, crisp writing. There is a chapter outline. Suggestions for further reading. Fourth to sixth grades.

811. Drury, John. *The Formation of Christian Europe*. Illus. Franco Vignazia. Minneapolis: Winston, 1980. unp. Illustrated History of the Church Series.

This overview of the years 600-900 begins with the occupation of northern Italy by the Lombards, who were both pagan and Arian Christian. Contains the lives of notables such as Pope Gregory, Columbanus, Amandus, and Maximus. Describes the widespread missionary activities in Europe; Charlemagne's empire; the spread of Islam into Spain. Events in each century are not in sequence and jump about in a sometimes confusing manner. This is a fact-packed text with big, humorous, bright pictures. Fourth to sixth grades.

812. Drury, John. *The Middle Ages*. Illus. Franco Vignazia. Minneapolis: Winston, 1981. unp. Illustrated History of the Church Series.

For the years 900-1300 the book includes the rise of the Holy Roman Empire and the feudal system, the founding of monastic orders, the Crusades, the Magna Carta, the Concordat of Worms, the Knights Templar, the beginning of Norman influence, scholasticism, Romanesque and Gothic art and architecture, and much more. Personalities described include Adalbert, Emperor Otto III, Hildebrand, Anselm, Bernard of Clairvaux, Thomas à Becket and Henry II, Francis of Assisi, and Thomas Aquinas. Has colorful and entertaining illustrations. Fourth to sixth grades.

813. Drury, John. *Protestant and Catholic Reform*. Illus. Antonio Molino. Minneapolis: Winston, 1981. unp. Illustrated History of the Church Series.

Contains a gingerly treatment of Luther, Zwingli, Menno Simons, and other Protestant reformers and is carefully non-condemning. Reformers within Roman Catholic church who press for a return to holiness include Cisneros, Ignatius Loyola, Thomas More, Philip Neri, Teresa of Avila, etc. Describes their conflict with Orthodox church, the changing political trends toward absolute monarchy and increasing oppression of peasants, the rise of Church of England, Puritans, Jansenism, Jesuits, etc. The period covered is 1500-1700. Clever, huge pictures in exceedingly bright colors caricature their subjects. Fourth to sixth grades.

814. Fellows, Lawrence. *A Gentle War: The Story of the Salvation Army*. New York: Macmillan, 1979. 88p.

Discusses the worldwide mission of the Army but emphasizes the American branch's current activities. Begins with the founding of the movement by William and Catherine Booth and their daughter, Evangeline in an interesting but disjointed anecdotal style. Has a bibliography, index, and photographs. Sixth grade and up.

815. Kleeberg, Irene Cumming. *Separation of Church and State*. New York: Watts, 1986. 64p. A First Book Series.

Discusses the United States Constitution, the Jeffersonian "wall of separation" that was designed to divide religion from government, and what factors tend to make this "wall" move back and forth over the years. Contains some religious history of the United States from 1620 on and facts about countries with established churches. Examines ongoing problematical themes leading to legal action such as public Christmas creches, prayer in public schools, and the possibility that Christmas and Thanksgiving might be considered unconstitutional holidays. This fascinating, important subject is handled unevenly and sometimes unclearly. It is poorly organized. Black-and-white photographs and art reproductions. Has a glossary and index. Fifth grade and up.

816. Macaulay, David. *Cathedral: The Story of Its Construction*. Illus. author. Boston: Houghton Mifflin, 1973. 77p.

Precise, entrancingly detailed pen-and-ink drawings show every stage in the building of a splendid, fictitious medieval French cathedral. Each step, from the architect's plan through the installation of the rose window, is carefully described along with the problems and dangers of construction and the craftsmen and materials that are involved. Has a glossary. Fifth grade and up.

817. Marty, Martin. *Christianity and the New World: From 1500 to 1800*. Illus. Merle Peek. Minneapolis: Winston, 1984. 127p. Illustrated History of the Church Series.

This three-hundred-year chronicle begins with Columbus's 1492 voyage and the Spanish conquest of the New World and extends to the period immediately following the Revolutionary War. It deals mostly with the North American Colonies and a bit with Canada and South America. Includes Catholic missions, the eighteenth-century Great Awakening, the origin and history of immigrant denominations, Deism, Colonial American Jews, church architecture, the religions of Washington, Jefferson, and Franklin. The writing is factual, critical, often wry. It is neither denominational nor evangelistic. The illustrations are a strange mixture of old prints and drawings with large, flat, cartoon-style pictures that are too young for the text. It has many short sections for easier reading. Fifth grade and up.

818. Norwood, Frederick A. *Young Reader's Book of Church History*. Illus. Tom Armstrong. Nashville: Abingdon, 1982. 176p.

Within the framework of a college professor's telling a group of modern children stories of Christianity's development, selected events and personalities, such as St. Francis, David Livingstone, John Bunyan, the Crusades, the Reformation, Henry VIII, American denominations, etc., are discussed. The book is more for pleasure reading than for reference. Has occasional black-and-white drawings and a bibliography. Fourth to sixth grades.

819. Watson, Percy. *Building the Medieval Cathedrals*. Minneapolis: Lerner, 1976. 51p. Cambridge Topic Book Series.

A thorough study of Norman Romanesque cathedrals built in England in the eleventh and twelfth centuries. Includes detailed information on and diagrams of the interior and exterior construction and furnishings; masons, carpenters, metal workers, glaziers, artists, and many other craftsmen involved; structural problems. Some material on Early Gothic cathedrals as well. Profusely illustrated with black-and-white photographs, drawings, maps. Has an index. Fifth grade and up.

820. Weiss, Ann E. *God and Government: The Separation of Church and State*. Boston: Houghton Mifflin, 1982. 132p.

Federal aid to parochial schools, cults' rights, religious tax exemptions, and the Moral Majority are among topics examined in a clear, informative, meticulous manner. Thought-provoking introduction encourages serious consideration of these issues by all religious groups. Has a bibliography and index. Sixth grade and up.

Fiction

821. Douglas, Lloyd. *The Robe*. Boston: Houghton Mifflin, 1942. 695p.

Tribune Marcellus, commander of the Roman soldiers at the Crucifixion, wins Jesus' robe in a dice game. Haunted by this strange and compelling man, Marcellus retraces Jesus' career in Galilee and eventually joins the persecuted Christian sect in Rome. He flouts Caligula and is executed. The book has a fine sense of setting, is suspenseful. Good readers sixth grade and up.

822. Paterson, Katherine. *Rebels of the Heavenly Kingdom*. New York: Dutton, 1983. 232p.

Armies of the Taiping Tienkuo--the Heavenly Kingdom of Great Peace, which is a version of Christianity venerating the High God and Elder Brother, Jesus--sweep across China, crushing the Imperial Manchu forces during the rebellion of 1850-53. Mei Lin, a young woman warrior, and Wang Lee, a peasant boy, are the heroine and hero. It is powerfully written. Sixth grade and up.

823. Smith, Claude Clayton. *The Stratford Devil*. New York: Walker, 1984. 192p. Walker's American History Series for Young People.

A somber account based on the early history of the Puritan settlement in Stratford, Connecticut, and the hanging of Goody Bassett as a witch in 1651. Ruth at age twelve lives with a kindly widow and is unaware of her true parentage. After being rescued from a wolf's attack by an Indian, she is given its pelt, which she treasures. When she is twenty-two she marries the schoolmaster, and he is accidentally poisoned. The community, obsessed with witches and wolves, blames Ruth for his death, for an Indian attack, of having a pact with wolves preying on their livestock, and of causing a woman to become ill. She is executed. Contains convincing details of rigorous daily life and the strong grip of narrow, prejudiced religion. The dark, portentous mood is complemented by formal, old-fashioned language. Sixth grade and up.

824. Speare, Elizabeth George. *The Witch of Blackbird Pond*. New York: Dell, 1958. 249p.

Sixteen-year-old Kit loses her home in tropical, relaxed Barbados and must seek shelter with her aunt's repressed Puritan family in chilly seventeenth-century Connecticut.

Hostility toward Quakers is shown in the persecution of a gentle, courageous old woman whom Kit befriends. The horror of the witch hunt overwhelms Kit when she herself becomes the victim. Very well written and researched historical romance. Fifth grade and up.

825. Vernon, Louise A. *The King's Book*. Illus. Allan Eitzen. Scottdale, Pa.: Herald, 1980. 127p.

Nat, the fourteen-year-old son of one of the translators of the King James Bible, is involved in mysteries concerning secret Catholics, the imprisonment of his father, and the new Bible itself. Has interesting details of setting and is rapidly paced. Fifth grade and up.

826. Wildsmith, Brian. *The True Cross*. Illus. author. New York: Oxford, 1977. unp.

A spare text with a legendary tone describes the planting of a sprig from the Tree of Life in the mouth of Adam's corpse. The sprig flourishes into a tree with miraculous healing properties. The tree is used for Jesus' cross and buried. When unearthed several centuries later, it still performs miracles. Exuberantly illustrated in lavish, eyefilling colors and patterns. Kindergarten to third grade.

IX
JUDAISM

827. Burstein, Chaya M. *The Jewish Kids Catalog*. Illus. author. Philadelphia: Jewish Publication Society of America, 1983. 224p.

Treasure trove of information, from the meaning of names through places to see in Israel. Nuggets on bar and bat mitzvahs; Jewish history; Yiddish, Hebrew, and Ladino; the year and its holidays; parties, crafts, and recipes; the holy books; dances and songs (with music); Bible stories and folktales; and much more. The text is spirited, enjoyable, educational, with black-and-white photographs, diagrams, maps, and witty drawings. It contains a short dictionary of people and terms and an index. Fourth to sixth grades.

828. Charing, Douglas. *The Jewish World*. Morristown, N.J.: Silver Burdett, 1983. 48p.

Excellently reproduced color and black-and-white photographs, diagrams, charts, drawings, and calligraphy illuminate a thorough coverage of the Jewish people today. Includes geographical distribution, basic beliefs, Orthodox and Progressive divisions, prayer, the synagogue, sacred books, symbolism, holidays, customs, and the effect of Judaism on worldwide religion and ethics but little history. Has a glossary, calendar, book list, art galleries and museums, helpful United States information centers, and an index. Fourth grade and up.

829. Drucker, Malka. *Celebrating Life: Jewish Rites of Passage*. New York: Holiday, 1984. 96p.

Ceremonies, superstitions, and traditions surrounding birth, adolescence, marriage, and death presented in warm, touching text. Shows the involvement of the whole Jewish community in these special times of life. Greeting and naming the baby, circumcision, bar and bat mitzvahs, the ketubah and other wedding customs, the get (bill of divorcement), ethical will, etc. Contains prayers, a glossary, and an index and has black-and-white photographs. Fifth grade and up.

830. Ganz, Yaffa. *Follow the Moon: A Journey Through the Jewish Year.* Illus. Harvey Klineman. New York: Feldheim, 1984, unp.

Begins with a section on Rosh Chodesh and the moon. Then discusses the weather, activities, holidays, birth and death dates of Biblical notables, historical events, Bible stories, and the astral constellation associated with each month, from Nissan through Adar. Interesting text is highlighted with cheerful color pictures. Also has a glossary of Hebrew and Yiddish words. Kindergarten to fourth grade.

831. Ganz, Yaffa. *Who Knows One? A Book of Jewish Numbers.* Illus. Harvey Klineman. New York: Feldheim, 1981. unp.

An attractively presented, high-level counting book offers a variety of Judaic information associated with each number. Included are 10, 12, 13, 18, 39, 40, 49, 70, 120, 613, as well as 1-9. Each has its Hebrew symbol and Arabic numeral. Many jolly cartoon-style pictures in color. Contains a glossary of Hebrew words and a list of Hebrew numbers and their associated Hebrew letters. Kindergarten to third grade.

832. Gilbert, Arthur, and Oscar Tarcov. *Your Neighbor Celebrates.* New York: Friendly House, 1957. 118p.

A thorough and interesting presentation of Judaism to non-Jews. Includes the history and celebration of holidays; synagogue building, holy objects, and services; the Bar Mitzvah and Confirmation. Orthodox, Conservative, and Reform Judaism described in an explanatory note. The work exhibits an ecumenical tone. Contains black-and-white photographs, a glossary, and a holiday calendar. Fourth grade and up.

833. Goldreich, Gloria. *A Treasury of Jewish Literature.* New York: Holt, 1982. 244p.

This literary survey begins with the Bible: excerpts from the Torah (Joseph's story), the Prophets (Isaiah), the Writings (Psalms, Proverbs, etc.), and the Apocrypha (Zebulun, Gad). Includes quotations from the Talmud,

Siddur, Zohar; Hasidic and Yiddish tales; poetry; and Holocaust material. Talks about the works of modern authors such as S.Y. Agnon, Philip Roth, Bernard Malamud, and Arthur Miller. There are short explanatory introductions to each section and a glossary, bibliography, and index. Sixth grade and up.

834. Halpern, Solomon Alter. *The Prisoner: And Other Tales of Faith*. New York: Feldheim, 1968. 216p.

Written in a lively, readable style, the book contains short stories with didactic themes that deal with a variety of subjects. It is based upon careful, scholarly research. Bible stories include Abraham successfully defying Nimrod, Moses tenderly being lifted from his basket by Pharaoh's daughter, Gideon, Ruth, Esther, and more. There are folktales of sages and miracles and modern adventures that are obvious and amateurish. It has a topical index and an appendix with background notes for many of the stories. Fifth grade and up.

835. Karlinsky, Ruth Schild. *My First Book of Mitzvos*. Spring Valley, N.Y.: Feldheim, 1985. unp.

In large, clear black-and-white photographs cheerful and attentive boys and girls at home and at Hebrew school illustrate mitzvos from netilas yadayim the first thing in the morning to reciting Shma Yisrael the last thing at night. Many deal with how to treat others: loving friends, honoring parents, welcoming guests, respecting the elderly, giving to the poor. Effective explanatory text for preschool through second grade.

836. Kipper, Lenore C. *The Alef-Bet of Jewish Values: Code Words of Jewish Life*. Illus. Jana Paiss. New York: Union of American Hebrew Congregations, 1985. 44p.

Twenty-three moral principles such as truth, justice, holiness, peace, wisdom, forgiveness are examined. The Hebrew word for each is given, how it applies to Jewish living, and often a story, quotation, or example to clarify the precept. Jewish identity, God and prayer, community and personal values are the themes stressed. The book is decorated with handsome drawings. Fifth grade and up.

837. Samuels, Ruth. *Pathways through Jewish History*. Rev. ed. New York: KTAV, 1977. 409p.

From Abraham's departure from Ur through the Entebbe rescue, the history of the Jews is encapsulated in a brisk and interesting narrative. Copious black-and-white maps, photographs, drawings, a glossary and an index are included. Fifth grade and up.

838. Segal, Yocheved. *Our Sages Showed the Way*. Vol. 1. Rev. ed. Illus. Naama Nothman. New York: Feldheim, 1982. 192p.

Forty-three very short tales (aggadoth) from the Talmud and other holy books of the Sages are grouped according to theme and extol virtues such as trusting in God, honoring parents, respecting others, honesty, hard work, love of the Torah. Some deal with famous figures such as Rabbi Akiva; others tell about ordinary, pious people. Virtue is always rewarded. The tales have a succinct folktale charm. Sources are given. There are sketchy pictures in three colors. Third to sixth grades.

839. Wood, Angela. *Judaism*. London: Batsford Academic and Educational, 1984. 72p. Dictionaries of World Religion Series.

Informative encyclopedic entries on many aspects: rites and ceremonies, prayers, theology, ethics, customs and family life, relations with non-Jews, scriptures, Zionism, etc., are written in long but not difficult sentences. There are black-and-white photographs and drawings, a historical time chart, a bibliography, and an index. Fifth grade and up.

ANTI-SEMITISM

840. Arnold, Caroline. *Anti-Semitism: A Modern Perspective*. New York: Messner, 1985. 224p.

Concentrates on the period since World War II but includes some material from other eras, such as the Middle Ages, nineteenth-century Russia, and Germany under Hitler. Discusses anti-Semitic oppression in the Soviet Union, Poland, Czechoslovakia, France, Austria, West Germany, Italy, Latin America, the Middle East, and the United States. Many specific instances are cited. There is a section on organized American hate groups; the concluding chapter on hope for change is very short. This is a serious, fact-filled, chilling book. It contains black-and-white photographs, an index, and a reading list. Sixth grade and up.

Fiction and Biography

841. Arrick, Fran. *Chernowitz!* Scarsdale, N.Y.: Bradbury, 1981. 165p.

Fifteen-year-old Bobby suddenly becomes the target of anti-Semitic prejudice when Emmett, the class bully, begins harassing him and influences other boys to follow along. Bobby ignores name-calling and swastikas, but Emmett's deliberate attempt to kill his cat sparks a devastating plan of revenge. Obvious but effective problem novel shows insidious effect of thoughtless prejudice on all involved. Sixth grade and up.

842. Holman, Felice. *The Murderer*. New York: Scribner's, 1978. 152p.

A twelve-year-old Jewish boy is bewildered by the casual but inevitable persecution by his Polish Catholic classmates in a small Pennsylvania mining town during the Depression. Especially puzzling is the term "Christ-killer." A young rabbi offers gentle, sensible counseling. It contains a vivid evocation of time and place, with details of the cheder, the Bar Mitzvah, and family life, and sharp characterization. A plea for tolerance is the natural outgrowth of the story. Fourth to sixth grades.

843. Hull, Eleanor. *The Summer People*. New York: Atheneum, 1984. 217p.

Although Jenny and her family are the only Jews at the Glen, a summer colony, they are welcomed by all. Jenny's best friend is a Baptist, Ann; and Episcopalian James wants her to marry him. However, when a Jew for Jesus wants to establish his headquarters in the resort, the majority of property owners vote against his proposition. Although Jenny finds the man obnoxious, too, she is mightily offended by what she considers prejudice. Ann manages to insult her, also, and she flounces off, disliking everyone. Eventually she forgives them. Much ado about very little. Sixth grade and up.

844. Weinstein, Frida Scheps. *A Hidden Childhood: A Jewish Girl's Sanctuary in a French Convent, 1942-1945*. New York: Farrar, 1985. 151p.

Poignant, unusual memoir of seven-year-old Jewish girl

sent from Paris to convent school in the country to protect her from the Germans in World War II. She is lovingly cared for there, and not surprisingly becomes absorbed in Roman Catholicism. Her parents refuse permission for her baptism, and she must remain on the fringe of the Catholic experience. Effective stream-of-consciousness style seems to come directly from the young child's mind. The cool tone belies the underlying confusion and loneliness of a displaced person. Fifth grade and up.

JEWISH LIFE

845. Ashabranner, Brent. *Gavriel and Jemal: Two Boys of Jerusalem.* New York: Dodd, 1984. 95p.

Portraits of fourteen-year-old Jemal, a Palestinian Arab, and twelve-year-old Gavriel, an Israeli Orthodox Jew, are drawn against the tension-filled background of modern Jerusalem. Describes the religious customs, family life, and education of each boy, with some history, geography, variety of population, and daily activities of Jerusalem itself included. An accurate, easy-to-read, absorbing book that contains black-and-white photographs of families and city scenes. Fifth grade and up.

846. Eisenberg, Phyllis Rose. *A Mitzvah Is Something Special.* Illus. Susan Jeschke. New York: Harper, 1978. 31p.

Lisa learns the official meaning of mitzvah (a big blessing) from her round, comfy, strudel-baking grandmother and discusses mitzvahs further with her fashionable, flute-playing Grandma Dorrie. Eager to perform one herself, she finds a way. Appreciates the value of different but equally loving life styles. Written in a warm, homey tone, the book has amusing black-and-white full page sketches. Kindergarten to third grade.

847. Goldstein, Andrew. *My Very Own Jewish Home.* Rockville, Md.: Kar-Ben, 1979. unp.

A little girl conducts a tour of her home and tells about the mezuzah, the special books, the dining room with its Shabbat candlesticks and kiddush cups, the kitchen where challah and holiday cookies are baked, and her own bedroom with its dreidles, grogger, tzedakah box, etc. An easy text with sharp black-and-white photographs. Preschool to second grade.

848. Groner, Judyth Saypol. *My Very Own Jewish Community.* Rockville, Md.: Kar-Ben, 1984. unp.

Attractive presentation of places in the greater Washington, D.C., area that are especially important for Jewish families. Includes a community center, day school, library, kosher market, book and gift shop, synagogues, cemetery, home for the aged. The book uses simple text and has clear black-and-white photographs. Preschool to second grade.

849. Lawton, Clive. *I Am a Jew.* New York: Watts, 1985. 32p.

A broad study of ten-year-old Ilana and her family, English Jews, that covers family life, dietary laws, Shabbat, the synagogue and religious school, holiday celebrations, family tree, Jewish calendar, fact page, and glossary. Good color photographs and an informative, easy-to-read text are hampered by a rather cluttered layout. Third to sixth grades.

850. Pomerantz, Barbara. *Bubby, Me, and Memories.* New York: Union of American Hebrew Congregations, 1985. unp.

Following the death of her beloved grandmother, a small girl's parents explain gently that everything must die eventually and that Bubby will never be coming back. Along with her sadness, the child remembers with happiness the walks, stories, cooking sessions, and other joys that she and Bubby shared. Describes the mourning customs at home and in the synagogue. Has thoughtful, poignant black-and-white photographs. Preschool to third grade.

Fiction

851. Chaikin, Miriam. *How Yossi Beat the Evil Urge.* Illus. Petra Mathers. New York: Harper, 1983. 42p.

A Hasidic boy's attention is constantly wandering as the rebbe lectures in the yeshiva. Also, he has stolen a piece of honey cake at home. Discouraged, he feels the Evil Urge in his personality is overwhelming his Good Urge and that he is not reaching God in prayer. Then his special gift for joyful worship is revealed on the Sabbath at the synagogue. A sympathetic, amusing penetration of a young boy's thoughts and actions. Good description of a Hasidic family. The spare text is augmented with witty black-and-white pictures done in primitive style. Third to fifth grades.

852. Chaikin, Miriam. *Lower! Higher! You're a Liar!* Illus. Richard Egielski. New York: Harper, 1984. 133p.

Molly, ten, is smart and self-satisfied and talks to God through her bedroom window. When the neighborhood bully takes timid Estelle's bracelet, a scared Molly faces up to her and gets it back. A fine portrayal of child's typical, self-centered, naive but truly genuine religious feelings. Molly's kosher, devout family is lively and likable, and her friends true to life products of Brooklyn in the late 1930s. Third to fifth grades.

853. Cushnir, Howard. *The Secret Spinner: Tales of Rav Gedalia*. Illus. Katherine Janus Kahn. Rockville, Md.: Kar-Ben, 1985. 48p.

In four short stories children in a Jewish suburban day school are taught little lessons by an elderly, caring, inventive Romanian rabbi. In the first, disturbed by their lack of charity, the rabbi concocts a talking tzedakah box from a computer. In the second, worried about their lack of consideration for others, he makes a shy girl the only one to see the prophets during a school Sukkot sleep-out. In the third, upset because Ari is mean to his little brother, the rabbi greases Ari's dreidle so that it shoots down a drain, and only little Tzvi's arm is small enough to reach for it. In the fourth, appalled by trash on the campus, the rabbi invents a garbage-eating machine. Forced plots and contrived characters, but the Rav is appealing and the writing adequate. Plenty of peppy black-and-white drawings. Second to fifth grades.

854. Hautzig, Esther. *The Seven Good Years: And Other Stories of I.L. Peretz*. Illus. Deborah Kogan Ray. Philadelphia: Jewish Publication Society of America, 1984. 94p.

Ten short stories adapted from the Yiddish originals include tales of wealth, poverty, miracles, long-suffering, conscience, and faith rewarded. Many have a folktale quality. Hazy black-and-white drawings in which the figures seem frozen in time and space reinforce the quiet depth of the text. For thoughtful, imaginative readers fifth grade and up.

855. Herman, Ben. *The Rhapsody in Blue of Mickey Klein*. Owings Mill, Md.: Stemmer, 1981. 143p.

Suffering from adolescent growing pains and a vivid imagination, twelve-year-old Mickey sweeps through life in

1939 Baltimore. He is thrown out of Hebrew school for reading a pornographic book, becomes friends with a fiery black preacher, studies for his Bar Mitzvah, has adventures with his uncle, and loses his father. Nostalgic, funny, touching, and authentic. Sixth grade and up.

856. Kaplan, Bess. *The Empty Chair*. New York: Harper & Row, 1975. 243p.

Ten-year-old Rebecca, sensitive child in a poor Canadian Jewish family, is devastated by her mother's death in childbirth and is reluctant to accept a stepmother. Deals with the meaning of death in Judaism, Jewish customs, perennial problems of Jews in a Christian culture. The book takes place in the 1930s; the emotions portrayed have poignancy and are appealing and universal. Has a glossary of Yiddish words. Fourth to sixth grades.

857. Ruby, Lois. *Two Truths in My Pocket*. New York: Fawcett, 1982. 116p.

This is a collection of short stories that generally expresses the Jewish experience. Micah and Chava are rabbi's children in a small Vermont town; to his horror the rabbi discovers his daughter wants to carry on the family rabbinical tradition, but his son does not. Mildly retarded Tracy is the only truly observant Jew in her uncaring family. Bobby falls madly in love with his English teacher and surprisingly gets valuable help from a young Catholic priest on how to break the spell. After Lauren dates a Gentile boy, she appreciates the valuable closeness of her own family. A Black Jewish teenager is received coldly by the youth group. When her great grandmother dies, a girl realizes she never tried to understand her aged relative. It is well written but often blatantly didactic. Fifth grade and up.

858. Schur, Maxine. *Schnook the Peddler*. Illus. Dale Redpath. Minneapolis: Dillon, 1985. 37p.

Sweet, short tale of a boy in rural Russia who keeps a dreidle dropped by an absent-minded peddler, who is an object of ridicule in the community. Suffering strong pangs of conscience, the boy finds the man sheltering in the synagogue, is gently forgiven and wisely counseled, and respects the peddler from then on. An effective story with strong, capably done black-and-white drawings that reflect the thoughtful mood. Contains a glossary. Fourth to sixth grades.

859. Taylor, Sydney. *All-of-a-Kind Family* (1966, 192p.). *All-of-a-Kind Family Downtown* (1972, 187p.). *All-of-a-Kind Family Uptown* (1958, 160p.). *Ella of All-of-a-Kind Family* (1978, 133p.). New York: Dell.

Depicts the growth of five little girls as the family moves about New York City before and after World War I, in the days when a trip to Coney Island was the ultimate treat. Eventually a little brother is added to the loving, close group. Religious holidays are explained, and their celebration described tenderly. Demonstrates wholesome traditional values in a sentimental, nostalgic way. Describes close friendships with non-Jewish neighbors and classmates. Has appealing black-and-white drawings by various artists. Third to sixth grades.

860. Vogiel, Eva. *A Problem Called Chavi*. Illus. Harvey Klineman. New York: Feldheim, 1985. 152p.

Shifra, a student at a Jewish girls' school in Newfield, England, wants to befriend Chavi, the new girl who is defensive and withdrawn but a brilliant writer. It takes an automobile accident and a Hanukkah play to bring them together. Depicts the daily life of well-to-do, observant British community. The plot is designed for obvious happy ending, but the writing is lively and skillful. Contains black-and-white sketches. Fourth to sixth grades.

861. Weilerstein, Sadie Rose. *Ten and a Kid*. Illus. Janina Domanska. Garden City, N.Y.: Doubleday, 1961. 187p.

A white kid mysteriously appears in Elijah's chair at the Pesach seder of a poor Lithuanian family. Subsequently many of their fondest wishes--feathers for bedding, a suitor for daughter Esther, school for eager Reizel--begin coming true during the following year. Family life, holiday customs, and the joy of small blessings are warmly and touchingly portrayed in a sprightly, affectionate style with matching black-and-white drawings. Has a glossary. Fourth to sixth grades.

862. Wolitzer, Hilma. *Wish You Were Here*. New York: Farrar, 1984. 180p.

The coming-of-age story of Bernie Segal, who learns to accept his mother's remarriage, finds his first girl friend, and copes with two sisters while working through his grief for his dead father. His final step is to take his father's first name officially in a synagogue ceremony. Describes a close-knit, loving family. Fifth grade and up.

JEWS AND CHRISTIANS

Fiction

863. Blume, Judy. *Are You There God? It's Me, Margaret.* Scarsdale, N.Y.: Bradbury, 1970. 160p.

Eleven-year-old Margaret is the child of a Christian mother and Jewish father. Her maternal grandparents are estranged from the family, and her paternal grandmother, a loving and possessive woman, is constantly pressing her to be Jewish. Although Margaret does not affiliate herself with either side, she has a warm personal relationship with God. A realistic, understanding, appealing work. Fifth and sixth grades.

864. Goddard, Alice L. *David, My Jewish Friend.* Illus. Siegmund Forst. New York: Friendship, 1967. 62p.

This is a helpful vehicle for interfaith understanding. Curious about the religious life of her friend David, Christian Margaret learns about Jewish beliefs, visits the synagogue, joins in some holiday celebrations, and is reminded that Jesus as a Jew experienced all these things. She is encouraged by David's parents and her own. Contains drawings. Third to fifth grades.

865. Potok, Chaim. *Davita's Harp.* New York: Knopf, 1985. 371p.

Depicts Davita's girlhood from age seven through early adolescence. Her father's background is Christian, her mother's Orthodox Jewish, but both have been driven by childhood traumas into the Communist Party. Davita is bright, solitary, neglected, and anxious. She seeks stability, and Judaism draws her into its warm fold, although a beloved aunt tries hard to win her to Christianity. Although it is introspective and rather slow moving, it is well and strongly written. Good readers sixth grade and up.

866. Smith, Doris Buchanan. *Laura Upside-Down.* New York: Viking, 1984. 148p.

Atheist Laura, Jewish Zipporah, and Fundamentalist Christian Anna are close, caring, ten-year-old friends. Some conflict ensues, as Anna believes her friends as non-Christians will go to hell, and Zipporah resents their ignorance of Jewish customs, but they cherish one another nevertheless and give a fine series of ecumenical holiday parties for Halloween, Thanksgiving, Hanukkah, and Christmas. Done in a non-judgmental, thoughtful, funny, and convincing manner. Third to fifth grades.

867. Sussman, Susan. *There's No Such Thing as a Chanukah Bush, Sandy Goldstein*. Illus. Charles Robinson. Niles, Ill.: Whitman, 1983. 48p.

Feeling deprived and uncomfortable amid all the fourth-grade preparations for Christmas, Robin asks her mother for a Chanukah bush and is gently denied. Surprisingly, her grandfather invites her to his union Christmas party, and she has a wonderful time enjoying the secular side of the holiday. She prays that a new friend will win the big Christmas tree and learns that sharing the holiday does not make one a Christian, just as inviting a Catholic girl to a Chanukah celebration does not make her a Jew. This is a lively and understanding book. Contains drawings. Kindergarten to fourth grade.

RABBIS

Fiction

868. Hurwitz, Johanna. *The Rabbi's Girls*. Illus. Pamela Johnson. New York: Morrow, 1982. 158p.

Depicts a year of joy and sorrow for eleven-year-old Carrie, her mother, five sisters, and her rabbi father. They encounter the sting of prejudice both from their Christian neighbor and a Jew who condemns them for consulting a non-Jewish physician, but generally life is enjoyable until a killer tornado strikes their small Ohio town. Then Papa exhausts himself tending his congregation after the storm and dies. A gentle and moving portrayal of family life, customs, superstitions, holidays, and ceremonies, combined with the duties and special problems of a rabbi. It is done in a serious, straightforward style. Has black-and-white pencil drawings of plain, sturdy people. Fourth to sixth grades.

869. Portnoy, Mindy Avra. *Ima on the Bima: My Mommy Is a Rabbi*. Illus. Steffi Karen Rubin. Rockville, Md.: Kar-Ben, 1986. unp.

The daily life of a young woman rabbi as seen through the eyes of her five-year-old daughter with descriptions of home life and holiday celebrations. Duties include counseling, performing weddings, leading Shabbat services, teaching religious school. It is written winningly from child's viewpoint and has realistic, attractive illustrations in black and white. Preschool to second grade.

SYNAGOGUE

870. Olivestone, Ceil, and David Olivestone. *Let's Go to Synagogue*. Illus. Arien Zeldich. New York: SBS, 1981. unp.

A little boy enjoys his experiences in the synagogue. This is a brief, basic story with winsome blue, red, and gold pictures. Has a glossary for parents. Preschool.

871. Sugarman, Joan G. *Inside the Synagogue*. Rev. ed. New York: Union of American Hebrew Congregations, 1984. unp.

Clear black-and-white photographs illustrate this fact-filled, simply written text about all aspects of the synagogue: the Holy Ark and parochet; the Torah, mantle, decorations; menorah; eternal light; artwork; siddur and its prayers; music; the rabbi. Contains a glossary. Kindergarten to fourth grade.

MISCELLANEOUS

872. Ginsburg, Marvell. *The Tattooed Torah*. Illus. Jo Gershman. New York: Union of American Hebrew Congregations, 1983. unp.

Based upon actual incidents in Czechoslovakia during World War II and afterward. A little Torah, perfect for children to carry, is happily living among regal large Torahs in Brno when Nazi soldiers roughly remove them from the synagogue, dump them in a warehouse, and tattoo them with identification numbers. After the war Little Torah is rescued by an American Jew and once again leads a joyful life in a Hebrew school. Flat black, white, and gold drawings. Kindergarten to fourth grade.

873. McDermott, Beverly Brodsky. *The Golem: A Jewish Legend.* Illus. author. Philadelphia: Lippincott, 1976. unp.

Has a striking format with powerful, frightening illustrations in black and burning colors perfect for this eerie folktale of the clay man created by a rabbi to protect the Jews of Prague. When the ghetto is stormed and burned by Gentiles, the Golem grows huge and vengeful. Horrified at the folly of opposing evil with more evil, the rabbi destroys him. Kindergarten to fourth grade.

874. Singer, Isaac Bashevis. *Elijah the Slave.* Illus. Antonio Frasconi. New York: Farrar, 1970. unp.

An old Hebrew legend in which Elijah is sent from heaven to a poverty-stricken scribe afflicted with a paralyzed hand. First he heals the scribe and then demands to be sold into slavery for a huge sum of money to make the scribe wealthy. He rewards his rich purchaser by building him a miraculous palace. Splendid illustrations, primitive in feeling and dazzling in design and color. Kindergarten to third grade.

875. Singer, Isaac Bashevis. *The Golem.* Illus. Uri Shulevitz. New York: Farrar, 1982. 85p.

To protect an exemplary Jew who is being unjustly accused by her unscrupulous father of kidnapping a little Christian girl, God sends a messenger to a pious rabbi ordering him to construct a giant clay man. The Golem's mission is to find the child and confound the Jew's persecutors. He succeeds but then wants to become human instead of sinking back into the earth. A pleasant and humorous story with folktale cadences and appropriately weird black-and-white illustrations. Third to sixth grades.

HOLIDAYS

General

876. Adler, David A. *A Picture Book of Jewish Holidays.* Illus. Linda Heller. New York: Holiday, 1981. 32p.

The Sabbath, Rosh Hashanah, Yom Kippur, Sukkot, Simchat

Torah, Hanukkah, Purim, Pesach, and ten other holidays are presented for very young children, with a bit of history and some celebratory customs for each. The text and clever, decorative illustrations in olive, blue, and gold are perfectly matched. Contains a glossary and calendar. Preschool to second grade.

877. Brinn, Ruth Esrig. *Let's Celebrate!* Illus. Stephanie Mensh. Rockville, Md.: Kar-Ben, 1977. 72p.

Fifty-seven crafts for small children that use basic materials such as popsicle sticks, empty spools, aluminum foil, brown bags, etc. to make decorative items for holidays. Included are candlesticks for Shabbat, a Rosh Hashanah shofar, a fruit mobile for Sukkot, a Maccabee puppet for Hanukkah, etc. Also includes recipes for uncooked snacks. Has simple directions and patterns in blue and white. Kindergarten to second grade.

878. Brinn, Ruth Esrig. *Let's Have a Party: 100 Mix-and-Match Party Ideas for the Jewish Holidays*. Illus. Madeline Wikler. Rockville, Md.: Kar-Ben, 1981. 79p.

Invitations, decorations, games, place cards, menus and recipes, and favors for Rosh Hashanah, Sukkot, Hanukkah, Tu B'Shevat, Purim, Pesach, Yom Ha'atzmant, Lag Ba'omer, Shavuot, Shabbat are given with easy-to-follow directions that can be used at home or school. Also has lists of party manners, holiday symbols and a good general subject index. Done in a very bright format with simple drawings. Third to sixth grades.

879. Brinn, Ruth Esrig. *More Let's Celebrate!* Illus. Katherine Janus Kahn. Rockville, Md.: Kar-Ben, 1984. 72p.

Fifty-seven easy crafts for Shabbat, Rosh Hashanah-Yom Kippur, Simchat Torah, Hanukkah, Tu B'shevat, Purim, Pesach, Shavuot, Lag Ba'omer, and Yom Ha'atzmant that call for everyday materials like egg cartons, tissue paper, shoe boxes, etc. They include a spice box, a miniature table top succah, Moses bath toy, birdfeeder, and so on. Done in a purple and white format with diagrams and drawings. Kindergarten to second grade.

880. Cashman, Greer Fay. *Jewish Days and Holidays*. Illus. Alona Frankel. New York: SBS, 1979. 61p.

The reasons for, dates of, and celebratory customs of eleven holidays told in a colorful, readable text and illustrated with amusing, creative, stylized pictures.

Supplementary encyclopedic information appears in side columns. Kindergarten to fourth grade.

881. Cedarbaum, Sophia N. *A First Book of Jewish Holidays*. Illus. Marlene Lobell Ruthen. New York: Union of American Hebrew Congregations, 1984. 72p.

Twins Debbie and Danny participate in celebrations of Shabbat, the High Holy Days, Sukkot, Simchat Torah, Hanukkah, Tu B'shivat, Purim, Pesach, and Shavuot at home, in the synagogue, and in school. The history of the holidays is touched upon, but the emphasis is on religious services, including confirmation of boys and girls at Shavuot, and holiday customs and foods--areas appealing to young children. It is detailed yet simply written and has songs and blessings. Depicted in a comfortable American setting in large three-color drawings. Preschool to early elementary.

882. Greenberg, Judith E., and Helen H. Carey. *Jewish Holidays*. New York: Watts, 1984. 66p.

A very well presented, clear, thorough introduction to the subject that would be of interest to anyone. Gives the background and celebration of the High Holy Days, the Harvest Holidays, the festivals, Passover, Shabbat, and the modern historical holidays. Some recipes and crafts are included. It is illustrated with a few black-and-white photographs that are of moderate interest. Contains an index and bibliography. Third to sixth grades.

Fiction

883. Ganz, Yaffa. *Savta Simcha and the Cinnamon Tree*. Illus. Bina Gewirtz. New York: Feldheim, 1984. 96p.

Savta Simcha has a deep faith in Hashem and a magical touch with plants, birds, and animals. She and her brother Nechemya and Ezra, an orphan boy, have various cozy little adventures in and about Jerusalem at Purim, Pesach, Lag Ba'omer and Tisha B'Av. The lively pictures are in color and black and white. Third to sixth grades.

884. Rabinowitz, Sholom. *Holiday Tales of Sholom Aleichem*. Illus. Thomas di Grazia. New York: Atheneum, 1979. 145p.

With bittersweet humor seven wry short stories deal with Jews in a Ukrainian village. Each centers about a holiday celebration that ends in disaster or disappointment. The sukkah roof collapses, a boy uses a crooked dreidle to bilk his friends, a greedy child bites the stem off the esrog, etc. Has vivid characterization. Evocative black-and-white drawings of mischievous boys and sturdy adults. Fifth grade and up.

885. Sofer, Barbara. *The Holiday Adventures of Achbar*. Illus. Nina Gaelen. Rockville, Md.: Kar-Ben, 1983. 63p.

Achbar, an observant Jewish mouse living in Detective Schuster's house, solves seven mysteries, each one associated with a Jewish holiday. Every time he must attract the detective's attention to an important clue leading to the answer. The plots are slight and improbable. Has black-and-white drawings. Third and fourth grades.

886. Weilerstein, Sadie Rose. *The Best of K'Tonton*. Illus. Marilyn Hirsch. Philadelphia: Jewish Publication Society of America, 1980. 94p.

Sprightly fairy tales about a Jewish Tom Thumb who is basically a good boy but much too inquisitive. His adventures often center about holiday celebrations. He is mixed into the dough for the Purim hamantashen, rides a spinning dreidle out the door and down the street, dangles from his father's lulav in the synagogue, and so on. All the stories have gentle morals. Contains large, action-filled black-and-white drawings and a glossary. Kindergarten to fourth grade.

887. Weilerstein, Sadie Rose. *What the Moon Brought*. Illus. Mathilda Keller. Philadelphia: Jewish Publication Society of America, 1970. 159p.

Celebrations of Rosh Hashanah, Yom Kippur, Succot, Purim, Shabbat, Pesach, and other holidays form the backgrounds for sweet, old-fashioned little stories about two small sisters from a comfortable, loving home. Done in a simple style with large type. Since it was originally published in 1942, some of the material is outdated, but that does not detract from its appeal. Has vintage black-and-white drawings. Preschool to second grade.

Individual Holidays

BAR AND BAT MITZVAH

888. Greenfeld, Howard. *Bar Mitzvah*. Illus. Elaine Grove. New York: Holt, 1981. unp.

Describes the roots of the belief that a boy assumes the full responsibility for religious practices as they are found in the Midrash, Talmud, Pirke Avot; a boy's responsibilities concerning the minyan, tallit, and tefillin, depending upon his branch of Judaism; a boy's training for the ceremony and its celebration. There is a brief section on bat mitzvah, the girl's equivalent ceremony. Done in a lucid, dignified style in an attractive format with bold scratchboard drawings. Fifth grade and up.

889. Metter, Bert. *Bar Mitzvah, Bat Mitzvah: How Jewish Boys and Girls Come of Age*. Illus. Marvin Friedman. New York: Clarion, 1984. 55p.

A basic, preparatory explanation of how bar and bat mitzvah developed and what they entail. Includes the ceremony, the new duties and privileges, and the celebration afterward. The memorable significance of this special day is stressed. It is easy to read and understand and illustrated with attractive brown-and-white sketches. Fourth grade and up.

890. Rosoff, David. *Growing Up: A Bar Mitzvah Story*. New York: Feldheim, 1984. 200p.

In the framework of a bare story about two boys, twelve and fifteen, going to their cousin's bar mitzvah, the book gives a wealth of facts about its significance. Included is a lengthy section on the correct usage of the tefillin. It is serious, theological, authoritative in tone. Contains an annotated glossary and an appendix of brief biographical sketches of various sages. Fifth grade and up.

Fiction

891. Asher, Sandy. *Daughters of the Law*. New York: Dell, 1980. 157p.

Although her late father rebelled against his Jewishness because of his suffering in the Holocaust and refused to allow the family to attend synagogue, a reluctant Ruthie is being pressed hard by her aunt to return to her faith and have bat mitzvah. When her mother finally tells her the full story of the past, Ruthie overcomes her terror and returns proudly to Judaism. Sixth grade and up.

892. Kaufman, Stephen. *Does Anyone Here Know the Way to Thirteen?* Boston: Houghton Mifflin, 1985. 157p.

Myron dreads his approaching bar mitzvah for various reasons: he is paired with Gary, who thinks he is a wimp, and he feels ignorant and uncomfortable about Judaism. But a combination of circumstances--meeting a rabbi's sympathetic daughter, making an important hit in a Little League game, knocking out Gary, and despite losing four teeth just before the ceremony, continuing with his haftorah anyway--gives him new confidence. In the end his growing appreciation of his Jewishness leads him to choose a Hebrew high school. The plot and most of the characters are contrived to make an obvious point, but Myron is wry and likeable. Fourth to sixth grades.

893. Konigsburg, E.L. *About the B'nai Bagels.* New York: Dell, 1969. 172p.

Mark, twelve, is "seriously in the business of being Hebrew." He is preparing for his bar mitzvah while playing on a Little League team sponsored by the sisterhood and managed enthusiastically by his mother, with the help of his brother. He learns to become a man through both experiences. Funny and fast moving with sharp dialogue and characterization. Fourth grade and up.

894. Provost, Gary, and Gail Levine-Freidus. *Good if It Goes.* Scarsdale, N.Y.: Bradbury, 1984. 146p.

Twelve-year-old David is horrified because he will have to go to Hebrew school twice a week to prepare for his bar mitzvah and thus jeopardize his shrimp league basketball career and his budding romance with a Catholic girl. After his beloved grandfather explains the significance of the ceremony in Jewish tradition, David eventually becomes absorbed in his preparations and proud of his heritage. Has snappy dialogue and lighthearted tone. Fifth grade and up.

895. Rosenblum, Richard. *My Bar Mitzvah.* Illus. author. New York: Morrow, 1985. unp.

Richard and his family launch preparations for the ceremony by picking huckleberries in the Catskills to make the wine. City scenes follow: wine in clay crocks in the basement; boys misbehaving in Hebrew school; goodies being cooked; a new suit being fitted; the synagogue packed with relatives, co-workers, neighbors, and friends. Afterward the congregation descends on the house for monumental refreshments and gift-giving. This lively narrative captures the happiness, tradition, and importance of this milestone in a boy's life as it depicts a middle-class family in 1941. Busy pen and ink drawings showing mischievous children and proud, self-satisfied adults capture the spirit of the occasion perfectly. Third to sixth grades.

HANUKKAH

896. Adler, David A. *Hanukkah Fun Book*. New York: Bonim, 1976. 47p.

Riddles, mazes, memory quizzes, scrambled words, rebuses, number puzzles, tricks, hidden words, and other games deal with the Magen David, shamash, dreidles, miracle of the oil, etc. Contains drawings. Third grade and up.

897. Adler, David A. *Hanukkah Game Book*. New York: Bonim, 1978. 48p.

Antiochus, dreidles, Maccabees, candles, menorahs, and other aspects of the season are enlivened by word identification and memory games, riddles, mazes, a crossword puzzle, board games to cut out, etc. Has drawings. Third grade and up.

898. Adler, David A. *A Picture Book of Hanukkah*. Illus. Linda Heller. New York: Holiday, 1982. 32p.

Principally a simple, lively retelling of the historical events in which Mattathias, his son Judah, and the Maccabees confound Antiochus and cleanse and rededicate the Temple. Contains a few facts about holiday celebrations at the end. It has well-designed, witty illustrations in earth tones of doll-like figures of robed Jews and helmeted, barefoot Greek soldiers. Preschool to third grade.

899. Behrens, June. *Hanukkah*. Chicago: Children's Press, 1983. 32p.

Much holiday information about special foods, the Maccabee story, the eight-day miracle of the sacred oil, lighting the menorah, games, gifts, songs, worship service at the Temple. Has adequate color photographs that follow one family's celebration at home and in the synagogue. Third grade and up.

900. Chaikin, Miriam. *Light Another Candle: The Story and Meaning of Hanukkah*. Illus. Demi. New York: Clarion, 1981. 80p.

Along with a concise account of the Jews' suffering under

Antiochus and the Maccabees' triumph, the growth of the holiday itself is detailed. Jews throughout the world and throughout the centuries have celebrated with joy and determination, sometimes in secret, in a variety of ways. There are sections on the history of the Temple and the Law. Has precise, elegant, humorous drawings in black, white, and red, a glossary, bibliography, and index. Third grade and up.

901. Charette, Beverly Rae. *The Story of Chanukah for Children*. Illus. Dick Keller. Milwaukee: Ideals, 1981. unp.

The history of the Syrian defilement of the Temple, the oppression of the Jews, and the defeat by the Maccabees, along with the miracle of the oil, are told in simple verse form. Also describes holiday customs such as latkes, menorah-lighting, dreidles, songs, gifts. Large, busy, undistinguished color pictures. Preschool and kindergarten.

902. Drucker, Malka. *Hanukkah: Eight Nights, Eight Lights*. Illus. Brom Hoban. New York: Holiday, 1980. 95p. Jewish Holidays Book Series.

A lucid explanation of the historical events surrounding the holiday followed by chapters on the meaning and lighting of the candles, dreidle and word games, foods and recipes, various types of menorahs, Hanukkah symbols and crafts, celebrations throughout history and the world. Done in a sprightly style, with black-and-white photographs and drawings. Third grade and up.

903. Fisher, Aileen. *My First Hanukkah Book*. Illus. Priscilla Kiedrowski. Chicago: Children's Press, 1985. 31p.

Short, simple verses, from four to thirteen lines long, express cheery thoughts about crisp potato pancakes, merry dreidle games, glowing menorahs, shiny gelt, the long-ago miracle in the Temple, etc. Brightly colored, flat pictures of children preparing for and enjoying the holiday. Preschool to second grade.

904. Gellman, Ellie. *It's Chanukah!* Illus. Katherine Janus Kahn. Rockville, Md.: Kar-Ben, 1985. unp.

Gila and little Josh use objects associated with Hanukkah to find shapes, identify colors, count from one to eight. They also play holiday games and eat snacks. The book has extremely bright, well-defined artwork. Preschool.

905. Goffstein, M.B. *Laughing Latkes.* Illus. author. New York: Farrar, 1980. unp.

This very short tribute to Hanukkah in which deceptively simple, appealingly animated black-and-white drawings show delighted potato pancakes approving dreidle games, the saving of the Temple and Judah Maccabee, Golda Meir and other mothers frying latkes, and a Hanukkah gift book. Preschool to second grade.

906. Greenfeld, Howard. *Chanukah.* New York: Holt, 1976. 39p.

Well-written and interesting short history of the joyous eight-day holiday celebrating the defeat of Antiochus by the Maccabees, the purification of the Temple, and the miraculous supply of undefiled oil. The history begins with the forced Hellenization of Jews and cruel repression of Judaism and details the Israelites' victorious struggle for religious freedom. Done in a handsome format. Fourth grade and up.

907. Saypol, Judyth Robbins, and Madeline Wikler. *My Very Own Chanukah Book.* Rockville, Md.: Kar-Ben, 1977. 32p.

Lively retelling of Antiochus-Judah Maccabee-cleansing of the Temple story for early elementary ages. Includes candlelighting ritual, suggested Hanukkah meditations on miracles, legends, freedom, gift giving, dreidle and bingo games, recipes for latkes and doughnuts, and songs with music and words in transliterated Hebrew and Yiddish. It is in a good-looking brown, orange, and white format. Kindergarten to third grade.

908. Shostak, Myra. *Rainbow Candles: A Chanukah Counting Book.* Illus. Katherine Janus Kahn. Rockville, Md.: Kar-Ben, 1986. unp.

A ponytailed little girl counts the candles in the menorah day by day, gets presents, spins her dreidles, mixes latkes, receives her coins, and generally enjoys the holiday. The book has clear numerals, with sets of objects to be counted multiplying daily. Contains gay, bright pictures. Preschool to kindergarten.

909. Simon, Norma. *Hanukkah.* Illus. Symeon Shimin. New York: Crowell, 1966. unp. Crowell Holiday Book Series.

Recounts the conflict between Antiochus and Mattathias and the Maccabees; the legend of the miraculous oil; the lighting of the menorah and other holiday customs; Hanukkah in Israel in factual, explanatory style. There are artistic, pensive black-and-white and three-color scenes of the past history and present celebration. Third to fifth grades.

Fiction

910. Aleichem, Sholem. *Hanukkah Money*. Illus. Uri Shulevitz. New York: Greenwillow, 1978. 32p.

A tough and funny short tale of two little brothers gloating over the Hanukkah gelt they have extracted from their father and uncles. Although meager, they consider it so munificent that they cannot even add it all up. This is a small gem of family life in a Russian village setting and is perfectly illustrated with stout, kerchiefed women; stooped, bearded men; stumpy, jug-eared children, done in muted tones of brown and gold. The effect is humorous and full of life. Kindergarten to fourth grade.

911. Burstein, Chaya. *Hanukkah Cat*. Illus. author. Rockville, Md.: Kar-Ben, 1985. unp.

A cold, orange-striped kitten arrives at Lenny's house on the first night of Hanukkah and upsets the family by getting into everything. But when Lenny gets lost while trying to find the kitten a new home, she guides him safely back to his own house and finally becomes a family member. Interwoven in the cozy plot are the Judah Maccabee story, the candle-lighting, and a dreidle game. The text is lively; the drawings are done in orange and black wash. Kindergarten to fourth grade.

912. Chaikin, Miriam. *Yossi Asks the Angels for Help*. Illus. Petra Mathers. New York: Harper & Row, 1985. 52p.

On the eve of the first night of Hanukkah Yossi manages to lose his two dollars of gelt with which he planned to buy his sister and parents gifts. Praying fiercely, he hopes the angels who come when the first Hanukkah candle is lit will help him find his money. In the end he uses his God-given common sense instead. The book has penetrating characterization, dry humor, and black-and-white pictures done in primitive style. Third to fifth grades.

913. Hirsh, Marilyn. *I Love Hanukkah*. Illus. author. New York: Holiday, 1984. unp.

A little boy's grandfather tells him the story of Mattathias, Judah Maccabee, the cleansing of the Temple, and the menorah miracle. His mother explains the candle lighting. The story also incorporates the significance of the dreidle, gifts, potato pancakes. Big, cheerful family figures and crowded, lively Bible story scenes are done in low-key colors. Preschool to second grade.

914. Sherman, Eileen Bluestone. *The Odd Potato: A Chanukah Story*. Illus. Katherine Janus Kahn. Rockville, Md.: Kar-Ben, 1984. unp.

Since Rachel's mother died, her father no longer wants to celebrate holidays. Nevertheless Rachel does the best she can to prepare for Hanukkah. Unable to find her mother's menorah, she uses a potato for the candles. Her efforts bring her father out of his shell at last. The work has strong, expressive pictures of the family in sad and happy times. Kindergarten to third grade.

915. Singer, Isaac Bashevis. *The Power of Light: Eight Stories for Hanukkah*. Illus. Irene Lieblich. New York: Farrar, 1980. 87p.

Each tale is associated with a Hanukkah event, but they vary in tone and setting. Some are miraculous, some realistic. Subjects range from a Yiddish-speaking parakeet, to a ghost demanding a holiday celebration, to teenagers hiding in the bombed-out Warsaw ghetto and secretly lighting Hanukkah candles. Illustrated with strong, glowing, primitive-style pictures. Fifth grade and up.

HIGH HOLY DAYS

916. Drucker, Malka. *Rosh Hashanah and Yom Kippur: Sweet Beginnings*. Illus. Bram Hoban. New York: Holiday, 1981. 95p. Jewish Holidays Book Series.

The concepts of the tefillah, teshuvah, tzedakah, and their concomitant soul-searching, asking forgiveness, and self dedication to a holier life are clearly and practically expressed and serve as an inspiration for anyone beginning a new year. Includes holiday history, prayers, rituals, customs, recipes, crafts, games, a glossary, reading list, index, and black-and-white photographs and drawings. Fifth grade and up.

917. Greenfeld, Howard. *Rosh Hashanah and Yom Kippur*. Illus. Elaine Grove. New York: Holt, 1979. 31p.

Breadth and depth of Judaic ethics are apparent in a serious, factual discussion of the High Holy Days. Rosh

Hashanah opens the new year and begins a solemn, ten-day period of self-examination, repentance, and gratitude. Yom Kippur ends the period with prayer, fasting, and ceremony. Done in a dignified format with black-and-white scratchboard decoration in formal patterns. Fifth grade and up.

918. Saypol, Judyth Robbins, and Madeline Wikler. *My Very Own Rosh Hashanah Book*. Rockville, Md.: Kar-Ben, 1978. 32p.

The purpose and customs of the holiday presented for young children. The shofar, tzedakah, home and synagogue services, folktales, anecdotes, blessings, and prayers with music are explained in short sentences in large type. The drawings are in orange and blue. Kindergarten to fourth grade.

919. Saypol, Judyth Robbins, and Madeline Wikler. *My Very Own Yom Kippur Book*. Rockville, Md.: Kar-Ben, 1978. 32p.

Serious, contemplative holiday interpreted for small children in terms of forgiving others and asking forgiveness of God and other people for sins such as rudeness, lying, and unfairness. Discusses special services such as Kol Nidre and Neilah in the synagogue and at home. Contains blessings and songs with music and appropriate folk tales. Has three-color drawings. Preschool to fourth grade.

Fiction

920. Chaikin, Miriam. *Finders Weepers*. Illus. Richard Egielski. New York: Harper, 1980. 120p.

Molly's High Holy Days become a time of fear and guilt because at Rosh Hashanah she has found a gold ring and not returned it to its owner. Her baby brother is hospitalized and she feels it is her fault. Once the ring is returned just before Yom Kippur, the baby feels better and Molly is greatly relieved. Fine details of family life in Brooklyn just before World War II. This is a funny, warmhearted book with realistic characters. The black-and-white drawings are quiet in feeling. Third to sixth grades.

921. Cohen, Barbara. *Yussel's Prayer: A Yom Kippur Story*. Illus. Michael J. Deraney. New York: Lothrop, 1981. unp.

A beautifully told story. Although he cannot attend shul

because he must care for the cattle herd, Yussel fasts and prays on Yom Kippur. In spite of the prayers rising from the congregation in the synagogue, the gate of heaven will not open until Yussel plays a melody to God on his flute. This pure, true devotion seals the Book of Life for the year. Contains strong, handsome pictures. First to fourth grades.

922. Fass, David E. *The Shofar That Lost Its Voice*. Illus. Marlene L. Ruthen. New York: Union of American Hebrew Congregations, 1982. 41p.

A fantasy in which a delighted Avi is asked to blow the shofar for the children's services on the High Holy Days. While he is practicing the various sounds, the shofar becomes puzzlingly mute. Suddenly Avi shrinks to a tiny size and passes through the shofar into a perfect world. There he must convince the shofar spirit to send its music again into his imperfect world. Illustrated with black-and-white drawings. Fourth to sixth grades.

PASSOVER

923. Adler, David A. *Passover Fun Book*. New York: Bonim, 1978. 48p.

There are rebuses, magic tricks, riddles, fill-in-the-blanks, quizzes, crossword and other puzzles, and identification games associated with aspects of the holiday such as matzot, wine cups, Had Gadya, etc., as well as drawings. Third grade and up.

924. Adler, David A. *A Picture Book of Passover*. Illus. Linda Heller. New York: Holiday, 1982. 32p.

Follows Moses' life in Egypt, ending with the Hebrews crossing the Red Sea. Describes the ways of celebrating the holiday in short, punchy text. Good humored, subtly colored pictures of short, sturdy, solemn people arranged in stylized patterns. Preschool to second grade.

925. Auerbach, Julie Jaslow. *Everything's Changing--It's Pesach!* Illus. Chari Radin. Rockville, Md.: Kar-Ben, 1986. unp.

Cheery four-line verses tell about how Passover activities are different from everyday ones: different china, matzah instead of toast, reading (the Haggadah) at the table, drinking wine, playing hide and seek (for the afikomen) indoors, etc. Perky drawings in black and white and yellow show a little girl having fun. Preschool to second grade.

926. Chaikin, Miriam. *Ask Another Question: The Story and Meaning of Passover*. Illus. Marvin Friedman. New York: Clarion, 1985. 89p.

A comprehensive, vivid, and gracefully written book that traces the roots of the holiday even before the Exodus to the Festival of the Paschal Offering. It tells the story of Moses and his teachings to the Israelites, describes the evolution of the celebration and the Haggadah throughout history, including Passover in the Holocaust, gives specific details and symbolism of the seder, and describes holiday customs among Marranos, Falashas, Samaritans, Soviet Jews, and other groups. Songs include "Had Gadya" and "Who Knows One?" There are a glossary, an annotated reading list, an index, and three-color drawings. Third to sixth grades.

927. Drucker, Malka. *Passover: A Season of Freedom*. Illus. Bram Hoban. New York: Holiday, 1981. 95p. Jewish Holiday Books Series.

A condensation of Exodus is followed by thorough, felicitous detailing of Passover customs: scrubbing the house, searching for hametz, the seder with all its special traditions and holiday foods, holiday songs, and Passover blessings. In addition, there are craft ideas for Haggadah covers, Elijah's cup, and the like, games, a glossary, reading list, index, and black-and-white photographs and drawings. Third to sixth grades.

928. Galbreath, Naomi. *The Story of Passover for Children*. Illus. Kurt Avdek. Chicago: Children's Press, 1984. unp.

This "interreligious version," which may be more appropriate for Christian children studying Passover than for Jewish children, relates the story of Moses and how Passover is celebrated today and includes a page on Jesus and the Last Supper. Has strong, stern, swirling color pictures. Kindergarten to second grade.

929. Greenfeld, Howard. *Passover*. Illus. Elaine Grove. New York: Holt, 1978. 32p.

A crisp summary of the conflict between Pharaoh and the Israelites from the preservation of the infant Moses through the parting of the Red Sea introduces the three-thousand-year-old holiday which celebrates a major turning point in Jewish history. Preparation of the home and the seder meal with its special foods and traditional order are detailed with clarity and joy. Includes dramatic scratchboard illustrations in black and white. Fourth grade and up.

930. Hirsh, Marilyn. *I Love Passover*. Illus. author. New York: Holiday, 1985. unp.

A little girl asks her mother to tell the history of Passover, which she does on a basic, brief level for small children. The next day the seder is celebrated in a cozy family setting with relatives gathered about the table. Traditions include the symbolism of the various foods, the hiding of the afikoman, and the opening of the door for Elijah. Contains large, busy sketches in muted colors. Preschool to second grade.

931. Marcus, Audrey Friedman, and Raymond A. Zwerin. *But This Night Is Different: A Seder Experience*. Illus. Judith Gwyn Brown. New York: Union of American Hebrew Congregations, 1980. unp.

The special ways--foods, songs, blessings, rituals, emotions--in which the Passover seder differs from other holidays and activities are listed for small children with joyful pictures of the preparations and celebration. Preschool to second grade.

932. Rosen, Anne, and Jonathan Rosen and Norma Rosen. *A Family Passover*. Philadelphia: Jewish Publication Society of America, 1980. unp.

A complete, clear, interesting account of why Pesach is celebrated, as told by a ten-year-old girl. It describes the ceremonies from buying new clothes to the seder at Grandma's. There are homey black-and-white photographs that reflect the joy and solemnity of the occasion. Kindergarten to fourth grade.

933. Simon, Norma. *Passover*. Illus. Symeon Shimin. New York: Crowell, 1965. unp. Crowell Holiday Book Series.

The enslavement of the Hebrews in Egypt and their deliverance by God and Moses is briefly told. The section on Passover customs of today describes special foods such as dumplings, sponge cake, sweet grape wine, matzot, etc.; the beautifully set table with a Haggadah at each place; and the disappearing afikoman. Includes Samaritan and

Israeli celebrations. The book emphasizes the human right to freedom throughout. Has strong, realistic two-, three-, and four-color pictures. Fourth to sixth grades.

934. Tabs, Judy, and Barbara Steinberg. *Matzah Meals: A Passover Cookbook for Kids*. Illus. Chari R. McLean. Rockville, Md.: Kar-Ben, 1985. 72p.

The recipes are graded according to difficulty and safety (no-cook; chopping, slicing, or baking; boiling or frying) and whether meat, dairy, or parve. Gives traditional seder foods, plus additional soups, salads, appetizers, meats, international matzah dishes, sweets, and beverages and depicts seder crafts, a typical table setting, symbols, and history. It is enlivened by many pen and ink drawings. Kindergarten and up.

Fiction

935. Cohen, Barbara. *The Carp in the Bathtub*. Illus. Joan Halpern. New York: Lothrop, 1972. 48p.

Although their mama is renowned for her Passover gefilte fish, Leah and Harry won't touch it. They always make a pet of the main ingredient, a live carp which lives in their bathtub for a week before the holiday cooking begins. This is an unusual, touching story, done in a simple, expressive style in both text and large black-and-white drawings. First to fifth grades.

936. Groner, Judye, and Madeline Wikler. *Where Is the Afikomen?* Illus. Chari R. McLean. Rockville, Md.: Kar-Ben, 1985. unp.

A little girl searches under the seder plate, on top of the bookshelf, in Elijah's cup, under Daddy's kippah, etc., and finally finds the afikoman. Handsome, crisp, stylized drawings of familiar home scenes are highlighted by bright colors. Preschool.

937. Hurwitz, Johanna. *Once I Was a Plum Tree*. Illus. Ingrid Fetz. New York: Morrow, 1980. 160p.

Although she believes firmly in God, ten-year-old Geraldine, child of liberal, non-observant Jews, feels an emptiness without a guiding religion like that of her Catholic friends. A kindly German-Jewish family includes Gerry in a Passover seder, and she begins to feel a strong link with her heritage. The book gives an excellent sense of the time (1947) and place (Bronx apartment house) and has well-realized characters. Fourth to sixth grades.

938. Klass, Sheila Solomon. *Nobody Knows Me in Miami*. New York: Scribner, 1981. 149p.

A poor Orthodox family in 1937 Brooklyn allows Miriam, their lively ten-year-old, to choose if she wishes to be adopted by her wealthy Reform aunt and uncle in Florida, and leave her gentle, devout, loving parents and older sister. The story revolves around the Passover celebration, which is explained and described in detail. Fourth to sixth grades.

939. Miller, Deborah Uchill. *Only Nine Chairs: A Tall Tale for Passover*. Illus. Karen Ostrove. Rockville, Md.: Kar-Ben, 1982. unp.

Nineteen friends and relatives of all ages try to sit at a seder table where there are only nine chairs. They pile on top of one another in a disastrous pyramid, dipping parsley with fishing rods and covering themselves with matzah crumbs until a solution is finally found. Contains vivacious black-and-white drawings. Preschool to second grade.

940. Shulevitz, Uri. *The Magician: An Adaptation from the Yiddish of I.L. Peretz*. Illus. author. New York: Macmillan, 1973. 32p.

A succinctly told tale of Elijah the prophet. A mysterious, tatterdemalion magician arrives in a small village on Passover eve and asks to be the guest of a poor, elderly couple who have nothing to eat. When he provides them with an elegant feast, they rush to the rabbi in fear that his power is evil. Has dark, moody black-and-white drawings through which bundled-up peasants move wonderingly as the magician smilingly performs his tricks. Kindergarten to fourth grade.

941. Zusman, Evelyn. *The Passover Parrot*. Illus. Katherine Janus Kahn. Rockville, Md.: Kar-Ben, 1983. unp.

In a pleasantly cluttered middle-class home filled with seven children and a big green parrot the family prepares to celebrate Passover with their guests. Along with little Leba, the parrot learns the four questions in Hebrew and then steals the afikomen, adding excitement to the seder. The slight story is enlivened by busily detailed, appealing pictures. Kindergarten to third grade.

PURIM

942. Chaikin, Miriam. *Make Noise, Make Merry: The Story and Meaning of Purim*. Illus. Demi. New York: Clarion, 1983. 90p.

This imaginative, well-told narrative of Esther is introduced by a brief recounting of the Exile. Has the history of the inclusion of the Book of Esther into the Bible and the first laws governing the holiday. Today's customs include gifts to the poor, reading the scroll, special foods and drink, noisemaking, costumes, and plays. Also mentions the secret celebrations during World War II. Has a glossary and reading list and is lavishly decorated with meticulous, animated, witty purple-and-white illustrations. Third to sixth grades.

943. Greenfeld, Howard. *Purim*. Illus. Elaine Grove. New York: Holt, 1982. unp.

A dignified retelling of Esther's story followed by a short description of holiday customs: reading the Megillah, noisemaking, giving plays, and feasting. Striking format combines black-and-white illustrations with strong, foreshortened figures arranged in panels with large, handsome typeface. Fourth grade and up.

Fiction

944. Chaikin, Miriam. *Getting Even*. Illus. Richard Egielski. New York: Harper & Row, 1982. 120p.

Ten-year-old Molly's holiday is spoiled because her friend Tsippi has disappointed her. To even the score Molly tells another girl that Tsippi's parents are Communists, and much sorrow follows. Molly eats non-Kosher Chinese food, her little brother gets sick, and she is miserable with guilt. When Tsippi forgives her, Molly thanks God fervently. The setting is Brooklyn, at the beginning of World War II, and concerns a close family of observant Jews who have realistic personalities. Contains sturdy black-and-white drawings. Third to sixth grades.

945. Cohen, Barbara. *Here Come the Purim Players!* Illus. Beverly Brodsky. New York: Lothrop, 1984. unp.

An eagerly awaited Purim troupe of local actors performs before an audience of all ages gathered at Reb Zalman's house in the Prague ghetto. Comments from the crowd enliven the play, as the story of Esther and Haman is told simply and well. There are impressionistic illustrations in luminous colors. Kindergarten to third grade.

SHABBAT

946. Chaikin, Miriam. *The Seventh Day: The Story of the Jewish Sabbath.* Illus. David Frampton. Garden City, N.Y.: Doubleday, 1980. 47p.

The commandment to remember the Sabbath and keep it holy is explained by a short retelling of Exodus and Genesis, with an emphasis on God's rest on the seventh day. The history is followed by a detailed description of Sabbath customs, rituals, and prayers. The reverent prose is done in rolling cadences; there are powerful black-and-white woodcuts. Third to sixth grades.

947. Drucker, Malka. *Shabbat: A Peaceful Island.* Illus. Bram Hoban. New York: Holiday, 1983. 95p. Jewish Holidays Book Series.

Loving, in-depth examination of Shabbat's many aspects includes its evolution throughout Jewish history, synagogue services, rituals and symbolism, special Sabbaths, laws to be remembered and observed, food and recipes, crafts, folktales, word games. There is an appendix of forbidden acts, a reading list, glossary, and index, in addition to black-and-white photographs and drawings. Fourth grade and up.

948. Gellman, Ellie. *Shai's Shabbat Walk.* Illus. Chari R. McLean. Rockville, Md.: Kar-Ben, 1985. unp.

Walking with his teddy bear, a little boy sees various things that remind him that Shabbat is a time for resting, singing, hearing stories, and sharing with friends. The illustrations have simple figures in bright, basic colors. Preschool.

949. Lipson, Ruth. *Shabbos Is Coming.* Illus. Nurit Tzarfati. New York: Feldheim, 1985. unp.

Little girl in Jewish playschool tells about her daily activities at school and home as the family prepares for the Sabbath. Each day of the week has a special activity: learning about the Torah parasha, ironing the Shabbos tablecloth, cleaning, shopping, cooking, sharing the holy day with others. Depicts a comfortable, middle-class setting in gentle, conversational text with tidy drawings in four colors. Preschool and kindergarten.

950. Zwerin, Raymond A., and Audrey Friedman Marcus. *Shabbat Can Be*. Illus. Yuri Salzman. New York: Union of American Hebrew Congregations, 1979. unp.

Big, bright pictures of sweet-faced little boys and girls from happy homes and a gentle, easy text express many Sabbath joys. Describes familiar experiences with friends and family at home, in the synagogue and outdoors and stresses the Sabbath feeling in the heart. Preschool to second grade.

Fiction

951. Aronin, Ben. *The Secret of the Sabbath Fish*. Illus. Shay Rieger. Philadelphia: Jewish Publication Society of America, 1978. unp.

Childless Tante Masha, a kind widow in a small Russian village, wishes she could bring some gift to the poor people there. Elijah, disguised as a fishmonger, suggests she prepare a prize fish with the history of the Jews in mind as she blends various symbolic ingredients. The result is gefilte fish. This clever folktale has large black-and-white cartoon-style drawings. Third to fifth grades.

952. Clifford, Eth. *The Remembering Box*. Illus. Donna Diamond. Boston: Houghton Mifflin, 1985. 70p.

In 1942 nine-year-old Joshua spends almost every Sabbath with his grandmother, who lives alone. After sharing the holiday preparations and celebrating with "tears from the soul," they love to examine the treasures in an old trunk of souvenirs. When the grandmother senses that death is approaching, she prepares a special remembering box for Joshua. The grandmother's character and loving relationship with her grandson are stressed and reflect the Sabbath peace. Has realistic, almost photographic black-and-white illustrations. Third to fifth grades.

953. Leavitt, June. *The Flight to Seven Swan Bay*. Illus. Chana Galatzer. New York: Feldheim, 1985. 232p.

A small seaplane carrying observant Jews of all ages and an experienced woodsman-pilot crashes in a remote Canadian lake en route to a tiny Jewish community in the far north. The group must survive on nature's bounty alone until rescue, but they manage to celebrate the Sabbath properly, even in the wilderness. This absorbing book has an excellent sense of setting, details of woodcraft. Fifth grade and up.

954. Miller, Deborah Uchill. *Poppy Seeds, Too: A Twisted Tale for Shabbat*. Illus. Karen Ostrove. Rockville, Md.: Kar-Ben, 1982. unp.

Scrawling pen-and-ink drawings show an eccentric group of people who are dissatisfied with leaden loaves of whole wheat bread haphazardly blending white flour, honey, eggs, raisins, and poppy seeds. They are inventing challah. Next they create a cover and a board to protect it. There are captions in the form of short verses, a recipe, and blessings. Preschool to second grade.

955. Pomerantz, Barbara. *Who Will Lead Kiddush?* Illus. Donna Ruff. New York: Union of American Hebrew Congregations, 1985. unp.

A little girl whose parents are divorcing feels more secure after her father explains that she and her mother will be able to lead kiddush without him. Also, she will be visiting him often on Friday nights, and they will still be sharing the ceremony together. The continuity of the ritual and his assurance that he will always love her are comforting. Contains black-and-white drawings. Preschool to second grade.

956. Schwartz, Amy. *Mrs. Moskowitz and the Sabbath Candlesticks*. Illus. author. Philadelphia: Jewish Publication Society of America, 1983. unp.

Mrs. Moskowitz, a stout elderly lady in sensible shoes, is unhappy about giving up her house and moving into an apartment. But when her son brings her two tarnished candlesticks, a flood of happy memories is unloosed. After she polishes them, they need a tablecloth, a clean floor, a bunch of flowers, a challah, etc., etc., until the whole apartment is suddenly neat and ready for her to invite the family for the Sabbath. Gives a clear, warmhearted explanation of the Sabbath customs and has homey black-and-white pencil drawings. Kindergarten to third grade.

SUKKOT

957. Chaikin, Miriam. *Shake a Palm Branch: The Story and Meaning of Sukkot*. Illus. Marvin Friedman. New York: Clarion, 1984. 88p.

A thorough examination of the holiday includes its two-fold purpose commemorating the wandering of the Israelites in the wilderness and the first harvest festival in the Promised Land, its evolution over the centuries from the early sacrifices and water-pourings to today's special celebrations throughout the world, its traditional foods and songs. Discusses the addition of Simhat Torah. Contains a dictionary of Jewish terms, a Sukkot glossary, bibliography, and index. Skillful black-and-white drawings are emphasized with gold. Third to sixth grades.

958. Drucker, Malka. *Sukkot: A Time to Rejoice*. Illus. Bram Hoban. New York: Holiday, 1982. 96p. Jewish Holidays Book Series.

Authoritative discussion of the spirit, symbolism, and rituals of the holiday, with fine sections on the lulav and etrog, the building and decorating of a sukkah, seasonal recipes, and word games. Includes folk stories and blessings. Written in a clear, reverent manner, the book has a glossary, index, and black-and-white photographs and drawings. Fourth grade and up.

959. Saypol, Judith Robbins, and Madeline Wikler. *My Very Own Sukkot Book*. Rockville, Md.: Kar-Ben, 1980. 40p.

The history of the holiday celebrating the wandering in the desert, the harvest, and pilgrimages to Jerusalem. The building of a succah is associated with all three and the book describes the construction, decoration, and usage of the holiday succah. Several interpretations of the symbolism of the lulav and etrog are given. There are traditional blessings and songs in Hebrew and English, synagogue services, the significance of Sukkot and Thanksgiving in this lucid and attractive work. It has russet decorations of silhouetted scenes and symbols. Kindergarten to fourth grade.

Fiction

960. Adler, David A. *The House on the Roof: A Sukkot Story.* Illus. Marilyn Hirsh. Rockville, Md.: Kar-Ben, 1984. unp.

When an elderly gentleman builds a sukkah on the roof of his apartment building so that he and his grandchildren can celebrate Sukkot properly, his crabby landlady takes him to court. Big, action-filled pictures in autumnal colors fit the clever story perfectly. This is a reprint of the 1976 Bonim book. Preschool to third grade.

MISCELLANEOUS

961. Appelman, Harlene Winnick, and Jane Sherwin Shapiro. *A Seder for Tu B'Shevat.* Illus. Chari R. McLean. Rockville, Md.: Kar-Ben, 1984. 32p.

The seder for celebrating the New Year of the Trees in late January or early February recognizes the four seasons with four cups of wine and thanks God for the fruits of the vine and tree with three kinds of fruits and seeds to plant to renew the earth. The importance of conservation is stressed with anecdotes, the history of the holiday, blessings, tree lore, songs with music, suggestions for the seder plates, and other related activities. Contains cheerful drawings in green, black and white. Kindergarten and up.

962. Saypol, Judyth Robbins, and Madeline Wikler. *My Very Own Shavuot Book.* Rockville, Md.: Kar-Ben, 1982. 24p.

Describes the double celebration: of the harvest when the first fruits are brought to the Temple and of the giving of the Torah to the Jewish people. Includes simple versions of the Ten Commandments, Moses on Mt. Sinai, two Torah legends, the story of Ruth (traditionally associated with this holiday) along with customs and songs. Done in a handsome format, with monotone pages in various colors. Preschool to third grade.

963. Saypol, Judyth Robbins, and Madeline Wikler. *My Very Own Simchat Torah Book.* Rockville, Md.: Kar-Ben, 1981. 24p.

Short, direct sentences describe the contents of the Torah and its appearance, explain how the holiday celebrates its reading from beginning to end in the synagogue and then starts over again. Discusses the ceremonies of hakafot (parades), aliyah for the entire congregation, the consecration service, remembrance of Soviet Jews, etc. The book also contains Hebrew songs with music and is done in an attractive purple and white format. Preschool to third grade.

X
RELIGIONS

GENERAL WORKS

964. Ansley, Delight. *The Good Ways*. New rev. ed. Illus. Robert Hallock. New York: Crowell, 1959. 214p.

Many religions are described in very short chapters: animism and other primitive faiths, Egyptian, Old Testament, Greek, Hindu, Taoism, Islam, and Christianity. All these roads lead to God, but the way of Jesus is favored. Judgmental tone weakens an otherwise interesting and informally written work. Sixth grade and up.

965. Bailey, John, and Kenneth McLeish and David Spearman. *Gods and Men: Myths and Legends from the World's Religions*. Illus. Derek Collard, Charles Keeping, and Jeroo Roy. New York: Oxford, 1981. 143p.

A vivid, skillful retelling of traditional stories of creation, good and evil, heroes and prophets that includes many accounts of the Flood (Sumeria, India, China, Old Testament), Adam and Eve, Krishna and the serpent. David, Moses, Elijah, St. George, Sir Galahad, Mohammed, Rama, and Sikh Guru Gobind Rai are among the heroes. There are suitably powerful, but often frightening black-and-white drawings. Fifth grade and up.

966. Berger, Gilda. *Religion*. Illus. Anne Canevari Green. New York: Watts, 1983. 96p. Reference First Book Series.

A dictionary of the principal world religions includes a capsule history and theology of each, along with sects, ceremonies, important personages, scriptures, and general terms. Some definitions are brief, but many are encyclopedic. Done in crisp, factual style in a clear, well-defined format, but there are negligible illustrations. Fourth to sixth grades.

967. Farmer, Penelope. *Beginnings: Creation Myths of the World.* Illus. Antonio Frasconi. New York: Atheneum, 1978. 146p.

The origin of the world, man, food plants, death; the reasons for the Flood; the obtaining of fire for mankind; and eschatological prophecies, as seen through the eyes of many peoples, are described here. Includes Indian, Russian, Hawaiian, Native American, New Zealander, and many more, plus those from the Koran and the Bible. There is a thoughtful introduction to each section. The wide scope and powerful themes are well expressed in accompanying woodcuts and the text is smoothly written. Has a bibliography and footnotes. Fifth grade and up.

968. Gaer, Joseph. *How the Great Religions Began.* New and rev. ed. New York: Dodd, 1966. 424p.

Sprightly, easily understood accounts of the principal religions and their founders treat most beliefs fairly and stress the common ethics of them all. The principal weakness is the author's obvious preference for Protestantism over Catholicism. Some information is outdated. Sixth grade and up.

969. Haskins, James. *Religions.* Philadelphia: Lippincott, 1973. 157p.

A scholarly, matter-of-fact historical treatment of the five major faiths, with short biographies of Buddha, Jesus Christ, and Mohammed. Useful for comparing their parallel development, the book describes ritual practices, along with the gradual changes in the purity of the original beliefs. Includes the influence of sects on the youth of the 1960s. The material on traditional Christianity is not entirely accurate, but the other research seems to be careful. Has a bibliography. Sixth grade and up.

970. Moskin, Marietta D. *In Search of God: The Story of Religion.* New York: Atheneum, 1979. 142p.

The main themes are religious concepts rather than denominations. Capsule descriptions of the major faiths are given as part of the overall development of religion. Although the writing lacks a smooth flow, the treatment of the subject matter is exceptionally clear, fair, thoughtful, and comprehensive. Black-and-white photographs reproduce sculpture adequately but badly downgrade the paintings used. Sixth grade and up.

971. Moskin, Marietta D. *In the Name of God: Religion in Everyday Life*. New York: Atheneum, 1980. 185p.

A concentrated history of religion's influence on mankind, beginning with the first efforts to explain life's mysteries. Discusses religion's civilizing influence, religion and the state, religion and the sciences, religion and the arts. The material is thought provoking, impartial, easily understood. Sixth grade and up.

972. Rice, Edward. *American Saints and Seers: American-born Religions and the Genius behind Them*. New York: Four Winds, 1982. 229p.

A fact-filled examination of peculiarly American faiths, their founders, and principal leaders. Encompasses the Shakers, Mormons, Christian Scientists, Seventh Day Adventists; Jehovah's Witnesses and other millennial sects; Holiness, charismatic and Pentecostal groups; the Code of Handsome Lake, Ghost Dancers, and the peyote-using Native American Church; the evolution of the Black Muslims; and cults such as the Sanctified Sisters, House of David, People's Temple. This absorbing and perceptive work has biographical and historical information, done in an unbiased, reportorial tone. Contains a few black-and-white photographs and drawings, a bibliography, and an index. Fifth grade and up.

973. Ross, Floyd H., and Tynette Hills. *The Great Religions: By Which Men Live*. New York: Fawcett, 1956. 192p.

The underlying principles of Brahmanic Hinduism, Buddhism, Taoism, Confucianism, Shinto, Judaism, Christianity, and Islam are presented with clarity and evenhanded admiration. The divisions within each are explained; how these principles have been interpreted and often distorted is touched upon thoughtfully; all done with a refreshing ecumenical and spiritual tone. Contains an index. This was first published by Beacon under the title *Questions That Matter Most Asked by the World's Religions*. Sixth grade and up.

974. Wolcott, Leonard, and Carolyn Wolcott. *Through the Moon-Gate*. Illus. Vivian Berger. New York: Friendship, 1978. 36p.

Included in a short general history of China are thoughts of Confucius, Master Mo, Lao Tzu, Jesus, and Chairman Mao. Touches upon the influences of Taoism, Buddhism, Islam, and Christianity. There are folktales, poetry, songs, and woodcut illustrations. Third to sixth grades.

SPECIFIC NON-JUDEO-CHRISTIAN RELIGIONS

Bahai

975. Baha Ullah. *Bahai Prayers and Tablets for the Young*. Wilmette, Ill.: Bahai Publishing Trust, 1978. 30p.

Contains spiritually elevated prayers of Abdul-Baha and Baha Ullah praising God, asking for blessings upon babies and children, and beseeching guidance for them. The work is replete with fruit, flower, and tree imagery needing rain and sun as little ones need the nourishment of the maternal breast. Fifth grade and up.

976. Christensen, Deborah. *God and Me*. Illus. Pepper Oldziey and John Solarz. Wilmette, Ill.: Bahai Publishing Trust, 1980. unp.

God is all-glorious, mighty, giving, loving, unseen but reflected in creation. Children can respond to him by prayer and right living. Done in very simple text with big line drawings. Preschool to second grade.

977. Christensen, Deborah. *I Am a Bahai*. Illus. Pepper Oldziey and John Solarz. Wilmette, Ill.: Bahai Publishing Trust, 1984. unp.

The Bahai community, religious school, government, nineteen feasts, eleven holy days, four holidays, the Bab and Bahaullah, and houses of worship are described very simply in large type. Contains black-and-white photographs. Preschool to second grade.

978. Lee, Anthony A. *The Black Rose*. Illus. Rex John Irvine. Los Angeles: Kalimat, 1979. unp.

The multiplicity of human beings is celebrated by the variety of those adherents to the Bahai faith. They are short and tall, male and female, young and old, rich and poor, black, brown, yellow, and white. As Abdul-Baha goes with his followers through the Bowery in New York, children make fun of him, but he is not upset. When they visit him, he greets them warmly. The book has cheerful drawings in color and black and white. Kindergarten to second grade.

979. Lee, Anthony A. *The Cornerstone*. Illus. Rex John Irvine. Los Angeles: Kalimat, 1979. unp.

Bahais in America want their own house of worship. Abdul-

Baha gives them permission and instructions based on the number nine. He comes personally to Wilmette, Illinois, where he and his followers dig a ceremonial foundation, and he places the first stone for the temple. Written in an easy text, the work has sketchy, realistic pictures in color and black and white. Kindergarten to second grade.

980. Lee, Anthony A. *The Proud Helper*. Illus. Rex John Irvine. Los Angeles: Kalimat, 1979. unp.

While Abdul-Baha is imprisoned in Akka, he asks a woman visitor to help an ill friend of his. Appalled by the filth in the sick man's house, she runs away. She is told firmly that caring for him is a way of serving God, and she returns. The very simple text has action-filled drawings in black and white and color. Preschool to second grade.

981. Lee, Anthony A. *The Scottish Visitors*. Illus. Rex John Irvine. Los Angeles: Kalimat, 1980. unp.

This is a gentle lesson from Abdul-Baha concerning consideration for others. While the Master is visiting in London, a rude journalist disrupts a meeting to interview him. The ladies present are outraged, but Abdul-Baha draws the man aside, talks to him, makes him feel comfortable, and chides the ladies for their own rudeness. Has lively drawings in two-tones and color. Preschool to second grade.

982. Lee, Anthony A. *The Unfriendly Governor*. Illus. Rex John Irvine. Los Angeles: Kalimat, 1979. unp.

The Bahais are threatened by a governor who plans to shut all their shops, but he is suddenly demoted and called to Damascus. He is distraught that there is no one to help his wife and children. Abdul-Baha, leader of the persecuted, arranges to send them to the capital safely and thus returns good for evil. Done in simple langauge and drawings in black and white and color. Preschool to second grade.

983. Ostovar, Terry. *Fly through the Bahai Year*. Illus. author. Los Angeles: Kalimat, 1980. unp.

A cardinal flies over the Bahai temple and tells a butterfly about the eleven holy days of the religion and how they are celebrated. Done in a brief text, the book has simple, warm full-color and two-color drawings of children, gardens, and temple scenes. Preschool to second grade.

Buddhism

984. Bancroft, Anne. *The Buddhist World*. Morristown, N.J.: Silver Burdett, 1984. 48p.

The gentle, non-theistic quality of the well-reasoned enlightenment central to the Buddhist faith is discussed, along with the Theravada and Mahayana varieties of practice. Includes Tibetan beliefs, Zen, scriptures, art, holy places, monks, geographical distribution. The organization of facts is sometimes confusing, but it does have very good color photographs, drawings, and calligraphy as well as a glossary, lists of festivals, books to read, information centers in the United States, and an index. Fifth grade and up.

985. Barker, Carol. *Ananda in Sri Lanka: A Story of Buddhism*. Illus. author. London: Hamish Hamilton, 1985. unp.

The dry, information-packed, extensive text describes the family life, rice cultivation, and religious education in a poor Sri Lanka village. Facts about Buddhism: its principles, monks, festivals, history, dissemination, and Siddhartha's life are poorly integrated into the main story. It is, however, very handsomely illustrated in bright earth tones, with stylized figures arranged in rhythmic patterns, where everyday activities and beautiful worship services are shown. Fourth to sixth grades.

986. Rawding, F.W. *The Buddha*. Minneapolis: Lerner, 1975. 51p. Cambridge Topic Book Series.

Early life of Siddartha Gotama includes the birth myth and his early ministry after renouncing worldly pleasures at age twenty-nine. The book describes the culture and environment of ancient India and the expansion of the religion into eastern Asia, has an explication of the Middle Way, with its Four Truths and Eightfold Path, Five Precepts, and depicts the life of a monk. There are black-and-white photographs, drawings, maps, and diagrams, and an index. Fifth grade and up.

Fiction

987. Garrigue, Sheila. *The Eternal Spring of Mr. Ito.* New York: Bradbury, 1985. 163p.

A gentle, thoughtful account of a middle-aged Japanese-Canadian, fiercely loyal to his adopted country, who cannot face the disgrace of internment during World War II. Serene in his strong Buddhist faith and his belief in a steady progress toward Nirvana, he seeks a gradual death in a hidden cave. All this is seen through the sympathetic, respectful, and affectionate eyes of a young English girl. Sixth grade and up.

988. Coutant, Helen. *First Snow.* Illus. Vo-Dinh. New York: Knopf, 1974. 33p.

As Vietnamese refugees eagerly await the first sight of snow in New England, Lien asks her terminally ill grandmother what death means. She is sent outdoors to experience the transformation of a snowflake into a water drop which is absorbed by a tiny pine tree. Lien realizes that nothing is destroyed; only its form is changed. Depicts the Buddhist belief that life and death are but two aspects of the same phenomenon. Contains black-and-white drawings. Kindergarten to third grade.

Hinduism

989. Aggarwal, Manju. *I Am a Hindu.* New York: Watts, 1985. 32p.

The entire Hindu way of life as it is practiced by an Indian family living in London includes religious beliefs, worship at home and in the temple, food, clothing, household gods, holy books, customs, festivals, and other general information. Contains good color photographs, the Hindi script alphabet, the Hindu calendar, a glossary, and an index. First to fourth grades.

990. Bahree, Patricia. *The Hindu World.* Morristown, N.J.: Silver Burdett, 1982. 48p.

The variety of Hindu worship is well expressed in an overview of the faith including a brief history, main sects and deities, reincarnation and salvation, castes, family life and customs, holidays, sacred writings, model of a temple, arts, yoga, holy places. Deals principally with

India. Has fine photographs, mostly color, plus drawings and a map; a glossary, an index, a bibliography, important dates, and a time line. Fourth grade and up.

991. Bahree, Patricia. *Hinduism*. London: Batsford, 1984. 72p.

Clear, scholarly compendium of basic religious information in dictionary form. Includes deities, overall philosophy, worship methods, sacred writings, outstanding leaders, Indian culture and customs, history. There are a chronology, a bibliography, and an index, as well as plentiful black-and-white photographs. Fifth grade and up.

992. Edmonds, I.G. *Hinduism*. New York: Watts, 1979. 64p.

This fact-filled presentation includes deities such as Brahma, Vishnu, and Siva; ways to salvation; sacred scriptures and Puranas; reformed sects of Buddhists, Jains, and Sikhs; Hindu customs, culture, history, and geographical distribution. Also contains a time line, glossary, map, bibliography, index, and black-and-white photographs. Fourth grade and up.

993. Shetty, Sharat. *A Hindu Boyhood*. Illus. Mehlli Gobhai. New York: Evans, 1970. 61p.

Sharat and his friend Eswar dare a traditional curse by putting their hands on an Untouchable boy. This simply written and interesting book contains descriptions of daily life in 1946 rural India, along with basic precepts of the religion, caste system, holidays, customs. It also has a glossary. The drawings are done in golden brown tones. Third to sixth grades.

Fiction and Folktales

994. Bang, Kirsten. *Yougga Finds Mother Teresa: The Adventures of a Beggar Boy in India*. Illus. Kamma Svensson. New York: Seabury, 1983. 167p.

This vivid and touching book tells the story of a ten-year-old crippled boy who is purchased from a poor family in a small Indian village to serve as a companion and source of income (by his begging) for a kindly man who is realizing his life's dream of a pilgrimage to holy Benares. Much detail of Hindu gods and customs authenticates the journey. After the death of his adopted father, Yougga is rescued by Mother Teresa's Missionaries of Charity. Contains appealing line drawings. Fifth grade and up.

995. Beach, Milo Cleveland. *The Adventures of Rama*. Washington, D.C.: Freer Gallery of Art, 1983. 62p.

Adapted from the Ramayana, with exquisite illustrations from a sixteenth-century Indian manuscript, the book tells of Visha who chooses to be born as Rama, a king's son. With the aid of Hanuman and his army of monkeys and bears, Rama is able to rescue his beautiful wife, Sita, who has been kidnapped by the powerful demons who oppose him. The pictures in luminous soft colors of dainty women, lively monkey men, and horrible monsters have decorative beauty, along with rhythm, balance, and power. Fourth grade and up.

996. Bonnici, Peter. *The Festival*. Illus. Lisa Kopper. Minneapolis: Carolrhoda, 1984. unp.

While visiting his grandmother's village, Arjuna participates in the festival of the village temple. After a ritual bath the men dance and chant around the elephant-centered, elaborately decorated temple shrine, eat chapatis, and tell stories for a thoroughly satisfying holiday. A lovingly presented picture of rural Indian culture and warm family relationships, using simple text with a poetic lilt. The graceful illustrations in black, white, and tan bring a variety of village people into vibrant life. Preschool to second grade.

997. Bosse, Malcolm J. *Ganesh*. New York: Crowell, 1981. 192p.

After his father dies a white teenaged boy brought up in India as a Hindu returns to the United States to live with his Christian aunt and attend a rural high school. An object of curiosity at first, eventually he is accepted and even admired by his classmates. This is an effective presentation of Yoga, burial customs, Indian culture, Gayatri Mantra prayer, vegetarianism, fasting, and passive resistance that is quietly enthralling. Fifth grade and up.

988. Greene, Joshua. *A Gift of Love: The Story of Sudama the Brahmin*. Illus. Puskara dasa. Lynbrook, N.Y.: Bala, 1982. unp.

Sudama, a Brahmin priest and childhood friend of Lord Krishna, is happily living in poverty, but his wife persuades him to visit Lord Krishna with a modest gift of chipped rice to ask for help. He goes to the palace at Dwarka but asks for nothing. He is richly rewarded for his devotion but continues to live humbly, sharing his wealth. Uses a brown-and-cream format with drawings done in the Indian tradition of idealized, decorative art. Third and fourth grades.

999. Greene, Joshua. *Gopal the Invincible*. Illus. Sunita devi dasi. New York: Bala, 1984. unp.

This story is based on the Bhagavatapurana. Krishna, the Supreme Personality of the Godhead, is born as Gopal the cowherd on a mission to defend the righteous and destroy evil-doers. Even as a toddler he performs miracles and overcomes demons, although the villagers do not recognize his divinity. The clear text has a legendary tone and the brilliant illustrations, in the style of Indian paintings, are adorned with flowers, peacocks, blossoming trees, and idealized people. Third to fourth grades.

1000. Greene, Joshua. *Kaliya, King of Serpents*. Illus. Patrick Wire. New York: Bala, 1979. unp. The Childhood Pastimes of Krishna Series.

Depicts Lord Krishna as a beautiful little child helping the other boys herd the village calves and vanquishing the huge, twelve-headed snake that is polluting the river with his poison. The villagers are overjoyed that their beloved companion emerges safely from the battle. Employs rather formal but simple language and large, elegant, softly colored illustrations of a fire-spitting monster with half-human wives and a pale, sweet-faced Krishna. Kindergarten to fourth grade.

1001. Greene, Joshua. *Krishna, Master of All Mystics*. Illus. Dominique Amendola. New York: Bala, 1981. unp. The Childhood Pastimes of Krishna Series.

Based on the Bhagavata Purana, describes Lord Krishna as a five-year-old cowherd who is sharing a lunch in the woods with his fellows when Brahma, chief of the demigods, tests his divinity by stealing the boys and calves. Krishna replicates them so that the villagers will not grieve, and Brahma apologizes. Written simply and illustrated in an idealized Indian-style art with graceful lines and glowing colors. Each large picture is framed in a floral or abstract motif. Kindergarten to fourth grade.

1002. Greene, Joshua. *Sakshi Gopal: A Witness for the Wedding*. Illus. Tom Foley. New York: Bala, 1981. 17p.

The story is based on the Sri Caitanya-caritamrta. An elderly, wealthy brahmin promises his daughter in marriage to a poor young brahmin who has cared for him on a pilgrimage. To foil the older man's furious family, the young brahmin begs the deity, Gopal, to accompany him to his village and attest to the promise. Pleased by his piety, the Lord agrees. Has a stately style, and a brown-and-gold format with attractive full-page, one-dimensional, traditionally stylized drawings. Third grade and up.

1003. Jaffrey, Madhur. *Seasons of Splendor: Tales, Myths, and Legends of India*. Illus. Michael Foreman. New York: Atheneum, 1985. 128p.

Vividly retold stories of gods and miraculous morality tales of human beings, many associated with various Hindu festivals such as Dussehra, Holi, and Divali. Included are Krishna's childhood, Rama and the demon king Ravan, Lakshmi, Parvati, Shiva. Brilliantly colored illustrations, many full page, in a traditionally Indian style include plenty of gruesome monsters. There are also dainty black-and-white drawings and a glossary. Kindergarten and up.

Islam

1004. Aggarwal, Manju. *I Am a Muslim*. New York: Watts, 1985. 32p.

The basic tenets of Islam--the Five Pillars of the faith, rules for daily living, methods of prayer, the Mosque, calendar of the Muslim year, the Koran--are described and religious practices shown in the life of an eleven-year-old Pakistani boy and his family living in London. Has a glossary, Muslim facts and figures page, an index, and excellent color photographs. Third grade and up.

1005. Goldston, Robert. *The Sword of the Prophet: A History of the Arab World from the Time of Mohammed to the Present Day*. New York: Dial, 1979. 246p.

An absorbing, clearly written, sympathetic and thorough account of the Arabs and Islam from A.D. 570, the year of Mohammed's birth, to the present. The tolerance of

Moslems toward other religions is stressed over the jihad mentality, but both are explored. Although it has more history than religion, the two are closely intertwined. There are maps, an index, and an extensive bibliography. Sixth grade and up.

1006. Tames, Richard. *Islam*. London: Batsford, 1985. 72p. Dictionaries of World Religions Series.

From Abbasids to Zakat, an authoritative and interesting description of the Islamic way of life. Includes pithy sections on worship, theology, sects, history, daily living, the position of women, personalities, and so forth. Illustrated with maps and black-and-white photographs, it also contains a bibliography and an index. Fifth grade and up.

1007. Tames, Richard. *The Muslim World*. Morristown, N.J.: Silver Burdett, 1982. 47p.

Much information about the Islamic people presented in a large format splendidly illustrated with color photographs, maps, diagrams, and calligraphy. Includes history, geography, Muhammad, the Qur'an, mosques, theology, art, customs and daily life, and the Sufis. Has a glossary, a calendar, a bibliography, a list of Islamic organizations and of museums and art galleries with Islamic collections in the United States, and an index. Fourth grade and up.

Native American

1008. Armer, Laura Adams. *Waterless Mountain*. Illus. author and Sidney Armer. New York: Longmans, Green, 1931. 212p.

The adventures of a Navaho boy with unusual mystical qualities reflect the intimate, respectful relationship of Native American religion with nature's every aspect. Man's universal need to worship a higher being shines throughout Younger Brother's reactions to his experiences on the plains and mountains of his home and in the white man's city. This moving and poetic book has dark black-and-white pictures. Fifth grade and up.

1009. Baker, Betty. *And Me, Coyote*. Illus. Marie Horvath. New York: Macmillan, 1982. unp.

Based on the creation myths of California Native American

tribes. With persistent, self-important Coyote advising and helping him, the World Maker rises from the water and creates land, plants, animals, light, and people. His brother Blind Man creates ugliness and disease. Has a simple text with a storytelling tone and bold, vigorous black-and-white linoleum cut illustrations. Kindergarten to fourth grade.

1010. Baylor, Byrd. *A God on Every Mountaintop: Stories of Southwest Indian Sacred Mountains*. Illus. Carol Brown. New York: Scribner, 1981. 64p.

Mountains are holy ground for the Papago, Navajo, Pima, Maricopa, Zuni, Apache, and other tribes. They figure in a number of creation myths, flood stories, and everyday spiritual living. Each tribe has its own mountains with their inhabiting deities wielding magic protective power. In an exceptional format the text is arranged like free verse and is filled with symbols of rainbows, thunderbolts, turquoise, corn, squash, spiders, eagles, and other things evocative of Indian life in harmony with nature. The illustrations are boldly patterned in black and show chunky people, writhing snakes, sharp peaks--all full of verve and humor. All ages.

1011. Bierhorst, John. *The Sacred Path: Spells, Prayers, and Power Songs of the American Indians*. New York: Morrow, 1983. 191p.

A moving, dignified, and often exquisitely poetic work with beseechments that deal with life's major undertakings: birth, growth, love, travel, illness, weather, agriculture, hunting, and death. The tone varies from contrite to demanding and represents a wide scope of tribes in North and South America. It has been extensively researched and is illustrated with drawings of fetishes and prayer sticks. Contains notes, a bibliography, and a glossary of tribes, cultures, and languages. Fifth grade and up.

1012. De Paola, Tomie. *The Legend of the Bluebonnet*. Illus. author. New York: Putnam, 1983. unp.

This is a Comanche legend. In time of drought the Great Spirits demand the sacrifice of a valuable possession from the People, because they have become selfish and take from the earth but return nothing. An orphan girl assumes responsibility for the tribe's welfare and burns her beloved doll as the offering. Wherever she has scattered the ashes bluebonnets spring up and warm rain falls. The illustrations of subtle simplicity contrast soft earth browns and reds with skies of mauve pink and midnight blue. The figures are static and dignified. Kindergarten to third grade.

1013. Goble, Paul. *Buffalo Woman*. Illus. author. Scarsdale, N.Y.: Bradbury, 1984. unp.

The tribes of the Great Plains express their belief that the Creator wishes to make them one with the buffalo people who sustain them with food and hides and to teach them to be worthy of the herds' sacrifice. In this legend a great hunter is stalking a buffalo cow when she is transformed into a beautiful maiden. They fall in love and marry, but his people reject her as an animal. Sadly, she returns to the herd, and her husband asks to be changed into a buffalo bull so that he may join her. The strong colors of the West intensify the bold, rhythmic patterns of the illustrations, which express the beauty and order of the Native American universe. Kindergarten and up.

1014. Goble, Paul. *The Gift of the Sacred Dog*. Illus. author. Scarsdale, N.Y.: Bradbury, 1980. unp.

Buffalo have disappeared, and the people are tired and hungry. When a boy climbs to a high hilltop and prays to the Great Spirit for help, a magnificent, strange animal appears. He is called the Sacred Dog, and his mission is to help the people. A flood of these animals, which are horses, pours from a cave to live as relatives with all living things, according to the wishes of the Great Spirit. The vigorous pictures in bold colors have a flat, primitive perspective and show the flora and fauna of the West. Kindergarten to fourth grade.

1015. Goble, Paul. *The Great Race: Of the Birds and Animals*. Illus. author. New York: Bradbury, 1985. unp.

The Creator gathers all the four-legged and two-legged creatures on earth and organizes a race, whose winner will control the world. A magpie, unnoticed, rides on a buffalo's back and flies off at the end to win, bringing victory to the two-legged creatures. According to the Cheyenne and Dakota, this is how man became dominant. The Creator cautions him to be a careful steward of all the animals, as they are his relatives. While it contains strong, clean-lined, rhythmic pictures in sharp desert colors, the book has somewhat choppy text. Kindergarten to third grade.

1016. Goble, Paul. *Star Boy*. Illus. author. Scarsdale, N.Y.: Bradbury, 1983. unp.

A poetic Blackfoot legend in which a human maiden falls in love with the Morning Star, marries him, and bears a child. She disobeys his parents, the Sun and Moon, and is sent back to earth with her son, who is scarred as a result. This boy eventually ascends again to the sky, is healed and blessed, and returns to teach his people to honor the Creator. The exciting, fresh, creative illustrations in deep colors show the birds, flowers, animals, and terrain of the American West. Kindergarten to fourth grade.

1017. Hillerman, Tony. *The Boy Who Made Dragonfly*. Illus. Janet Grado. Albuquerque: University of New Mexico Press, 1986. 81p.

When the Zuni people first inhabit the Valley of the Hot Water, they are blessed by the Beloved Ones with great abundance, which they squander. They are punished by a drought and flee to the Hopi villages, leaving two young children behind. The boy cares tenderly for his sister and fashions a dragonfly to cheer her. Since they are pious and good, the insect intercedes for them with the gods, who send them food and eventually make them the leaders and priests of a chastened tribe. Beautifully told myth filled with authentic Zuni customs, culture, and philosophy that exemplifies a universal moral. Has finely done black-and-white drawings and notes. Fourth grade and up.

1018. McDermott, Gerald. *Arrow to the Sun: A Pueblo Indian Tale*. Illus. author. New York: Viking, 1974. unp.

The Lord of the Sun touches a maiden with his golden ray and conceives a son. Searching for his father, the boy is shot to heaven on a magic arrow, bravely endures terrible trials with lions, serpents, bees, and lightning, and returns to earth to bring the god's spirit to mankind. Modeled on Pueblo artwork, the illustrations are brilliant and electrifying. Preschool to third grade.

1019. White Deer of Autumn. *Ceremony--In the Circle of Life*. Illus. Daniel San Souci. Milwaukee: Raintree, 1983. 32p.

A Native American boy growing up in the city is visited by Star Spirit, who reveals the truths of his heritage.

He explains the Circle of Life, which has a quadrant for each race of man and a direction for each season and aspect of the sun. Thus the ceremony of Creation and the unity of all life are celebrated. Man's responsibility for stewardship of the earth is stressed. The appropriate, formal language gives the text a liturgical quality. The handsome, vigorous illustrations show scenes of natural beauty. Kindergarten to fourth grade.

Miscellaneous

1020. Aggarwal, Manju. *I Am a Sikh*. New York: Watts, 1985. 32p.

Describes the Sikh faith as experienced by a nine-year-old boy and his Punjabi family living in London. Short sentences and bright photographs portray worship in the Gurdwara (temple), the Adi Granth (holy text), the five Sikh symbols, traditions in clothing and food, holidays, the ten gurus, and the principles of the faith. Has a glossary, an index, and Sikh facts and figures in brief. Third to fifth grades.

1021. Matsubara, Hisako. *Cranes at Dusk*. New York: Doubleday, 1985. 253p.

An absorbing account of Kyoto during the time of the Japanese surrender in World War II centers on Saya, ten-year-old daughter of the Guji, a high Shinto priest. She is drawn to the Christian faith as it becomes suddenly popular after the war. Her father, an intellectual, deeply spiritual person, sees truth in all religions. This is a perceptive, concise, and affective work. Good readers fifth grade and up.

1022. Williams, Jay. *The Surprising Things Maui Did*. Illus. Charles Mikolaycak. New York: Four Winds, 1979. unp.

Maui, nephew of the Sea God, has extraordinary powers. He creates birds with beats from his drum, pushes up the sky, snares the sun in a net and makes it promise to move more slowly, pulls an island up from the ocean, and does other useful deeds. Written in an authentic, myth-telling tone, the book has magnificent illustrations in vibrant colors of handsome Polynesian people. Kindergarten to third grade.

CULTS

1023. Brancato, Robin. *Blinded by the Light*. New York: Bantam, 1978. 166p.

When her brother is swallowed up by the Light of the World cult, a college girl and her boy friend pretend interest in the group so that they can find and talk with him. When they succeed, they find he is completely converted. The manipulative techniques of cult operation are well described. The suspenseful plot is handled effectively in a crisp, convincing style. Sixth grade and up.

1024. Johnson, Joan. *The Cult Movement*. New York: Watts, 1984. 106p.

Defines a cult, as opposed to a denomination or a sect, as a religious group with a living leader claiming to be divinely inspired, an emphasis on unquestioning belief and obedience, and an exclusive life style and right to salvation. Concentrates mainly on the Unification Church, the Children of God, Synanon, the Peoples' Temple, and the Divine Light Mission. Discusses the appeal of cults to young people, mind control, deprogramming. Done in a critical and warning tone. Black-and-white photographs. Sixth grade and up.

1025. Miklowitz, Gloria D. *The Love Bombers*. New York: Delacorte, 1980. 199p.

An attempt to understand the magnetism of cults for young people of various backgrounds is presented as an open-ended story of a sensitive college student who joins the Adamites, a group resembling the Moonies, and resists the efforts of his sister and best friend to get him to leave. Effective, accurate depiction of cult recruitment techniques, living conditions, and the appeal of belonging to a close-knit, dominating society. Sixth grade and up.

1026. Veglahn, Nancy. *Fellowship of the Seven Stars*. Nashville: Abingdon, 1981. 175p.

Tired of being the dutiful preacher's daughter, sixteen-year-old Mazie joins a cult whose narrow view of God excludes the outside world almost entirely. Although she appreciates feeling loved, superior, and important, her sharp and witty intelligence discovers serious flaws in the Fellowship, and she finally escapes its clutches. This fast-paced book has humorous touches. It understands the cult appeal and the danger of a restrictive Christianity. Fifth grade and up.

RELIGIOUS HOLIDAYS

See also JUDAISM--HOLIDAYS

1027. Bragdon, Allen D. *Joy through the World.* New York: Dodd, 1985. 167p.

Splendid presentation of holiday celebrations throughout the world: Divali in India, Loy Krathong in Thailand, Hanukkah in Israel, Sinterklaas in the Netherlands, Santa Lucia in Sweden, Advent in Germany, Wigilia in Poland, Natale in Italy, the Twelve Days of Christmas in Britain, Los Posadas in Latin America, Christmas in North America, Grandfather Frost in Russia, and more. This spiritedly written work describes history, customs, foods, recipes, gifts, handicrafts. There are superb color photographs throughout. All ages.

1028. Burnett, Bernice. *First Book of Holidays.* Illus. Marjorie Glaubach. New York: Watts, 1955. 96p. Holidays (First Books) Series.

A combination of both secular and sacred holidays in a comprehensive list. Descriptions include good coverage of the history and customs of Christmas, Easter, Thanksgiving, St. Patrick's Day and brief mentions of the Holy Days of Obligation. There is a short section on major Jewish holidays. The cheerful, animated drawings are done in black, white, and red. Has an index and bibliography. Kindergarten to fourth grade.

1029. Cosman, Madeleine Pelner. *Medieval Holidays and Festivals.* New York: Scribner, 1981. 136p.

The traditional holiday year begins with Twelfth Night (Epiphany) with its wassails, fires, and mummers' plays, then Valentine's Day (three different St. Valentines are mentioned) with divinations and chivarees, Easter morris dancers and mystery plays, Midsummer Eve with its ancient fire customs rededicated to St. John, St. Swithin's Day honoring a pious bishop, Lammas (loaf mass) Day giving thanks for the harvest, Michaelmas for the dragon-fighting saint, Halloween, St. Catherine's Day with flaming wheels, and Christmas with its Yule log and boar's head. This lovingly researched and enthusiastically presented work also describes games, foods, ceremonies, and costumes. It has black-and-white drawings. Sixth grade and up.

1030. Larrick, Nancy. *More Poetry for Holidays*. Illus. Harold Berson. New York: Scholastic, 1973. 64p.

Short poems begin with New Year's Day and end with Christmas. They include both happy and thoughtful selections on Purim, Passover, Rosh Hashanah, Sukkot, Thanksgiving, Hanukkah. The choices for other holidays such as Easter are secular rather than religious. There are little black, white, and green drawings. Preschool to fourth grade.

1031. Livingston, Myra Cohn. *O Frabjous Day! Poetry for Holidays and Special Occasions*. New York: Atheneum, 1977. 205p.

Selections from eighty-one poets and eleven cultures from Old Testament times forward include Shakespeare, Schiller, Hopkins, Sandberg, Langston Hughes, etc., and maintain a high level of artistry. There is a section on Jewish and Christian holy days and has two pieces dealing with Buddha. Also contains title, author, first line, and translator indexes, and notes. Fifth grade and up.

1032. Millen, Nina. *Children's Festivals from Many Lands*. Illus. Janet Smalley. New York: Friendship, 1964. 191p.

Gathered directly from residents and missionaries of countries throughout the world, the coverage of games, customs, costumes, songs, greetings, foods, and history is comprehensive and authoritative. The festivals are divided into folk and Christian sections and then arranged by continent and country. Gay black-and-white drawings. All ages.

1033. Streb, Judith. *Holiday Parties*. Illus. Anne Canevari Green. New York: Watts, 1985. 64p.

Short descriptions of the history and symbols of Valentine's Day, Thanksgiving, Christmas, Hanukkah, and Halloween, followed by party plans for invitations, decorations, favors, foods, and games. Has small black-and-white drawings, a bibliography, and an index. Fourth to sixth grades.

Christmas

See also THE NEW TESTAMENT AND JESUS--JESUS' LIFE AND TEACHINGS --BIRTH

1034. Anderson, Joan. *Christmas on the Prairie*. New York: Clarion, 1985. unp.

A recreation of Christmas as it would have been celebrated by a blacksmith's family in multi-ethnic frontier Indiana in 1836. On Christmas Eve day the children misbehave in school, the mother shops in a general store, the family bakes cookies and calls on friends, the children hang stockings. This well-researched and interestingly presented book includes German, Dutch, and English customs. It has generally good and convincing black-and-white photographs. First grade and up.

1035. Barth, Edna. *Holly, Reindeer, and Colored Lights: The Story of the Christmas Symbols*. Illus. Ursula Arndt. New York: Seabury, 1971. 96p.

A careful study of both the pagan and Christian symbolism intertwined in Christmas celebrations. Discusses midwinter festivals, the Star of Bethlehem, the Christmas tree, traditional greens and flowers, manger scenes, Santa figures, the Magi, and so on, with fascinating historical details. The work has a bibliography, an index, and pages decorated with jolly black-and-white drawings accented with red. Third to sixth grades.

1036. Batchelor, Mary. *Our Family Christmas Book*. Nashville: Abingdon, 1984. 93p.

A melange of history, stories, crafts, customs, meditations, poems in a busy format generously illustrated with excellent color photographs, bright artwork in various styles, and black-and-white drawings. The topics include bells, carols, Christingles, celebrations in different countries, St. Nicholas, etc. Among the authors are Laura Ingalls Wilder, C.S. Lewis, and Leo Tolstoy. The book has an index. Kindergarten and up.

1037. *Christmas*. Huntington, Ind.: Our Sunday Visitor, 1978. 160p.

This is a British-produced, large, handsome collection of Christmas customs, music, paintings, crafts, cards, saints, cookery, and short stories whose best features are a reproduction of the beautifully illuminated Bedford Book of Hours showing the Nativity according to Matthew and Luke; holiday celebrations throughout the world, including unusual places such as Pakistan and New Guinea; and the Saints Nicholas, Wenceslaus, and Francis. Other sections tend to be cursory. There is a scholarly discussion of paintings, too few of which are shown in the illustrations. The didactic stories include a modern nativity, a Baboushka, and a Christmas miracle. It has an outstanding format and color reproduction of photographs, paintings, and a variety of artwork. Fifth grade and up.

1038. Cooney, Barbara. *Christmas*. Illus. author. New York: Crowell, 1967. unp. Crowell Holiday Book Series.

Simple accounts of the Nativity events, pagan festivals of Yule and Saturnalia, St. Nicholas and Santa Claus, and the Christmas symbols of fire and light. Discusses briefly Christmas customs and legends and emphasizes the birth of Christ. It has short sentences, large type, and graceful, joyful four-color pictures. Preschool to third grade.

1039. Cuyler, Margery. *The All-Around Christmas Book*. Illus. Corbett Jones. New York: Holt, 1982. 88p.

A clearly presented and interestingly written trove of holiday facts and ideas that includes history, both Christian and pagan; symbolism of greens and flowers; carols and cards; St. Nicholas and Santa; worldwide customs, recipes, crafts, and games. It also contains a bibliography, an index, black-and-white illustrations. Third to fifth grades.

1040. Gibbons, Gail. *Christmas Time*. Illus. author. New York: Holiday, 1982. unp.

A brief but satisfactory version of the Nativity. Modern Christmas customs stressing religious symbolism include evergreens, gifts, lights, church-going. Describes the St. Nicholas legend and Santa Claus in easy, factual prose and has exciting, skillfully designed, and brilliantly colored graphics. Preschool to second grade.

1041. Giblin, James Cross. *The Truth about Santa Claus*. New York: Crowell, 1985. 86p.

A well-organized and researched, crisply written account of the evolution of St. Nicholas, the Bishop of Myra, into modern day Santa Claus. The saint's biography, legends of his miracles (including several versions of the one about the bags of gold given to the poor sisters), and the celebration of St. Nicholas Day are described in this book, which also includes material on Father Christmas, the Christkindl, and the history of the Santa figure in America. It is illustrated with black-and-white drawings and prints. Third grade and up.

1042. Herda, D.J. *Christmas*. Illus. Anne Canevari Green. New York: Watts, 1983. 64p. A First Book Series.

This superficial treatment of the holiday tries to cover its history, worldwide customs, carols (includes backgrounds and words of thirteen well-known songs and hymns), gifts and decorations (mainly simple crafts), foods and recipes for sweets too quickly. It has a personal, rather preachy and condescending tone, black-and-white photographs, prints, and drawings, and an index. Third and fourth grades.

1043. Kalman, Bobbie. *We Celebrate Christmas*. Illus. Lisa Smith and Lynne Carson. New York: Crabtree, 1985. 57p. Holidays and Festivals Series.

A Christmas miscellanea that includes poems, stories, carols, and other Christmas music, customs in various countries, party ideas, foods, Santa Claus, la Befana, other gift-bringers and legends. It has big, crisply outlined, fresh color pictures of children amid Christmas joys and lively black-and-white drawings. Kindergarten and up.

1044. Kelley, Emily. *Christmas around the World*. Illus. Priscilla Kiedrowski. Minneapolis: Carolrhoda, 1986. 48p.

Using large type and short sentences, the book has mildly interesting descriptions of Christmas customs in Mexico, Sweden, Norway, Spain, China, Iraq, and Iran, plus highlights from four other countries. The busy black-and-white and color pictures are done in a flat style and cluttered format. Kindergarten to fourth grade.

1045. Moncure, Jane Belk. *Christmas Is a Happy Time*. Illus. Frances Hook. Elgin, Ill.: Child's World, 1980. 32p.

The simple text indicates that Christmas is a celebration of Baby Jesus' birthday, with children ringing handbells, lighting candles, presenting a Christmas pageant, singing carols, giving gifts, showing love. Has full-page pictures of beautiful children of various races in soft, rich colors. Preschool and kindergarten.

1046. Myra, Harold. *Santa, Are You for Real?* Illus. Dwight Walles. Nashville: Nelson, 1977. 32p.

Todd, a sad and puzzled little boy, doesn't understand the connection of Jesus' birth and St. Nicholas and secular Christmas customs. His father explains. Todd's part of the story is told in verse and illustrated with blocky, bright-eyed children. St. Nicholas' part is in prose, with contrasting traditional pictures. Preschool to second grade.

1047. Stevens, Patricia Bunning. *Merry Christmas: A History of the Holiday*. New York: Macmillan, 1979. 158p.

The absorption of pagan figures and festivals, the development of beloved traditions such as the Christmas tree and gift-bringing, the stories behind the composition of favorite carols, hymns and songs, and many other aspects of the holiday have been carefully researched and are presented as a fascinating history. The Nativity is the starting point. Contains a bibliography and an index. Fifth grade and up.

1048. Wiersum, Beverly Rae. *The Story of Christmas for Children*. Illus. Lorraine Schreiner Wells. Milwaukee: Ideals, 1979. unp.

The reason for gift-giving at Christmas (to show our love as God showed his) is explained to a family of small children by their parents by means of the Nativity story. Done in rhymed text, the book has saccharine, static pictures in muted colors. Preschool to second grade.

1049. Willson, Robina Beckles. *Merry Christmas: Children at Christmastime Around the World*. Illus. Satoma Ichikawa. New York: Philomel, 1983. 72p.

Exquisitely detailed, joyful illustrations glowing with color and vitality show children in Germany, the Netherlands, Poland, Czechoslovakia, Finland, Norway, Sweden, France, Italy, India, Japan, etc., busy with their special Christmas preparations and helping to commemorate Jesus' birth. Contains familiar and unfamiliar carols with music. Legends and customs for each country are described in the text. All ages.

CAROLS AND SONGS

1050. Baker, Laura Nelson. *The Friendly Beasts*. Illus. Nicolas Sidjakov. Berkeley, Calif.: Parnassus, 1957. unp.

This adaptation of the fourteenth-century carol tells of the animals who, while waiting for the arrival of Mary and Joseph at the Nativity stable, discuss the gifts that they will give the baby Jesus after his birth. The book includes music and witty pictures in stylized patterns overlaid with blocks of olive, orange, rose, and green. Preschool to second grade.

1051. Cusack, Margaret, illus. *The Christmas Carol Sampler*. New York: Harcourt, 1983. 32p.

Simple piano arrangements for thirteen of the most familiar carols and songs are uniquely illustrated with pictures of appliqued collage and three-dimensional fabric sculpture. Splendidly creative, varied, and artistic, the needlework subjects are a cityscape with a church, the infant Jesus surrounded by kindly beasts, a mother reading to her child, and more, all in rich colors and patterns. All ages.

1052. De Paola, Tomie, illus. *The Friendly Beasts: An Old English Christmas Carol*. New York: Putnam, 1981. unp.

An elegantly lettered version of the words and music, with beautifully balanced illustrations suffused with subtle color. The donkey, cow, and sheep are kind-eyed and passive, the doves proud, the Holy Family and worshippers dressed in flowing medieval robes. All exude quiet peace. Preschool to second grade.

1053. Domanska, Janina, illus. *Din Dan Don, It's Christmas*. New York: Greenwillow, 1975. unp.

The text of the Polish carol concerning a procession of birds to the Nativity stable is excitingly illustrated in the glowing colors and flat, black-outlined figures of stained glass. Drawn by a huge star, peasants, soldiers, girls and boys carrying huge pots of flowers, and the Magi all march past domed and steepled churches to the Holy Family. Preschool to second grade.

1054. Mohr, Joseph. *Silent Night*. Illus. Susan Jeffers. New York: Dutton, 1984. unp.

This romantically illustrated version with large, double-page scenes in subdued but rich nighttime colors of idealized figures--robed and feathered angels, turbaned Magi, a strong and gentle Joseph, youthful Mary, and plump infant--is infused with a mood of peace and quiet happiness. The work includes music. Preschool and up.

1055. Tennyson, Noel, illus. *Christmas Carols*. New York: Random House, 1981. unp.

Very detailed, action-filled, varied pictures, done in soft-toned color, of carol singers of all ages, bearded Magi on loaded camels, the stable with doves and angels, a Christmas banquet table, a country snow scene, and so forth surround the words of familiar carols and Christmas hymns. Preschool to second grade.

POETRY

1056. Barth, Edna. *A Christmas Feast: Poems, Sayings, Greetings and Wishes*. Illus. Ursula Arndt. New York: Houghton Mifflin, 1979. 156p.

This interesting variety of poetry stresses the religious aspect of Christmas but deals with many other areas as well. Shakespearean fragments, modern works for children, old rhymes, carols are all included. Has an interesting section on Yuletide superstitions. The book is decorated with small etchings. Fifth grade and up.

1057. Harrison, Michael, and Christopher Stuart-Clark. *The Oxford Book of Christmas Poems*. Oxford, England: Oxford University Press, 1983. 160p.

An outstanding collection that includes both classic works and well-known poets such as Longfellow, Kipling, and Auden, plus less familiar selections, all of a consistently high quality. The groupings are: the onset of winter and Advent; the Christmas season, including St. Stephen's Day; ways of celebrating the holiday; the New Year. Most have religious themes but reflect many moods. The work is illustrated with a variety of fine black-and-white and color pictures, some elegant and some humorous. Fifth grade and up.

1058. Livingston, Myra Cohn. *Christmas Poems*. Illus. Trina Schart Hyman. New York: Holiday, 1984. 32p.

Simple and charming new and old works by Langston Hughes, Christina Rossetti, Clement Moore, John Ciardi, Norma Farber, and more, tell of bells, Magi, shepherds, the Holy Family, etc. Illustrations in tones of brown, olive green and red show perky wooden toys and Christmas ornaments, sometimes watched by handsome, thoughtful children. Kindergarten to third grade.

1059. Livingston, Myra Cohn. *Poems of Christmas*. New York: Atheneum, 1980. 171p.

The spirit of Christmas is expressed with reverence, poignancy, beauty, and humor in a large collection of mostly short poems from many centuries and countries. Included are selections from the Bible, Heinrich Heine, Alfred, Lord Tennyson, Robert Frost, Ogden Nash, Eleanor Farjeon, and others, as well as traditional carols. There are author, title, first line, and translator indexes. Fifth grade and up.

STORIES

1060. Aoki, Hisako. *Santa's Favorite Story*. Illus. Ivan Gantschev. Boston: Alphabet, 1982. unp.

A useful amalgamation of Santa Claus and the Nativity. Perky animals find Santa asleep in a snowy forest and worry that he is too tired to bring Christmas. He explains cheerfully that the real Christmas is the celebration of the birth of God's son and tells them the Nativity story in simple language. They all return to Santa's house to prepare gifts and share the holiday. Illustrated with winsome watercolors filled with soft shapes such as cushiony snow drifts, fluffy trees, big-eyed creatures. Preschool to second grade.

1061. Aurelio, John. *The Beggars' Christmas*. Illus. Stan Skardinski. New York: Paulist, 1979. 66p.

In 1230 the bishop at Soissons orders that a creche be erected in the church. Outside, a blind man and a crippled beggar huddle around a weak fire and wonder bitterly about the meaning and location of Christmas. An angel grants each a wish. When they have returned to the present, they are greatly changed and support each other lovingly as they hasten to the church where they can feel Jesus' invisible touch. Contains strong, realistic black-and-white drawings of medieval scenes. Fifth grade and up.

1062. Aurelio, John. *The Boy Who Stole the Christmas Star*. Illus. Stan Skardinski. New York: Crossroad, 1981. 54p.

A satisfying fantasy in which mischievous Paul, son of an impoverished schoolmaster, learns that gifts won't come unless the Christmas tree has a star and there is an infant Jesus to go in the creche underneath. Consequently when his dumpy little guardian angel transports him to heaven, he interferes with the Nativity by snatching the Star of Bethlehem and the Magi's gifts for his own family. All ends well and miraculously. Has handsome pen-and-ink drawings. Fourth to sixth grades.

1063. Bacigalupa, Drew. *A Good and Perfect Gift*. Illus. Jeannie Pear. Huntington, Ind.: Our Sunday Visitor, 1978. 46p.

Manuelita, a fatherless child from a poor Mexican home, is bitterly disappointed because El Santo Nino has not brought her a father to enjoy, even just for the holiday. A little miracle occurs in answer to her prayer when a fugitive from the law shelters in their adobe hut for Christmas Day and carves three beautiful Nativity figures for her. This tenderly, poetically, convincingly told story has skillfully done black-and-white full-page drawings that portray the characters with gentle strength and realism and a glossary of Spanish words. Kindergarten to fourth grade.

1064. Berger, Barbara Helen. *The Donkey's Dream*. Illus. author. New York: Philomel, 1985. unp.

A donkey being led through a star-spangled night dreams he carries on his back a gleaming city, a sailing ship, an arching fountain, a giant rose, a lady "full of heaven." Arriving in a pink city with no place for them to stay, the blue-robed lady and her husband enter a cave, which fills with light upon the birth of her child. Children will need these beautiful symbols of the Virgin Mary interpreted. The book has a short, delicate, musical text and mystical, exquisite, lambent illustrations. Kindergarten and up.

1065. Briscoe, Jill. *The Innkeeper's Daughter.* Illus. Dennis Hockerman. Milwaukee: Ideals, 1984. unp.

Keturah, a girl born without fingers, hides in her father's stable on the night of Jesus' birth. As if in a dream she sees the rainbow rays of the star, childlike cherubs cleaning the stable and grooming the animals, Mary and Joseph and the new baby, the adoring shepherds and the Magi. When Mary invites her to hold the infant, she realizes her hands are healed. The unoriginal plot is told in a rather long text for its picture book format. Has big, softly colored, sentimental pictures with lots of animals. Third and fourth grades.

1066. Butterworth, Nick. *The Nativity Play.* Illus. Nick Inkpen. Boston: Little, Brown, 1985. unp.

The essence of every ingenuously earnest, charmingly jerrybuilt elementary school Christmas pageant is tenderly and hilariously portrayed. Softly colored, jolly pictures show angels with taped coat hanger wings, wise men in striped bathrobes and yarn beards, a six-legged (three-child) camel, a teacher joyfully pounding on a battered piano, and other typical scenes. The text tells the basic story with British humor. Preschool to third grade.

1067. Christian, Mary Blount. *Anna and the Strangers.* Illus. Charles T. Cox. Nashville: Abingdon, 1981. unp.

When Mary and Joseph are seeking a place to stay in Bethlehem, an innkeeper's young daughter suggests they rest in the inn stable. After the baby is born, the girl brings him a white linen cloth woven by her late mother. Although the gift seems small to Anna, Mary praises her for her loving generosity. Has black, blue, and white drawings of plain, sturdy people. First to fourth grades.

1068. Christian, Mary Blount. *Christmas Reflections.* Illus. Art Kirchoff. St. Louis: Concordia, 1980. unp.

A white family in the country and a black family in the city both prepare for Christmas. God's love and the Nativity are at the center of their holiday. Handsome drawings in brown, white, and gold mingle the symbols and events of today with those in Biblical Bethlehem. Preschool to second grade.

1069. *Christmas Classics for Children*. St. Louis: Concordia, 1981. 175p.

Stories reprinted from earlier Concordia books include "The City That Forgot About Christmas" (a mysterious old carpenter carves figures for a Nativity scene and reawakens the Christmas spirit in the townspeople), "Journeys to Bethlehem" (a fine retelling of Jesus' birth with dramatic illustrations), "Little Tree and His Wish" (a tiny tree becomes the manger bed), "The Mysterious Star" (as little boy looks for the Bethlehem star, his caring love for others reflects Jesus' love), "The Story of Silent Night" (after mice chew the organ bellows, the pastor and schoolmaster write a simple hymn to be sung to guitar accompaniment). Contains color pictures. Preschool to fourth grade.

1070. Claire, Anne. *Andro: The Star of Bethlehem*. Illus. Anne Rettig. Cincinnati: Standard, 1981. unp.

Andro has the worst singing voice of all the stars but loves to praise God with it anyway. As a reward he is appointed to shine on the birth at Bethlehem and light the path of the Magi. Cartoon-like angels and stars with faces in midnight blue skies. A rather uninspired work. Kindergarten to second grade.

1071. Cooney, Barbara. *The Little Juggler: Adapted from an Old French Legend*. Illus. author. New York: Hastings, 1961. 47p.

Based on a thirteenth-century French manuscript that is gracefully and touchingly retold in musical prose, this is the story of an orphaned young street juggler who plies his trade successfully in summer but is on the verge of starvation and freezing in winter. A kindly monk brings him to the monastery. Having no gift to bring the Virgin and Child at Christmas, he performs his tricks for them so vigorously that he faints. The statue comes to life and ministers to him. The meticulously designed illustrations in black and white and gay four-color are full of warmth and tenderness. Second to fifth grades.

1072. Corrin, Sara, and Stephen Corrin. *The Faber Book of Christmas Stories*. London: Faber, 1984. 192p.

A well-rounded collection of fourteen short stories by different authors in both modern and old-fashioned settings. Each has a Christmas legendary quality. Religious miracles occur in four. One deals with a Jewish child secretly enjoying the Christmas Eve revels. It is a humorous, poignant, warm-hearted, and satisfying work. Fifth grade and up.

1073. De Paola, Tomie. *The Clown of God: An Old Story*. Illus. author. New York: Harcourt, 1978. unp.

An orphan boy with juggling talents gains fame as a traveling entertainer until old age impairs his talent. Wishing to give the Virgin and Child a Christmas gift, he attempts to entertain them with his tricks and finds his skill has been miraculously restored. His whole-hearted gift is graciously received, showing that those who give happiness to others give glory to God. The colors, clothes, faces, and landscapes of Renaissance art are reflected in the elegantly designed illustrations. Kindergarten to fourth grade.

1074. De Paola, Tomie. *The Legend of Old Befana*. Illus. author. New York: Harcourt, 1980. unp.

Based on the Italian version of the folktale in which an old lady is too busy sweeping and scowling to enjoy the magnificence of the Nativity star or respond to the invitation to join the Magis' procession to Bethlehem. But after a child leading a camel tells her the Baby King will change the world and help the poor, she starts out with her broom and a basket of goodies to search for him. Each year on January sixth she flies across the sky, visiting children and leaving gifts. Entertaining, well-balanced illustrations in rose, blue, and brown show a jowly, grumpy-faced woman against a serene, stylized medieval background. Preschool to third grade.

1075. Farber, Norma. *All Those Mothers at the Manger*. Illus. Megan Lloyd. New York: Harper, 1985. unp.

A slight, sentimental poem about animal and bird mothers gathered about Mary in the stable. The whimsical cartoon illustrations show a bright-eyed pig, cats, chickens, sheep, cows, horses, and mice gazing affectionately and approvingly as Mary washes and wraps her infant. A wordless beginning depicts Mary and Joseph crossing a golden desert to Bethlehem, inquiring at the inn, and being directed to the stable. Preschool to second grade.

1076. Farber, Norma. *How the Hibernators Came to Bethlehem.* Illus. Barbara Cooney. New York: Walker, 1980. unp.

Crystal beams from the Bethlehem star slip into the dens, nests, and holes of all the winter-sleeping creatures, rousing them to join in the great parade of beasts wending their way to the stable to worship the infant Jesus. The poetic text is perfectly matched with illustrations suffused with beauty and mystery. Kindergarten to second grade.

1077. Gentile, Gennaro L. *The Mouse in the Manger.* Illus. Vernon McKissack. Notre Dame, Ind.: Ave Maria, 1978. unp.

Because his father won't give him more straw for his bed, Oscar Mouse leaves the family burrow in a huff. He creeps into the stable-cave where Mary has given birth and is moved to give the straw he has just gathered for himself to the baby Jesus to help cushion the manger bed. Mary has taught him true friendship, and he returns home a happier and wiser mouse. The contrived story has cartoon-like illustrations. Kindergarten to third grade.

1078. Hines, William. *The Camel Boy.* Illus. James McIlrath. Huntington, Ind.: Our Sunday Visitor, 1978. 74p.

The young slave of an arrogant innkeeper is close to the Holy Family from the time they arrive in Bethlehem until they flee to Egypt. Blessed by their friendship, he learns to forgive others and face life bravely. The fine rhythmic narrative, handsome format, and careful detail give the work interest and authority. Third to sixth grades.

1079. Kasuya, Masahiro. *The Tiniest Christmas Star.* Illus. author. Valley Forge, Pa.: Judson, 1979. unp.

The tiniest star is ignored in the parade of animals the other singing stars have called to the stable to worship the infant Jesus. Finally it finds a small flower with which to share the good news and carries a gift of sweet perfume to delight the baby. Has full-page pictures in deep, soft colors of glowing stars and charming animals. Preschool to second grade.

1080. Keats, Ezra Jack, illus. *The Little Drummer Boy.* New York: Collier, 1972. unp.

Mystical illustrations in rich, muted colors show a thin,

barefoot child following the Magi to the stable where he gives the infant Jesus a drum solo as a birthday present. The words and music of the song are included. Preschool to second grade.

1081. L'Engle, Madeleine. *The Twenty-four Days before Christmas: An Austin Family Story*. New York: Farrar, 1964. 48p.

Three young children celebrate Advent with traditional family activities as they await the coming of a new baby into the family. Seven-year-old Vicky makes an important sacrifice and prays that her mother will be at home Christmas eve instead of in the hospital. Depicts a comfortable country home background. Third to fifth grades.

1082. Marxhausen, Joanne. *The Mysterious Star*. Illus. Susan Stoehr Morris. St. Louis: Concordia, 1974. unp.

As little Jamie searches for his special Christmas star, his caring love brightens the lives of many people along the way. God's love is reflected in his kindnesses just as it was in the Star of Bethlehem. The color illustrations of cherubic children have Disneylike saccharinity. Kindergarten to second grade.

1083. Menotti, Gian Carlo. *Amahl and the Night Visitors*. Illus. Michele Lemieux. New York: Morrow, 1986. 64p.

A crippled boy and his mother, living in poverty, are visited by the Magi as they stop for food and rest during their search for the Christ Child. Driven by love and concern for her child, Amahl's mother tries to steal some of the king's gold. But when she hears of the special love the holy baby will bring to the world, she returns it. Amahl eagerly offers his handmade crutch as a gift to the newborn infant, and his lameness is cured. Large, dramatic watercolors filled with the mystery of that special night show the travelers in all their glittering splendor. The text, skillfully adapted from the opera libretto, is poetic and richly descriptive. All ages.

1084. Mikolaycak, Charles. *Babushka*. Illus. author. New York: Holiday, 1984. unp.

An unusually imaginative version of the Russian folktale in which a youthful, fairhaired Babushka is too houseproud to join the Magi as they seek the infant Christ.

When she is finally ready to go, she can never find the holy baby, though she searches the faces of children throughout the world, growing old and bent on her endless journey. Done in a simple narrative style with magnificent, strong, graceful illustrations, vibrantly colored and textured. All ages.

1085. Moore, John Travers. *The Story of Silent Night*. Illus. Bob Hyskell and Leonard Gray. St. Louis: Concordia, 1965. unp.

When mice destroy his organ bellows just before Christmas eve, Father Josef Mohr composes a Christmas poem and asks Franz Gruber to set it to music suitable for a guitar. A highly sentimentalized work, with illustrations resembling an animated cartoon. Second to fourth grades.

1086. Paterson, Katherine. *Angels and Other Strangers*. New York: Crowell, 1979. 118p.

Upbeat, sometimes dated, short stories of uneven quality in which Jesus becomes truly real at Christmastime and steps into the lives of all kinds of people, from desperate little children to sad young mothers to elderly widowers. Although generally well written, the points of the stories are sometimes forced. Fifth grade and up.

1087. Peterson, Cheryl, illus. *The Animals' Christmas*. Chicago: Random House, 1983. unp.

The cow, donkey, sheep, and dove in the Nativity stable plan their gifts to the newborn infant Jesus. Illustrated in realistic style showing animals in a sturdy barn of stone and timber, using soft colors. Preschool.

1088. Richards, Jack. *Johann's Gift to Christmas*. Illus. Len Norris. New York: Scribner, 1972. unp.

Johann, a mouse with a love of fine music, becomes the resident Oberndorf church mouse so that he can hear Herr Franz Xavier Gruber play the organ. Close to starvation in December of 1818, Johann munches the leather organ bellows. Since they will only be able to play a guitar on Christmas eve, Gruber and the pastor compose a simple new hymn, "Silent Night." Contains jolly scenes of alpenhorns, village bands, snowy peaks, and a lederhosened mouse family in black and white and color. Kindergarten to second grade.

1089. Robbins, Ruth. *Baboushka and the Three Kings*. Illus. Nicolas Sidjakov. Berkeley, Calif.: Parnassus, 1960. unp.

Done in a stunning format of wooden doll figures in primary colors and elegant typography. The Three Kings are searching for Jesus in a snowy Russian landscape and stop at the snug hut of an old lady to invite her to share their journey. By the time she is ready to heed the call of Jesus, it is too late to find him. Every Christmastime she wanders, searching, from village to village. Kindergarten to second grade.

1090. Robinson, Barbara. *The Best Christmas Pageant Ever*. Illus. Janet Gwyn Brown. New York: Avon, 1973. 80p.

The human experience of the Nativity is brought sharply into focus when the six rough and tough Herdman kids, hearing that refreshments are served in Sunday School, take over the Christmas pageant. To them the story of Jesus' birth is exciting and new, and they change the routine performance into something lively and meaningful. Scratchy, action-filled black-and-white drawings express the Herdmans' personalities. The writing is breezy, funny, and poignant. Third to sixth grades.

1091. Rogers, Jean. *King Island Christmas*. Illus. Rie Munoz. New York: Greenwillow, 1985. unp.

Fresh, endearing plot and pictures. The Eskimos of an island in the Bering Sea rescue their Christmas celebration when they brave angry waves to bring their new priest to land from a freighter anchored offshore. A joyful holiday follows. The Eskimos are a lively kaleidoscope of round-faced, colorfully bundled figures with red cheeks and noses against the cold white and blue of the Arctic background. Preschool to third grade.

1092. Royds, Caroline. *The Christmas Book: Stories, Poems, and Carols for the Twelve Days of Christmas*. Illus. Annabel Spenceley. New York: Putnam, 1985. 93p.

The Nativity stories include Baboushka, a retelling of Jesus' birth, and a Christian myth from Brittany. Also included are secular Christmas tales, along with poetry and hymns. The large, handsome volume is appealingly illustrated with innocent children, kindly adults, and charming animals in color and black and white. Preschool and up.

1093. Sawyer, Ruth. *Joy to the World: Christmas Legends*. Illus. Trina Schart Hyman. Boston: Little, Brown, 1966. 102p.

Artistically retold, unfamiliar folktales include Ireland's miracle of St. Cumgall in which monks are fed by mice, Spain's San Froilan's creche, and the Serbian story of a blessed blind boy. Unusual carols are included in between the legends. The humorous pictures in mustard, black, and white are elegantly detailed. Third grade and up.

1094. Schindler, Regine. *Hannah at the Manger*. Illus. Hilde Heyduck-Huth. Nashville: Abingdon, 1983. unp.

While begging in Bethlehem, a poor shepherd's daughter encounters Mary and Joseph. Afterward she mysteriously finds a valuable pearl- and gold-encrusted piece of cloth in her basket. That night she follows her father to the Nativity stable and covers the baby king with her beautiful cloth. Although the plot is unoriginal, the text is stately, with soft, introspective illustrations in muted colors of stocky people in medieval-looking garments. Kindergarten to third grade.

1095. Scholey, Arthur. *Baboushka: A Traditional Russian Folk Tale*. Illus. Ray Burrows and Corinne Burrows. Westchester, Ill.: Crossway, 1982. unp.

Because she feels she must sweep, polish, scour, and cook before she leaves her cottage to follow the Christmas star, a youthful Baboushka in a gay peasant dress sets out too late for Bethlehem. She is told by an angel that the Holy Family has already fled to Egypt. Throughout eternity she continues her search for the Christ Child and leaves toys for good children as she travels. In this spirited retelling the folk art-style illustrations are done in brilliant colors and patterns. Contains the "Baboushka Carol" words and music. Kindergarten to fourth grade.

1096. Schulz, Charles. *A Charlie Brown Christmas*. Illus. author. New York: Random House, 1977. unp.

Comic strip favorite Charlie Brown is appalled by the "big commercial racket" being made of Christmas. While most of his friends love every bit of the tinsel and greed, he wonders what Christmas is really about. Linus finally tells all the children the Nativity story, and they reassess their priorities. Uses the "Peanuts Gang" illustrations. Preschool and up.

Easter

See also NEW TESTAMENT AND JESUS--JESUS' LIFE AND TEACHINGS--HOLY WEEK AND RESURRECTION

1097. Barth, Edna. *Lilies, Rabbits, and Painted Eggs: The Story of the Easter Symbols*. Illus. Ursula Arndt. New York: Seabury, 1970. 64p.

Describes the origins and usage of both secular and religious symbols. Includes fire, eggs, bells, colors, animals, clothes, water, flowers, etc. It is well researched and written in a lively, readable style. Has small, lively two-color drawings throughout. Third to sixth grades.

1098. Berger, Gilda. *Easter and Other Spring Holidays*. Illus. Anne Canevari Green. New York: Watts, 1983. 66p. A First Book Series.

A thorough general coverage of the celebrations associated with spring's return such as May Day, the Persephone legend, Walpurgis Night, Hindu and Buddhist festivals, etc., as well as Jewish Tu b'Shevat, Purim, Passover, Shavuot, plus Christian Lent, Holy Week, Easter, Pentecost. The religious and secular symbolism includes eggs, rabbits, fire, and the lamb. Contains interesting crafts and recipes. Written in an impartial, non-sectarian tone with clear and lively exposition. Has black-and-white prints, drawings, photographs, and an index. Third grade and up.

1099. Fisher, Aileen. *Easter*. Illus. Ati Forberg. New York: Crowell, 1968. unp. Crowell Holiday Book Series.

Centers around the Christian celebration of the Resurrection and how the various symbols of spring and rebirth gradually became associated with it. The absorbing text is a brief retelling of the events of Holy Week and Jesus' subsequent appearances to his disciples. Dynamic, rather abstract illustrations are in color and black and white. Preschool to third grade.

1100. Gnat, Erv, illus. *The Story of Easter for Children*. Chicago: Children's Press, 1984. unp.

A sometimes confusing conglomeration of subjects includes spring flowers, birds, kittens, Easter symbols, the Nativity, Holy Week, new clothes, going to church. All are meant to express new life. It has a simplistic, rhymed text. The gleaming illustrations mix realistic, skillfully detailed nature scenes with toylike big-eyed lambs and fawns and also include scenes from Jesus' life. Preschool to second grade.

1101. Kalman, Bobbie. *We Celebrate Easter*. Illus. Maureen Shaughnessy. New York: Crabtree, 1985. 57p. The Holidays and Festivals Series.

Holiday snippets include all aspects of Easter: new life and the arrival of spring; the crucifixion and resurrection of Jesus; holiday games, crafts, and recipes; carnival customs throughout the world; methods of egg decoration; Lenten, Good Friday, and Easter stories and symbols. Large, lively pictures in color and black and white include children of various races celebrating amid spring flowers. Kindergarten to third grade.

1102. Livingston, Myra Cohn. *Easter Poems*. Illus. John Wallner. New York: Holiday, 1985. 32p.

Handsome, elaborate black-and-white graphics highlighted in spring green and violet present a variety of images for each poem. The subjects range through Easter mornings, silky rabbits, crosses on Golgotha, sea creatures celebrating the risen Jesus, and a plea for peace. The poets include Norma Farber, John Ciardi, and Joan Aiken. This is a varied and original collection. Kindergarten to fourth grade.

1103. Myra, Harold. *Easter Bunny, Are You for Real?* Illus. Dwight Walles. Nashville: Nelson, 1979. 32p.

All aspects of Easter are successfully integrated by a father answering his young children's questions about the place of bunnies and eggs in the Christian celebration of Jesus' resurrection. They are constructing a giant, treat-stuffed rabbit for use at school. Death and afterlife are also touched upon gently. Preschool to third grade.

Halloween

1104. Barth, Edna. *Witches, Pumpkins, and Grinning Ghosts: The Story of Halloween Symbols*. Illus. Ursula Arndt. New York: Clarion, 1972. 96p.

An explanation of the conversion of the Druid Celtic

festival of Samhain, honoring the Lord of the Dead, by the seventh-century Christian church into All Saints' Day, or All Hallows, honoring early Christian martyrs. The night before is called All Hallows' Eve. Also includes a lively discussion of witches, the devil, and other Halloween symbols in which the church has been entwined over the centuries, and how holidays honoring the dead are celebrated throughout the world. A thorough and fascinating work, with spirited black-and-orange drawings on every page. Third to sixth grades.

1105. Myra, Harold. *Halloween, Is It for Real?* Illus. Dwight Walles. Nashville: Nelson, 1982. 32p.

The discussion in a Christian family of the origin of Halloween includes its pagan Celtic roots as a festival to frighten away evil spirits and Christian attempts to convert it into a celebration of departed saints. The family decides to have a children's costume party during which the guests discuss the loss of loved ones and their belief in heaven. The work stresses the power of good over evil. Large, busy pictures of family and party activities alternate those in full color with those in orange and brown tones. Kindergarten to fourth grade.

Thanksgiving

1106. Anderson, Joan. *The First Thanksgiving Feast*. New York: Clarion, 1984. unp.

An imaginative, effective recreation of the Pilgrims' feast based on first-hand accounts and photographed at Plimoth Plantation, the living history museum of seventeenth century life in Plymouth, Massachusetts. The comments on their experiences in the new world made by both "saints" (the Separatists) and "strangers" (the opportunists who accompanied them on the Mayflower) give immediacy to a sprightly text. Lively black-and-white photographs show colonists' houses, agriculture, fishing, foods, feasting, dancing, and friendship with splendid Indians. Kindergarten and up.

1107. Bains, Rae. *Pilgrims and Thanksgiving*. Illus. David Wenzel. Mahwah, N.J.: Troll, 1985. 30p.

Basic facts of the Puritan Separatist movement away from the Church of England, the migration of the Puritans to Holland, the formation of a group of Puritans and Strangers to emigrate to the new world, their experiences in the Plymouth Colony (including the Mayflower Compact and the treaty with the Wampanoags), and the first Thanksgiving feast. The hardship of the voyage and early years are downplayed but good general information is conveyed in a straightforward text. Has somber watercolors and illustrations. Kindergarten to fourth grade.

1108. Baldwin, Margaret. *Thanksgiving*. Illus. Anne Canevari Green. New York: Watts, 1983. 64p. A First Book Series.

Concentrates on the Pilgrim experience: why they became Separatists, how they traveled to the new world, what happened in the early days of settlement. Good, authoritative details of their hardships, daily life, and contacts with Indians. Some mention of harvest and Thanksgiving festivals in general and the evolution of an official Thanksgiving Day in the United States. There is an extraneous chapter on games, crafts, and foods. The work has clear, fact-filled text and black-and-white prints, drawings, photographs, a bibliography and an index. Fourth grade and up.

1109. Barth, Edna. *Turkeys, Pilgrims, and Indian Corn: The Story of the Thanksgiving Symbols*. Illus. Ursula Arndt. New York: Seabury, 1975. 96p.

This rendition of the history and customs of the holiday, stressing the Pilgrims' life on the Mayflower and in the new world discusses the families, clothing, livestock, agriculture, and relations with neighboring Indians. Harvest festivals in Japan, India, England, etc., are briefly mentioned. Contains instructive line drawings in black, white, and gold, a bibliography, and an index. Third to sixth grades.

1110. Bartlett, Robert Merrill. *Thanksgiving Day*. Illus. W.T. Mars. New York: Crowell, 1965. unp. Crowell Holiday Book Series.

Discusses early Greek, Roman, Jewish, and European harvest celebrations before launching into a lively retelling of the Pilgrim adventure, with pictorial, accurate details. The first feast of thanksgiving is vividly described, and the second Pilgrim thanksgiving day, proclaimed after a time of great hardship, is also recounted, along with present ways of celebration. The drawings are in black, white, and jade green. Kindergarten to fourth grade.

1111. Cohen, Barbara. *Molly's Pilgrim.* Illus. Michael J. Deraney. New York: Lothrop, 1983. unp.

Sweetly didactic story of a Russian Jewish immigrant who is teased and misunderstood by her third-grade classmates, particularly when she brings a clothespin doll dressed like a Russian peasant rather than a conventional Pilgrim for the Thanksgiving scene at school. Her teacher explains that pilgrims are still seeking religious freedom in America and that Thanksgiving is based on the Biblical harvest holiday of the Tabernacles (Molly's Sukkos). Has strong, realistic black-and-white illustrations. Kindergarten to fourth grade.

1112. Dalgliesh, Alice. *The Thanksgiving Story.* Illus. Helen Sewell. New York: Scribner, 1954. unp.

A vivid account of the Mayflower voyage, the first difficult months in the Plymouth Colony, early encounters with friendly and hostile Indians, and the three-day feast of Thanksgiving to God. Contains bright, amusing illustrations done in the flat, rhythmic patterns of American primitive art. Kindergarten to fourth grade.

1113. Gibbons, Gail. *Thanksgiving Day.* Illus. author. New York: Holiday, 1983. unp.

Terse but adequate descriptions crisply illustrated in clear, intense colors, dynamic patterns, simplified forms tell the Pilgrim story. Includes the Mayflower voyage, the winter suffering, help from the Indians, the thanksgiving feast, and describes the modern-day celebration with its decorations, hymns, holiday foods, games, parades. Preschool to second grade.

1114. Hopkins, Lee Bennett. *Merrily Comes Our Harvest In: Poems for Thanksgiving.* Illus. Ben Shecter. New York: Harcourt, 1978. 32p.

A vivacious collection of twenty short, appreciative poems, celebrating autumn, feasting, Pilgrims and Indians, and Nature's bounty. The poets include Aileen Fisher, Marchette Chute, Robert Graves, and others. Has cheerful, amusing drawings. Kindergarten to fourth grade.

1115. Kessel, Joyce K. *Squanto and the First Thanksgiving.* Illus. Lisa Donze. Minneapolis: Carolrhoda, 1983. 48p.

A biography of the Christian Patuxet Indian Squanto which emphasizes his role in the survival of the Pilgrims during their first year in Plymouth by teaching them to farm and hunt, along with a description of the first thanksgiving feast. An easy reader that has plain brown-and-white illustrations. Kindergarten to third grade.

1116. Livingston, Myra Cohn. *Thanksgiving Poems*. Illus. Stephen Gammell. New York: Holiday, 1985. 32p.

Includes the works of Kaye Starbird, Eve Merriam, Jane Yolen, X.J. Kennedy, and others. Also has two Native American songs, Psalm One Hundred, and a hymn. Depicts various moods and topics: praise and thanksgiving, plus humor centering around family feasts and talking turkeys. Three-color illustrations vary from jolly cartoons to realistic portraits and landscapes, as they reflect the individual selection. Kindergarten and up.

1117. McGovern, Ann. *If You Sailed on the Mayflower*. Illus. J.B. Handelsman. New York: Scholastic, 1969. 80p.

Straightforward, interesting history begins with the Separatist movement, details the Mayflower voyage, describes landing on Cape Cod, the move to Plymouth, the rigors of the first winter, daily life, and events of first thanksgiving celebration. Has high spirited, cartoon-style green-and-white drawings. Kindergarten to fourth grade.

1118. Moncure, Jane Belk. *My First Thanksgiving Book*. Illus. Gwen Connelly. Chicago: Children's Press, 1984. 31p.

Contains simple rhymes about the Pilgrims and the Indians, stressing their friendship, the first harvest, and the thanksgiving feast, and about modern day holiday celebrations, including pumpkin pies, giving thanks, and sharing food with the needy. Flat, static illustrations of doll-like people are enlivened with bright, clear colors. Preschool to second grade.

1119. Prelutsky, Jack. *It's Thanksgiving*. Illus. Marylin Hafner. New York: Greenwillow, 1982. 48p.

Contains funny, brisk little poems on all aspects of the holiday. Includes the feasting Pilgrims and Indians, a gathering at Grandmother's, parades in the rain, overeating, leftovers, and so forth. Has cleverly detailed cartoon illustrations in autumn browns and oranges. Preschool to fourth grade.

1120. Rogers, Lou. *The First Thanksgiving*. Illus. Michael Lowenbein. Chicago: Follett, 1962. 31p.

The search for religious freedom sends the Pilgrims first to Holland and then to America, where there is room for them to establish their own way of life. Early experiences in the new land and good relationships with the Indians culminate in a munificent feast of thanksgiving to God. Basic facts are presented with interesting details and adequate color pictures reinforce the text. Kindergarten to third grade.

1121. Whitehead, Pat. *Best Thanksgiving Book*. Illus. Susan T. Hall. Mahwah, N.J.: Troll, 1985. unp.

Gives the essentials of the Pilgrim saga in short sentences combined with a harmonizing alphabet book (A for America, P for Peace, T for Thanks, etc.). The clear upper- and lower-case letters make for good concepts. There are merry, bright pictures of Pilgrim and Indian families cooperating. The book ends with the happy feast. Preschool and kindergarten.

Valentine's Day

1122. Gibbons, Gail. *Valentine's Day*. Illus. author. New York: Holiday, 1986. unp.

The founding of the holiday is attributed to St. Valentine, patron saint of lovers and beloved friend of many children, who used to bring him notes and flowers. Modern day Valentine customs, refreshments, parties, crafts are described. Has decorative line drawings in brilliant colors. Preschool to first grade.

1123. Kessel, Joyce. *Valentine's Day*. Illus. Karen Ritz. Minneapolis: Carolrhoda, 1981. 48p.

Discusses its evolution from a pagan holiday devoted to Lupercus and Juno into one dedicated by Pope Gelasius to a St. Valentine (probably one of the two Valentines persecuted by the Roman emperor Claudius), along with other history and customs. An early reader that has graceful black-and-white drawings touched with red. Kindergarten to third grade.

RELIGIOUS PUBLISHERS' DIRECTORY

Abingdon Press
201 Eighth Ave. South
P.O. Box 801
Nashville, TN 37202

Augsburg Publishing House
426 South Fifth St.
P.O. Box 1209
Minneapolis, MN 55440

Ave Maria Press
Notre Dame, IN 46556

Bahai Publishing Trust
415 Linden Ave.
Wilmette, IL 60091

Baker Book House
2768 East Paris Ave. S.E.
P.O. Box 6287
Grand Rapids, MI 49506

Bala Books
38 Dawes Ave.
Lynbrook, N.Y. 11563

Bethany Fellowship
see Bethany House

Bethany House
6820 Auto Club Rd.
Minneapolis, MN 55438

Bethany Press
P.O. Box 179
St. Louis, MO 63166

Broadman
127 9th Ave. N.
Nashville, TN 37234

Chariot
see David C. Cook

The Child's World
980 N. McLean Blvd.
P.O. Box 989
Elgin, IL 60121

Chosen Books
Lincoln, VA 22078

Concordia Publishing House
3558 S. Jefferson Ave.
St. Louis, MO 63118

David C. Cook
850 N. Grove Ave.
Elgin, IL 60120

Crossroad/Continuum
575 Lexington Ave.
New York, NY 10022

Crossway-Good News Publishers
9825 W. Roosevelt Rd.
Westchester, IL 60153

Dandelion House
see The Child's World

David and Charles
Box 57
N. Pomfret, VT 05053

Decker Press
Box 3838
Grand Junction, CO 81502

Faith and Life Press
718B Main st.
Newton, KS 67114

Philipp Feldheim, Inc.
200 Airport Executive Park
Spring Valley, NY 10977

Fortress Press
2000 Queen Lane
Philadelphia, PA 19129

Friendship Press
475 Riverside Dr.
New York, NY 10115

Geneva Press
925 Chestnut St.
Philadelphia, PA 19107

C.R. Gibson Co.
32 Knight St.
Norwalk, CT 06856

Guideposts Associates, Inc.
Carmel, NY 10512

Herald Press
Scottdale, PA 15683

Ideals
11315 Watertown Plank Rd.
P.O. Box 1101
Milwaukee, WI 53201

Jewish Publication Society of America
60 E. 42nd St., Suite 707
New York, NY 10165

Judson Press
P.O. Box 851
Valley Forge, PA 19482-0851

Kalimat Press
10889 Wilshire Blvd.
Suite 700
Los Angeles, CA 90024

Kar-Ben
11216 Empire Lane
Rockville, MD 20852

KTAV Publishing House, Inc.
75 Varick St.
New York, NY 10013

Liguori Publications
1 Liguori Drive
Liguori, MO 63057

Lion
10885 Textile Rd.
P.O. Box 985
Belleville, MI 48111

Liturgical Press
St. John's Abbey
Collegeville, MN 56321

Logos International
2500 Hamilton Blvd.
S. Plainfield, NJ 07080

Moody Press
820 N. LaSalle Dr.
Chicago, IL 60610

Multnomah Press
10209 S.E. Division St.
Portland, OR 97266

Thomas Nelson Publishers
Nelson Place at Elm Hill Pike
P.O. Box 141000
Nashville, TN 37214-1000

Our Sunday Visitor
200 Noll Plaza
Huntington, IN 46750

Paraclete
P.O. Box 1568
Orleans, MA 02653

Paulist Press
997 Macarthur Blvd.
Mahwah, N.J. 07430

Regal Books
Division of G/L Publications
2300 Knoll Dr.
Ventura, CA 93003

Resource Publications
P.O. Box 444
Saratoga, CA 95070

Fleming H. Revell Co.
Old Tappan, NJ 07675

SBS Publishing
14 W. Forest Ave.
Englewood, NJ 07631

Scarf Press
58 E. 83rd St.
New York, NY 10028

Servant Publications
P.O. Box 8617
Ann Arbor, MI 48107

Harold Shaw Publishers
P.O. Box 567
388 Gundersen Dr.
Wheaton, IL 60189

Standard Publishing
8121 Hamilton Ave.
Cincinnati, OH 45231

Stillpoint Publishing
P.O. Box 640
Meetinghouse Rd.
Walpole, NH 03608
(affiliated with Dutton)

Sweet Publishing Co.
3934 Sandshell
Ft. Worth, TX 76137

Tyndale House Publishers
336 Gundersen Dr.
P.O. Box 80
Wheaton, IL 60187

United American Hebrew Congregations
838 Fifth Ave.
New York, NY 10021

Upper Room
1908 Grand Ave.
P.O. Box 189
Nashville, TN 37202

Warner Press
P.O. Box 2499
Anderson, IN 46018

Victor Books
Scripture Press Publications
1825 College Ave.
P.O. Box 1825
Wheaton, IL 60187

Westminster Press
925 Chestnut St.
Philadelphia, PA 19107

Winston-Seabury Press
430 Oak Grove
Minneapolis, MN 55403
(affiliated with Harper and Row)

Word Books
4800 W. Waco Dr.
Waco, TX 76710

Zondervan
1415 Lake Drive S.E.
Grand Rapids, MI 49506

AUTHOR INDEX

TITLE INDEX

DATE DUE
